Digital Rights at the Periphery

THE GEOPOLITICS OF INFORMATION

Edited by Dan Schiller, Yuezhi Zhao, and Amanda Ciafone

For a list of books in the series, please see our website at www.press.uillinois.edu.

Digital Rights at the Periphery

Making Brazil's Marco Civil

GUY T. HOSKINS

Library of Congress Cataloging-in-Publication Data
Names: Hoskins, Guy T., author.
Title: Digital rights at the periphery : making Brazil's Marco Civil /
    Guy T. Hoskins.
Description: Urbana : University of Illinois Press, 2025. | Series:
    The geopolitics of information | Includes bibliographical
    references and index.
Identifiers: LCCN 2024060705 (print) | LCCN 2024060706
    (ebook) | ISBN 9780252046674 (cloth) | ISBN 9780252088773
    (paperback) | ISBN 9780252047992 (ebook)
Subjects: LCSH: Internet—Law and legislation—Brazil. |
    Computer networks—Law and legislation—Brazil. | Digital
    rights management—Brazil.
Classification: LCC KHD335.C65 H67 2025 (print) |
    LCC KHD335.C65 (ebook) | DDC 343.8109/944—dc23/
    eng/20250111
LC record available at https://lccn.loc.gov/2024060705
LC ebook record available at https://lccn.loc.gov/2024060706

For Kristi, Eva, Eloise, and Delia

*and in dedication to all those who strive
for more just and democratic means
of communication*

Contents

Acknowledgments

This book has at times felt like an interminable undertaking. The conceptual genesis of this book occurred in 2012, and I conducted field research in Brazil in 2014 and 2015, intermittently wrote these chapters between 2016 and 2023, and prepared the manuscript for completion in 2024. During the span of these twelve years, I have also become a father three times (to three remarkable girls), taught dozens of courses, defended a PhD, and muddled my way through a global pandemic. That these words now appear printed on paper is only possible owing to the contributions of some important people that merit acknowledgment here.

I recognize the generous financial support of the Social Sciences and Humanities Council of Canada (SSHRC), York University, and the Sylff Association, which provided me the time and resources necessary to carry out such an ambitious project. The travel funding provided by the latter group allowed me to do three weeks of field research in Brazil, a vital endeavor for this manuscript, as well as providing some of my fondest memories of recent years. That research trip allowed me to travel across a beautiful, fascinating country and meet a cast of people—protagonists in the story of the Marco Civil—whose gracious willingness to talk to me and introduce me to others made telling this story possible.

In terms of more personal acknowledgments, I thank my life partner, Kristi, for imbuing me with the self-belief to pursue a doctorate in the first place, for carrying the parenting burden during my academic jaunts, and for skillfully managing my episodic bouts of imposter syndrome. To my three wonderful daughters—Eva, Eloise, and Delia—thank you for motivating me to try and be the best version of myself (of which this book represents a small but vivid manifestation) and to Eva especially, thank you for the insights born of trying to have my ideas make sense to an inquiring child's mind. To my mother and father, Yolande and Julian, your love and support and your examples of hard work and sacrifice are the foundation on which I stand. I strive to make you proud and hope that this book does that to some small degree.

Although my home office has at times felt like an isolation tank, the ideas that this work comprises have, in fact, been presented and discussed at numerous academic conferences around the world that I have had the great privilege to attend. And I acknowledge the insights, support, and camaraderie of academic colleagues and friends, including Dwayne Winseck, Catherine Middleton, Sara Bannerman, Gregory Taylor, Fenwick McKelvey, Ben Birkinbine, Nathaniel Weiner, and Dan Joseph.

Danny Nasset at the University of Illinois Press has earned my enduring gratitude for believing in the potential of this work from an early stage and for supporting me through this long process. The two anonymous reviewers assigned to an early version of this manuscript also provided great encouragement and sharp insights, while the editorial, production, and design staff at the UI Press have been a pleasure to work with.

Finally, as a seemingly inexhaustible source of sage advice and patience in the development of this research, thank you to my friend and erstwhile doctoral supervisor, Greg Elmer.

This book draws upon some previously published work. Chapter 5 is derived in part from an article published in *Javnost: The Public*, volume 31, issue 2, 2024, © 2024 EURICOM, at http://www.tandfonline.com/10 .1080/13183222.2024.2346704. This material is made available with permission of the publisher.

Digital Rights at the Periphery

Introduction

Making the Marco Civil

The inequities and exploitations of informational capitalism have in recent years moved out of the shadows and become matters of lively public debate. These include the algorithmic amplification of harmful content, industrial-scale privacy violations, and abuse of market power. The harms caused by informational capitalism do not settle evenly around the globe, however. At the core of the system, the leading companies are headquartered, the technologies are developed, and the wealth and power are concentrated. At the periphery, the damage wrought is the greatest: amplified ethnic discord contributing to genocide in Myanmar; a toxic legion of trolls, bots, and disinformation marshaled by tyrants from the Philippines to Iran; and attempts to manipulate elections in Brazil, Bolivia, and India, among many others.

One of the preeminent responses to the repressive power of informational capitalism—by policymakers and activists—has been the enactment of digital rights. Indeed, since the late 1990s a cascade of more than fifty initiatives have been launched by legislatures, intergovernmental groups, and advocacy organizations. In their dominant guise, digital rights comprise a blend of reimagined traditional civil rights, in the form of privacy and freedom of expression, and "digital native" rights, such as access, openness, and network neutrality. One of the first comprehensive frameworks of digital rights to be passed into law anywhere was Brazil's Marco Civil da Internet (Civil Rights Framework for the Internet), which was heralded as a global template by luminaries such as World Wide Web inventor Tim Berners-Lee, and as a "magna carta for the web" by *The Economist* magazine (*Net closes*, 2014, March 29).

When I stumbled out of the doors to the Brazilian Chamber of Congress late at night at the conclusion of the historic vote in 2014 that converted the Marco Civil into law, I shared the sense of achievement. Watching the bill's congressional rapporteur, Alessandro Molon, locked in a victorious embrace with members of Brazil's civil society organizations, my feelings, too, were those of having witnessed an unlikely triumph. During five years of bitter partisan conflict, geopolitical machinations, and relentless interest-group lobbying, the prospect of the Marco Civil ever becoming law had seemed vanishingly small.

But it was in the process of trying to understand how the Marco Civil could have been approved in the face of such formidable opposition—by undertaking a critical policy analysis mapping those disputes—that I called into question the premise for celebration. Did the Marco Civil, in fact, represent a *civic* framework of rights, one that safeguarded the internet as a medium that nourishes rather than undermines Brazil's democracy? And could the bill truly be considered *universal*, a globally transferable legislative blueprint? Instead, the argument at the heart of this book is that in this particular manifestation and in their general, dominant form, digital rights accommodate rather than challenge informational capitalism. Moreover, although digital rights are oft-framed as universal in their scope and application, the enactment of digital rights is highly contingent upon local sociocultural context and political economic configurations.

This book, then, is about how digital rights are shaped by the logics of informational capitalism at the periphery of the system. And this matters because despite its massed concentration of economic power, the internet remains a potentially democratic medium of communication, and the Marco Civil and similar digital-rights frameworks are entrusted by civil society organizations and governments around the world as a means to realize that "vulnerable potential" (Coleman & Blumler, 2009, p. 9). In terms of harm reduction, too, concerns among lawmakers, citizens, and activists around online disinformation, platform monopoly and data privacy have achieved unprecedented visibility, and digital-rights frameworks that follow the Marco Civil's blueprint are presented as part of the solution. Finally, this account matters because of the gross inequities of informational capitalism's global political economy and the pressing need to better understand the particularities of the periphery and how the forces of informational capitalism and forms of resistance manifest themselves.

Ultimately, this book is animated by a set of inquiries designed to produce insights into the general and particular dimensions of this "battleground of information" (Jordan, 2015) and into the broad set of forces that constrains the civic potential of digital rights, and the manner in which those forces materialized in the particular context of Brazil's history, culture, and political economy and how those, in turn, shaped the form and significance of the Marco Civil.

Such particular insights include how the contributions of the Partido Pirata (Brazilian Pirate Party)—largely unheralded and certainly ignored by the architects of the Marco Civil—presented an alternative and much more substantive vision of what digital rights could mean in Brazil. The party's vision of digital rights was premised upon collectivist principles, broader social justice concerns, and structural reforms to the internet's infrastructure and political economy. Also, by undertaking a systematic analysis of the corporate consultation around the Marco Civil, this book casts a light onto the competing tangle of economic interests that delimited the bill's civic potential. These represent more than simply the inevitable friction of multistakeholderism, however, and the current volume shows how these corresponded more meaningfully to the dynamics of informational capitalism. Finally, although the revelations of whistleblower Edward Snowden undoubtedly represent the most widely recognized event discussed in these pages, their relevance in the context of the Marco Civil lacks any comparable understanding. Also demonstrated here is the connection across multiple dimensions: how Snowden's revelations forced the mechanics of informational capitalism out of the shadows and into the public eye, how that sudden visibility impelled the digital rights of the Marco Civil toward legislative approval, how the revelations created the conditions for the policy discourse of "data sovereignty," and how that placed Brazil on a geopolitical collision course with the United States.

Adjusting focus to account for the broader insights provided by this book, studying the Marco Civil illuminates how the dominant paradigm of digital rights serves to consolidate rather than check the exploitative logics of informational capitalism. Within the dominant approach to digital rights, there is a clear emphasis on individual rights and freedoms, especially in terms of expression and privacy, realized through technical and market-based solutions, such as network neutrality. Fundamentally, informational capitalism's core logics of commodification and control are unchallenged when the subjects of rights claims are atomized individuals, when those claims are pursued on the terrain of consumption, and when the liberties they safeguard serve as fuel for a system of accumulation and exploitation. Moreover, what is omitted from this paradigm is just as important as what is included. Conspicuously absent is any connection to broader social justice concerns, any focus on the internet's hypercommercial character or on public provision of content or services. Indeed, it is a core argument of this book that in order to recover the civic value of digital rights, we must draw upon the vitality of the communication rights tradition, to *marry together systemic reform of the communication environment with safeguards for individual rights* and to move beyond the smothered ambition of harm reduction to envision an internet that actually contributes to equity, justice, and a substantive democracy.

Introducing Informational Capitalism

In trying to appreciate how the dominant paradigm of digital rights has seen its civic value eviscerated and to assess the nature of the threats posed to internet users qua citizens that digital rights such as the Marco Civil are supposed to rebuff, it is essential to account for the salience of information and communication to contemporary capitalism.

That interrogation of capitalism has been addressed by multiple theorists and yielded a slew of prefixes: cybernetic (Robins & Webster, 1998), digital (Schiller, 1999), informational (Castells, 2000), communicative (Dean, 2005), networked (E. Fisher, 2010), cognitive (Moulier-Boutang, 2011), platform (Srnicek, 2017), and surveillance (Zuboff, 2019).

Selecting Castells's coinage of "informational" may appear arbitrary, as most of the concepts in the above list recognize the centrality of the commodification of information and communication networks to capitalist processes of production and accumulation and draw our attention to the concentrations of power and harms that follow. The concept of informational capitalism is arguably the most analytically satisfying, however. The following quote from one of the foremost theorists of informational capitalism discussing its spatial dimensions explains why:

> A global space is constituted by the interaction of global technological systems and transnational (economic, political, cultural) organizations and institutions. This space is characterized by global flows of capital, power, and ideology that create and permanently recreate a new transnational regime of domination. (Fuchs, 2009, p. 395)

The interrelationship between the technological apparatus of informational capitalism and its social-structural forms is a key dimension to understand. In the case of the Marco Civil, one of the reasons that it represents such a rich case study in the functioning of informational capitalism is the way in which different "institutions"—"political" (various ministries and agencies of the state), "economic" (media, telecoms, and web platforms), and "cultural" (civil society organizations)—battled to shape the Brazilian internet according to their preferred values and logics. Indeed, informational capitalism as an analytic schema does not limit its focus to web or technology companies but encompasses any actor that relies on informational resources to accumulate profit and/or to maintain power, including media conglomerates, telecom companies, state actors, and so forth.

Informational capitalism is a "global space" and establishes a "transnational regime" (Fuchs, 2009, p. 395). This observation is also integral to this study as Brazil exists at the periphery of an exploitative system from which power is wielded primarily from the center. Finally, Christian Fuchs notes that the system is characterized by flows of *capital, power,* and *ideology.* It is, indeed, one of the foundational arguments of this book that informational capitalism must be analyzed across both its material and symbolic dimensions: capital *and* ideology. Moreover, the flows of power underscore the importance of digital rights and their potential to serve as safeguards against the exploitations of informational capitalism yet at the same time remain highly vulnerable to the material and discursive power exercised within it.

Ultimately, it is under the conditions of this economic system that the development of any set of digital rights for the internet would be contested, a system in which the logics of profit and control prevail, a system in which an information network truly harnessed for civic ends would be anathema. Moreover, this particular set of disputes occurred in Brazil, a society and a market at the periphery of this system, a reality that shaped the nature of the Marco Civil and complicates the triumphant claims that its contents represent a *universal* framework of civic values for the internet. In effect, write once, run anywhere, as software developers might say.

Many Brazilian scholars have produced rich and detailed accounts of the Marco Civil's tumultuous five-year journey from a cherished vision of Brazilian technologists and activists to its passage into law, via unprecedented online consultations, intense corporate lobbying, and indefatigable civil society advocacy. These accounts center alternately on the legal novelties of the bill (Brito, 2015; Santarém, 2010), its innovative policy development (Abramovay, 2017; Papp, 2014), and the role played by civil society activism (Solagna, 2015). The Marco Civil has also formed part of other works by international scholars focused on the significance of the internet in Brazil's democratic practices (O'Maley, 2015). The common thread that runs through these works is in framing the Marco Civil as an improbable triumph for a "free and open" internet.

The uniqueness, however, of this account is, I contend, that the digital rights of the Marco Civil accommodate rather than challenge the systemic inequities of the internet that, in turn, derive from the logics of informational capitalism. Informational capitalism is a system advanced through discursive and material power, and we need to be attentive to both dimensions in order to understand how it sustains itself. As such, a dual analytical approach for using discourse and political economic analysis is applied here to examine how the Marco Civil was denuded of genuine civic potential. Finally, as informational capitalism is an uneven global system, understanding how it manifests itself at the periphery is needed in order to appreciate how the Marco Civil was not a smoothly replicable template but a fiercely contested and highly contextual phenomenon.

Defining Digital Rights

That digital rights elude ready definition is one of the few things on which scholars of the topic concur (Goggin et al., 2017; Isin & Ruppert, 2015; Karppinen & Puukko, 2020). The panoply of applicable names reveals the uncertainty: user rights, internet bills of rights, internet-related human rights, and rights of the digital era (Pettrachin, 2018). Partly, the lack of clarity derives from uncertainty around their intellectual lineage. Do they represent a reimagining of venerable rights, such as freedom of expression and assembly for the internet era, or a set of "digital native" rights, such as "the right to be forgotten"?

Is there a direct line to be drawn to the human rights tradition, or does the moral, political, and technological scope of digital rights represent a radical disjuncture? Do the champions of digital rights build upon the communication rights movement of the 1970s, or is that history largely disregarded? Can network neutrality be conceptualized as a right at all? What is the proper site of authority for digital rights claims: the platform or the state? These questions are important and will all be addressed, at least in part, in the pages of this book, but for now it suffices to delineate the concept of digital rights as it applies in this study.

What is difficult to contest is that the codification of digital rights—by civil society and government actors—represents *a programmatic response to the exercise of repressive power within informational capitalism*. Hintz and Milan (2011) chronicle the transition within cyberspace from "policies of liberation" to "policies of control" that included the rapid rise of digital state surveillance, the blocking of websites by authoritarian governments, and the throttling of web traffic by telecoms companies. Netizens developed a commensurate awareness that excessive state and private power on and through the internet should be checked by advancing an agenda of user rights.

That agenda of digital rights became a cascade of initiatives, enumerated at over fifty by one large-scale content analysis (Pettrachin, 2018). There is a huge variety in the type of initiatives that advance an agenda of digital rights, from manifestos devised by advocacy organizations (e.g., the Association for Progressive Communication's Internet Rights Charter, one notable attempt to align the internet with the values of human rights in 2006), to intergovernmental statements (the Charter of Rights and Freedoms for the Internet of the Internet Governance Forum in 2014), to national legislation (e.g., Brazil's Marco Civil da Internet in 2014). Moreover, a small cluster of groups has emerged within civil society whose principal remit is the advancement of digital rights. These include the international Access Now group, the Pakistani Digital Rights Foundation, and the Centre for Digital Rights in Canada. Other better-established civil society organizations (CSOs) that possess a more varied agenda but also advocate for digital rights include the Electronic Frontier Foundation, Pirate Party (across multiple independent, national chapters), and Article 19 (with the latter two prominent in the case of the Marco Civil). Within this complex network of organizations and initiatives, there is more diversity than coherence.

Research shows, however, that there appears to be a dominant paradigm in terms of the nature of the digital rights that are promoted (Gill, Redeker, & Gasser, 2015; Isin & Ruppert, 2015; Padovani, Musiani, & Pavan, 2010; Pettrachin, 2018). A dominant framework for digital rights has emerged that combines a reimagining of traditional civil rights for the internet, in the form of privacy and freedom of expression, with digital native rights in the form of access, openness, and innovation. This agenda also exhibits an uneasy tension between rights claims based upon the figure of the citizen and those focused upon the consumer. More critically, we can also identify that it is a framework individualized by "the trope of freedom" (Franklin, 2013, p. 143) and is populated by individualized liberties and technical and market-based fixes. Crucially, the agenda for digital rights continues to represent a core part of the policy mix for platform regulation in jurisdictions throughout the world (as discussed further in the concluding chapter to this book). For readers less familiar with policy terms, such as network neutrality and safe harbors, the appendix to this book briefly defines them and explains their final resolution within the Marco Civil law.

Tracking Power through Structure and Symbols

To identify the theoretical and methodological approaches required to unpick the entwinement of the digital rights paradigm and informational capitalism in the case of the Marco Civil, we must first take a step back and identify what it is that lies at the heart of this study. This attempt at diagnosis can show that the Marco Civil is fundamentally a story about power: an examination of how it is exercised by actors when an object in dispute—the internet—one that possesses great economic and civic value, is opened up for contestation to an array of conflicting interests. From this it follows that we must find the means to provide the fullest possible account of that power, across both its structural and symbolic dimensions.

Theoretical Approach

One analytical toolkit that takes the study of power as its defining focus is critical political economy. Defined succinctly by Smythe as research on "the power processes within society" (1960, p. 563), a critical political economic analysis implies a commitment to grasping the social totality and as such is both explanatory and prescriptive. One subset of the "mother discipline," the political economy of communication, is attentive to both the ownership structures of particular media and also the way in which beliefs and myth are presented therein that challenge or reinforce particular sets of social relations (Mosco, 2009). The political economy of communication is therefore particularly apt for analyzing the phenomenon of informational capitalism. It not only permits an appraisal of the economic power of actors, such as web platforms and media conglomerates, but then also to theorize the implications of those inequities for social relations writ large.

Although a founding tenet of the political economy of communication is that it attends to both "the symbolic *and* the material" (Comor, 2011, p. 44), the fact that its primary units of analysis tend to be institutions means that it tilts heavily toward a macrolevel focus that can elide the microlevel processes that underpin them. Mosco indeed warns that this zealous focus on institutions can mean that the "presumed power of media giants takes on its own mythic characteristics" (2005, p. 163).

One way to address this imbalance is to employ a discursive analysis alongside the political economic, one that is more attentive to the symbolic dimension of power. This is essential for this study for two reasons. The first is that we need to establish how informational capitalism sustains and legitimates itself through discourse and particularly how the dominant paradigm of digital rights has been shaped by this dimension of power. The second is the need to analyze the particular discourses that were present in the development of the Marco Civil because, as Streeter notes, "policy discourse is properly understood, not just as a kind of mystification of power relations coming from elsewhere, but as a *constitutive* part of those power relations" (2013, p. 495).

Although many scholars operating in the political economy and discourse traditions might consider the two approaches to be incommensurate, others have exploited their potential overlap. The work of Newman (2013; 2019) examining the contestation of network neutrality in the United States and of Streeter on communication policy (1996) and the cultural construction of the internet (2011) both pair discursive and political economic analysis to great effect. Efforts have indeed been made by the likes of Sum and Jessop (2013) to codify this pairing into a coherent and structured research model, a "cultural political economy." I, however, do not recognize the need to adopt one holistic model but, instead, to accept the value of an eclectic analytical approach for a dynamic object of study, selecting from a box of lenses to achieve the sharpest focus.

Accordingly, this book draws from critical discourse analysis (CDA) (Fairclough, 2003; Wodak & Meyer, 2009) and post-Marxian discourse analysis (Dahlberg, 2010; Laclau & Mouffe, 2001) in order to appreciate the constitutive role of discourse in this case. As Wodak and Meyer (2009) make clear, "discourse is structured by dominance; that every discourse is historically produced and interpreted" (p. 3). The manner in which the dominance of informational capitalism is legitimated through discourse is indeed a foundational component of this book.

According to post-Marxian discourse analysis, meanwhile, discourse functions as a mode of power to assign a preferred set of meanings to otherwise empty "signifiers" and to exclude alternative interpretations (Laclau & Mouffe, 2001). This approach sensitizes my analysis to the role of meta-signifiers, such as "freedom," "openness," "efficiency," and "neutrality," that are central to the discourse of digital rights, in general, and the Marco Civil, in particular. Indeed, my appreciation of the role of such signifiers owes a foundational debt to Fisher, whose analysis of the "digital discourse" (2010) has done much to guide my own thinking.

Methodology

The research presented in this book harnessed the benefits of triangulation with the application of three qualitative methodologies: discourse analysis, semi-structured elite interviews, and document analysis. These methodologies were applied to events from the time period 2009 through 2014 and are structured in a sequential exploratory research design, with the insights gained from each phase informing the execution and analysis of the one that followed.

Phase 1

Qualitative semi-structured elite interviews represented the primary methodology involving nineteen interviews with protagonists selected from the principal stakeholder groups responsible for the development of the Marco Civil, as well as a further four background interviews with academic and legal observers. The in-situ interviews took place in Rio de Janeiro, São Paulo, and Brasília in March 2015 and were conducted in either Portuguese or English. One interview with the secretary of legislative affairs at the Ministry of Justice occurred in 2018 using video conferencing software. All translations of Portuguese-language interviews, blog posts, and academic and media texts in this book are my own.

The interviewees were identified using a purposive sampling strategy based on their responsibilities within organizations that were prominent in the Marco Civil process. My interview sample included representatives of civil society organizations, telecommunications, media and web platforms, and government ministries. With two exceptions, all of these individuals agreed to be named. In the case of the anonymous participants, we agreed that I would refer to them in this work simply as "senior executives" in their respective industries (the web technology sector and telecommunications).

The interviewees were from three principal groups:

Civil society, seven individuals. Three researchers from the research laboratory Centro da Tecnologia e Sociedade (CTS) at the think tank Fundação Getulio Vargas (FGV), one founding board member from Brazil's Internet Steering Committee (CGI), two directors and one campaigner from communication and consumer rights organizations that advocated for the Marco Civil (Intervozes, IDEC, and Proteste), and one independent activist who led early campaigns to establish civil rights for the internet.

Corporate sector, five public policy executives/in-house counsel. Two from the media sector (Grupo Globo and Grupo Folha), one from the web technology sector (US web company), and two from the telecommunications sector (one from the long-distance carrier Embratel and one from the industry association Sinditelebrasil).

Within government, seven individuals. The Marco Civil's congressional rapporteur; the national secretary for information technology policies of the Brazilian government; a senior policy adviser at the state telecoms regulator, Anatel; the public consultation manager for the Marco Civil at the Ministry of Justice; a senior technology policy adviser for the Workers' Party (PT); and two holders of the office of secretary of legislative affairs at the Ministry of Justice.

Phase 2

Critical discourse analysis allows identification of the discourses used by the principal actor blocks that participated in the development of the bill, to identify the agendas or "logics," brought to bear on the process, or, in essence, the *politics* of internet policymaking. The CDA focuses on a dataset of mainstream press articles generated through keyword searches of Marco Civil da Internet and of Marco Civil of the *Folha de São Paulo* and *O Globo* newspapers from 2009 through 2014 using the Factiva database, as well as a selection of blog posts, press releases, op-eds, public speeches, and records of public online participation. The results of this CDA and the earlier interviews then informed the subsequent and final phase.

Phase 3

Document analysis forms the final phase by tracking the codification of the Marco Civil through its various legal drafts from the initial framework jointly proposed by the Ministry of Justice and the Getulio Vargas Foundation in 2009 to the final text approved by the Brazilian Senate in April 2014. By overlaying the data from the preceding two phases of analysis, I chart how particular provisions in the bill were changed according to the agendas pursued by the different actor blocks—as well as the impacts wrought by external events, such as the US National Security Agency (NSA) surveillance revelations—ultimately showing how the logics of informational capitalism were manifested in the digital rights of the Marco Civil.

Overlaying these three phases, a political economic analysis was applied to the findings that emerge, assessing how and why key economic sectors attempted to influence the scope and form of the Marco Civil and how they correspond to the logics and mechanics of informational capitalism. Political economy becomes, therefore, the glue that binds the three methodologies into a coherent whole.

The Road Ahead

To establish the context for this study, chapter 1 lays out an analytical framework to understand the functions and scope of informational capitalism. The first of four principal sections examines the logics of informational capitalism—grouped into two broad brackets of commodification and control—showing that despite its expansive nature, the system possesses a coherent core and consistent internal drives. These demonstrate how the civic safeguards codified in the Marco Civil serve more to facilitate than disrupt informational capitalism. Also identified are the core sectors within informational capitalism that overlap with stakeholder categories in internet policymaking. This provides a template to evaluate the actions of key actors around the Marco Civil, how they advocated for or resisted elements of the bill, and why.

The dynamics of informational capitalism is the second principal focus and examines the tensions and synergies between actors within the system. This accounts for the mechanics employed by these actors to advance their agendas, as well as the resistance exerted by actors external to the system. The resulting tensions help to explain the divergent policy positions adopted with regard to the Marco Civil.

Surveying the zones of informational capitalism is the third main section, an effort to address the most significant gap within existing accounts of the system, that of its core-periphery nature. This is essential to establish because Brazil's status at the periphery of informational capitalism was pivotal to the way the Marco Civil developed and the significances that can be assigned to the provisions within the law.

The final section moves away from political economy to establish how informational capitalism sustains and legitimates itself through discourse and particularly how the paradigm of digital rights has been shaped by this dimension of power. This section traces the development of digital rights to show how alternate visions for digital rights became marginalized. This is essential because it shows the arc of digital rights can be traced through the Marco Civil and how its tenets go with the grain of informational capitalism.

The next three chapters of this study present a chronological account of the policy development of the Marco Civil, examining the contestation of digital rights at the periphery of informational capitalism.

Chapter 2 primarily adopts a discourse focus in order to understand the narratives that were formative in delimiting the Marco Civil's civic potential from its inception. The first section picks up the threads laid out at the end of the previous chapter to show how cyberutopian discourses valorizing user freedom and expression used by blogger activists were prominent in the Marco Civil's prehistory. These championed web platforms and therefore guided a focus toward the perils of state censorship but precluded focus on the internet's political economy. Also identified are the technocratic and neoliberal discourses that constituted the bill's unofficial genesis.

When the Marco Civil became a government project, an "interpretive community" (Streeter, 1996) of young lawyers in intellectual property (IP) further circumscribed the bill's civic potential. The chapter then critically interrogates the processes of public and multistakeholder consultation that imbued the bill with democratic legitimacy, showing how the debate was framed in a way that precluded any genuine challenge to the logics of informational capitalism.

Chapter 3 employs a different lens to predominantly focus on the material power exerted by the core actors of informational capitalism to shape the bill according to their interests as it reached the Brazilian Congress. I operationalize the dynamics of my analytical framework to show how the telecoms sector, web platforms, broadcast media, and the IP-rights lobby alternately formed alliances of convenience, or advanced bitter rivalries, with regards to the core provisions in the Marco Civil.

This chapter focuses particularly on the measures of network neutrality and limited third-party liability. In the former case I contend that the paradox of network neutrality is that the more fiercely the telecoms sector resisted the measure, the more civil society groups were convinced it was a core civil right and discounted more substantive alternatives. The contestation of safe harbors or limited third-party liability for platforms is charted, and the chapter argues not only that safe harbors serve as a shallow proxy for freedom of online expression but reveals how its limited civic value was further diminished in order to win the support of the Globo media group.

Chapter 4 examines how the Marco Civil was finally freed from congressional deadlock by the Snowden revelations of US surveillance in Brazil, with President Dilma Rousseff using the bill as a core plank of her policy response. This sparked an intensification of conflict between rival sectors of informational capitalism, as all interested parties sought to secure their agendas during the bill's end game, resulting in a further dilution of the Marco Civil's civic value.

A defining tension in this period was how the government advanced the contradictory policies of data sovereignty and digital rights. The former was a resurrection of a recurring historical narrative of technological sovereignty and a legacy of Brazil's peripheral status. It focused on political economic and infrastructural measures to advance Brazil's power within informational capitalism but came into conflict with the expressive digital rights of the Marco Civil. This chapter also shows how Brazil's security services and the telecoms sector were able to secure coveted amendments for data retention and future business models, constituting major new restrictions on the civic rights of Brazil's internet users.

Chapter 5 considers the Marco Civil's early legacy in the context of President Jair Bolsonaro's election victory and his subsequent policy assault on digital rights in Brazil. Systematic attacks on freedom of expression online, widespread electoral disinformation campaigns, the violation of network neutrality through zero-rating schemes, legislative proposals to criminalize content moderation, and the continued market dominance of

US platforms all characterized the first years of the Marco Civil in Brazil. Here also considered are the implications for digital rights of the global rise of far-right populism and its use of social media.

The concluding chapter recaps the principal contributions offered by this book: an analytical framework for informational capitalism, a genealogy of digital rights, a legislative history of the Marco Civil, and an emphasis on understanding both the political economic and sociocultural particularities of the periphery. Moreover, by evaluating the Marco Civil in the context of the widely chronicled "techlash" that began to unfold from 2020, we can reflect on the fate of the digital-rights paradigm and contemplate how civic safeguards can adapt to the next phase of global capitalism.

1

Understanding Informational Capitalism

Logics, Dynamics, Zones, and Discourses

Is ours a new kind of society, as was
[industrial] capitalism, or is it just
a form of capitalism, perhaps to be
called informational capitalism?
—Vincent Mosco

The first task for this book is to draw the fullest picture possible of the phenomenon of informational capitalism. It is, after all, the core argument of this study that the proper context for understanding the significance of the Marco Civil is the system of informational capitalism: to advance that argument, we must know what that system is.

The panorama of contemporary capitalism and the centrality of information and communication described by such theorists as Castells (2000), Srnicek (2017), and Zuboff (2019) comprises multiple vignettes, and this chapter draws from all of them. Some accounts use the lens of class and labor (Dyer-Witheford, 2015; C. Fuchs, 2009; Scholz, 2016), discourse analysis (Fisher, 2010), the political economy of telecommunications (Schiller, 1999, 2007), or critical legal studies (Cohen, 2019). Not one of them, in isolation, however, offers a broad-spectrum analysis of the system of informational capitalism, one that can reconcile its multiple dynamics, identify its key actors and core logics, and appreciate the co-constitution of its political economy and discourses.

Partly, we can attribute the absence of such an account to the expansive nature of the system and the fact that its activities overlay numerous academic fields. Informational capitalism thus lends itself to a siloed analysis.

But, in the absence of the proper tool, sometimes we must build our own. To that end, what follows is a provisional attempt at a schematic of informational capitalism, engaging with the key accounts in such overlapping fields as critical legal studies, political economy of communication, critical media studies, surveillance studies, and critical discourse analysis. There are four principal sections to this framework: logics, dynamics, zones, and discourses.

The *logics* of informational capitalism—grouped into two broad brackets of commodification and control—show that for all of its variety, the system possesses a coherent set of internal drives that impel it "further in its flight into the future" (Dyer-Witheford, 2015, p. 188). This must be properly understood to show how the civic safeguards codified in the Marco Civil do not imply a disruption of informational capitalism but, in fact, facilitate its continued expansion.

The *dynamics* of informational capitalism refer to the tensions and synergies that exist among the various sectors that make up the system. This takes into account the *mechanics* employed by these actors to further their interests, as well as the forms of *resistance* adopted by external actors—activists, civil society organizations, social movements—that sometimes impede the fulfilment of those interests. Although the broad logics of informational capitalism remain consistent, the manner in which they are advanced by different actors is not always complementary. The resulting tensions explain many of the material manifestations of informational capitalism and, particularly, the antagonistic positions adopted within the Marco Civil's policy development.

Accounting for the *zones* of informational capitalism is an effort to address the most significant gap within existing accounts of the system: that of its core-periphery nature. While the notion of "core-periphery is well established within theories of global capitalism generally (Wallerstein, 1974), the presence of this tiered structure within informational capitalism is underdeveloped. This is crucial to understand for this study because Brazil's status at the periphery of informational capitalism, and its enduring position at the margins of global capitalism generally was a defining factor in shaping how the Marco Civil process unfolded.

Finally, the chapter switches lenses to establish how informational capitalism sustains and legitimates itself through *discourse* and, particularly, how the dominant understanding of digital rights has been shaped by this dimension of power. I draw upon Fisher's (2010) contribution of the "digital discourse": his identification of a weave of narratives based on the material characteristics of networked ICTs that serves to legitimate new modes of accumulation and the social atomization of neoliberalism. The digital discourse emphasizes networked autonomy, expression, participation, and openness. The chapter shows how this discourse was decisive in shaping the development of digital rights in a way that accommodated, rather than challenged, the operational logics of informational capitalism. Before building out these struts, however, we should begin with a brief account of the emergence of the system of informational capitalism.

The Informational Turn in Contemporary Capitalism

By the 1980s three decades of embedded liberalism and Keynesian economics were beginning to be usurped by a policy framework referred to as the Washington consensus, which was defined by "fiscal austerity . . . free trade, inward investment deregulation, privatization, market deregulation, and a commitment to protecting private property" (Centeno & Cohen, 2012, p. 319).

The mission to envelop multiple spheres of precapitalist activity into the domain of the market from the mid-1980s saw corporate investment in data-processing networks boom in the United States, and successive waves of liberalization prompted greater investment and technological development, in a virtuous cycle (Schiller, 2007, p. 83). Corresponding processes of digitization and media convergence in the early 1980s heralded deregulation of cable television and telephony, enabling massive mergers and industry concentration (Mattelart et al., 2000, p. 83).

Accompanying the election of the two principal architects of neoliberalism, US President Ronald Reagan and British Prime Minister Margaret Thatcher, there began an all-out assault on the noncommercial provision of information (Harvey, 2015; Schiller, 2007). This was premised on the enormous promise of informational commodification, as Streeter makes clear: "From the point of view of the power structure of capitalism, information had the extraordinary advantage of being something you could imagine as thinglike and therefore as property, as something capable of being bought and sold" (2011, p. 76). One of the central elements of this strategic shift was the focus on the protection and enforcement of intellectual property. The globalization of IP norms reached its apogee in 1994 with the establishment of the World Trade Organization (WTO) and the Trade-Related Aspects of Intellectual Property Rights (TRIPS) agreements.

As we trace these developments into the 1990s, we can observe a familiar dynamic of domestic American communications policy being transposed to the international arena to facilitate the global growth of information products and services seen as imperative to US economic renewal. For many societies in the global south, changes were imposed aggressively by

US agencies and the World Bank (Powers & Jablonski, 2015, p. 41; Schiller, 1999, p. 47).

Despite the internet's well-chronicled, noncommercial origins with the US Advanced Research Projects Agency Network (ARPANET) pioneers (Abbate, 1999), by the mid-1990s, as Dyer-Witheford recounts, "changes in US state policy steadily created a privatized, deregulated, business-friendly information-superhighway. . . . These high-level changes sent commercial ventures cascading through the entire system" (2015, p. 89).

Accompanying the commercialization of the internet were the rise and consolidation through corporate mergers of the Big Five US movie studios bound by an IP regime that permitted it "an iron grip on informational assets capable of being deployed and transformed in many ways" (Drahos & Braithwaite, 2002, p. 179). Landmark legislation of this era that further sedimented the corporate control of communications was the Telecommunications Act of 1996, which served to entrench a monopoly market in the apparent service of greater competition (McChesney, 2013, p. 110), and the Digital Millennium Copyright Act in 1998, designed to protect the IP assets of digital-media companies (Lessig, 2006).

A frenzy of speculative technology investment comprised the dot-com bubble, from approximately 1995 to 2000, based on the rise of ad-tech and e-commerce ventures (Crain, 2021). Following the dot-com bubble's spectacular implosion, one of its key legacies was the creation of a digital advertising infrastructure in which the tracking and profiling of consumers begat a surveillance-based internet economy (Zuboff, 2019).

Logics: Control and Commodification

A cursory analysis of the informational turn in contemporary capitalism reveals a range of processes that facilitate the production, accumulation, and the consolidation of resources and power. I call these the "mechanics" of informational capitalism, and according to the schema that this section develops, they correspond to the two central logics of informational capitalism: *control* of information, with the goal of *commodifying* it. It is important to understand that these logics do not represent an either/or proposition; instead, they are both always operative. Appreciating their duality is akin to a figure/ground illusion; when you cast your gaze on one, the other fades from view (while remaining demonstrably present).

Identifying these as the core logics of the system is not only an analytical expedient. It forces one to be cognizant of the exploitation and injustice inherent in this mode of accumulation. The control of information—extracted from both the public and private spheres—and its conversion into a commodity form for the purposes of profit creation—leeches the democratic virtue from communication, impoverishes the commons, and robs citizens of their agency.

Commodification: IP, Datafication, Informationalized Production

Informational capitalism is a commodifying force to the extent that it extends the reach of the market into ever more domains of human activity using both technological and legal means. According to Harvey (2005): "Commodification presumes the existence of property rights over processes, things and social relations, that a price can be put on them, and that they can be traded subject to legal contract" (p. 165). In other words, the process of commodification describes how use value is transformed into exchange value. The dual character of the commodity, in terms of its relationship to production and exchange, is also essential to understand in the context of information, as Schiller explains: "First there are those instances where information is the final product; second are those in which information is an intermediate component of production" (2007, p. 21).

Intellectual Property

The codification of property rights through the intellectual property (IP) regime is one of the core aspects of the commodification of information and "the legal form of the information age" (Boyle, 2008, p. xiv). It is in the field of critical legal studies, unsurprisingly, where one notes the significance of IP most keenly (Cohen, 2019; Drahos & Braithwaite, 2002; Lessig, 2006). It should be noted from the outset that featuring IP under the heading of "commodification" rather than "control" is a matter of expedience that does not negate the dual character of the IP regime as both the enclosure *and* marketization of information.

The classic argument invoked in favor of intellectual property in its *ideal* form is that it ensures the provision of public goods. More specifically, patents encourage technological innovation, and copyright supports a vibrant cultural sphere, while trademarks enable the production of high-quality consumer goods. Analyses of informational capitalism, however, chronicle the many ways in which the reality of IP law and its enforcement fall far short of these laudable ideals and serve, instead, to reinforce a system of accumulation that results in critical damage to the "commons of society" (C. Fuchs, 2011, p. 89).

The propertization of information through the IP regime is, indeed, integral to the functioning of informational capitalism. It is a rote claim but bears repetition here that information is "non-rivalrous." One person's consumption does not diminish the capacity of another to enjoy it. This scenario becomes especially vivid when we consider the digitization of information and the ability to reproduce it at near-zero cost and how this problematizes the enormous profit potential of immaterial goods.

Scarcity must be therefore imposed in order to effectively commodify information, and this becomes the essential function of IP. And in what amounts to a vicious cycle of commodification, as the economic value of informational commodities steadily increases, so, too, does the incentive to further extend the legal protections presented by property rights. Cultural works are commodified through the application of evermore stringent copyright protection leading to "corporations in effect . . . owning and controlling culture" (Berry, 2008, p. 37). This protection represents the "private interest perspective" of copyright in the name of giant technology and media companies, such as Disney, IBM, Sony, and so forth (Drahos & Braithwaite, 2002, p. 169).

Patents, meanwhile, are applied to an almost exhaustive range of informational resources, from software to genetic sequences in seeds and drugs. The internationalization of these norms in such form as the TRIPS agreement and the World Intellectual Property Organization (WIPO) represents the legal framework of capitalist accumulation. Such an extension of property rights is a tremendous boon for the media industry, agribusiness, and the pharmaceutical sectors—overwhelmingly represented by corporations in the global north and, especially, the United States (Mirrlees, 2016)—but constitutes an enormous impoverishment of the resources previously held in common by humanity.

The alternative to this process of commodification is the information commons, a trove of intellectual resources made available to everyone to access freely. Wittel (2012) characterizes the commons as "a space that enables counter-commodification—not just on a personal but on a global level. It demonstrates how creative work can flourish without the chains of intellectual property regulations" (p. 331). In his efforts to create a theory of "information politics," Jordan (2015), meanwhile, has developed the concept of a distributive commons premised on the "simultaneous complete use" of information that negates its commodification (p. 206).

The construction of institutional support for this space, in the form of the Creative Commons, was undertaken in 2001 with the founding principle of expanding the availability of creative works while still securing recognition and rights for creators. As a counterpoint to the proprietary maximalism of corporate-oriented IP law, the Creative Commons is championed notably by the likes of its founders, Lessig (2006) and Boyle, for its "distributed creativity" (2008, p. 184), while Benkler (2006) lauds its "commons-based peer production." The approach has not found universal favor, however, and several critical voices acknowledge its unfortunate coherence with broader capitalist logics (Berry, 2008; C. Fuchs, 2011; A. Taylor, 2014).

Datafication

The other principal form of commodification, as both a mode of exchange and input into production, that comprises informational capitalism is associated with a different set of actors. Whereas the commodification of information inherent to IP is a core business strategy pursued by the major content producers and/or copyright holders—movie, recording, and games studios, digital games—as well as agribusiness, technology, and pharmaceutical corporations, we now need to turn our attention to the entities that profit principally from the commodification of data. These are the platform companies that are Big Tech: Alphabet, Meta, Microsoft, Apple, and Amazon. Common to many of them is a business model predicated upon the capture and storage of the traces of digital acts performed by internet users. This data is then converted into a commodity tradable between companies to facilitate online advertising and marketing. Data also corresponds in this way to Schiller's "intermediate component in production," as it is used to guide the provision of services in order to amass even more data. Information, in this context, has indeed become "the new oil of the Internet and the currency of the digital world" (Powers & Jablonski, 2015, p. 96).

With incredible foresight, Robins and Webster (1998) stated that the trajectory of "cybernetic capitalism" was leading to a scenario in which "potentially all social functions are to be incorporated and metamorphosed into information commodities." The process of "datafication"—one where actions are converted into quantifiable, digital forms—is the current manifestation of that vision. Although datafication can be applied in any field of human endeavor, it is those actions that occur in the digital domain that are particularly apt for this conversion because they take place on platforms that are designed to facilitate total data capture. It is, after all, a commonplace observation that the users of Google are not its customers but its product (Vaidhyanathan, 2013, p. 3).

Van Dijck (2013) analyses the term "connectivity" to describe the valuable resource generated by users of social-media platforms, as their digital actions, particularly, the "affective traffic coming from 'like' and 'favourite' buttons" (p. 162), are converted into economic capital for the owners of the sites. The concept of the "biopolitical public domain" from Cohen (2019) offers another useful way to think about datafication as "an act of imagination tailored to the political economy of informational capitalism" (2019, p. 50).

When data is converted into an economic resource, it can be sold to data brokers and ad networks, compiled into profiles, and used to facilitate highly targeted "behavioural advertising" (Crain, 2021). The data is both sold directly as a commodity and is used as a means to "refine the process of delivering audiences . . . to advertisers" (Mosco, 2009, p. 137), thereby also functioning as "an intermediate component of production." The fortunes derived from these practices are great, and the likes of Meta, Alphabet, and ByteDance command jaw-dropping market capitalizations. A flurry of accounts have emerged in recent years identifying the oppressive and discriminatory potential of data-based, algorithmic systems for already marginalized peoples (Eubanks, 2019; Noble, 2018; O'Neil, 2017). Perhaps, the most sweeping assessment of data commodification and its implications is evident in Couldry and Mejias's coinage of "data colonialism," a system in which a cabal of interconnected technology companies—"the social quantification sector"—"capture and translate our life into data as we play, work and socialise that can be used to sell our lives back to us, albeit in commodified form" (2019, p. 68).

Informationalized Production

Any broad consideration of the commodification processes of informational capitalism requires a return to Schiller's point regarding its dual character and the importance of information as "an intermediate component of production." Schiller himself (1999; 2007) and Dyer-Witheford (2015) contributed an understanding of how the ability of corporations to capture, store, and transmit information instantly and without regard to distance has enabled a globalized regime of capitalist accumulation. According to the latter's description, "electronic value chains, high-tech agribusiness and speculative electronic commodity markets" constitute key elements of informational capitalism (p. 121). Indeed, he cites data showing that the marginal economic worth of the information communication technology (ICT) sector relative to agriculture, resource extraction, and retail, among others, demonstrates "the real significance of ICT capital is what it has done for capital *in general*" (p. 141, emphasis added). Couldry and Mejias (2019, p. 54) also remind us that it is easy to overstate the economic importance of the "social quantification sector" in relation to the broader economy. Accordingly, the financial sector cannot be ignored as Cohen (2019) notes: "Within the political economy of informational capitalism . . . many other, ostensibly more tangible activities have come to be understood as . . . inputs to the extractive activities of finance capital" (p. 26).

The integration of data-processing technologies into manufacturing represents a potent case study of the importance of information as an intermediate part of the production process. In his typology of forms of platform enterprises, Srnicek (2017) names industrial platforms as one of the key emerging forms. Through the industrial internet of things, "material goods become inseparable from their informational representations" (Srnicek, 2017, p. 65).

In sum, then, we can observe how the architects of informational capitalism—identified primarily as the copyright holders, web corporations, and high-technology industries—commodify information in the form of culture and technology through the framework of intellectual property, the datafication of personal expression and social relations online, the harnessing of immaterial labor, and the way that global, instantaneous flows of information facilitate accumulation across the totality of capitalism. Considered next is the other foundational logic of informational capitalism—control—and how it is employed by the actors already introduced, as well as one hitherto underexamined in this section: the state.

Control: IP Law, Surveillance, Code

Control, in the form of IP law, surveillance, and the enclosure of digital spaces through code, facilitates the commodification of information, and the ensuing accumulation strengthens the capacity of those actors that seek to impose yet more control. As seen in short order, the equation is complicated a little when the role of the state is introduced. Its status as a facilitator of commodification—by compelling global legislation strengthening the IP regime, deregulation of communications and media industries, conducting industrial espionage, or funding high-technology enterprises—is a means to further entrench control in the form of geopolitical hegemony.

The IP Regime (Law)

Venturing now into the specifics of control, this section starts as did the last, by examining intellectual property. Whereas the earlier references to IP centered on the *fact* of commodification, here we concern ourselves with IP's application to control the *flow* of these commodities in such a way so as to maximize remuneration for rights holders.

Two of the most prominent works criticizing the early excesses of the IP regime are *Information Feudalism: Who Owns the Knowledge Economy?* (Drahos & Braithwaite, 2002) and *The Public Domain: Enclosing the Commons of the Mind* (Boyle, 2008). Both are inspired by the parallels between earlier historical phases and their practices of unjust enclosure with those parallels imposed upon the contemporary information commons through IP law. Two principal mechanisms of IP control are highlighted here: one facilitated by law, the other by technology. The latter is discussed first.

According to Lessig's famous maxim in *Code* (2006), "Code can and will displace law as the primary defence of IP in cyberspace" (p. 175). His overall thesis pertains to the implications for democracy as mechanisms of communicative control are covertly engineered into the internet. The copyright-protection provisions featured in the US Digital Millennium Copyright Act of 1998 and other moves to build mechanisms of control into digital artifacts and platforms that, in order to protect the rights of IP holders, generated alarm among many observers.

Schiller, for instance, claims that "exclusionary corporate control over information as private property is predicated on interweaving police powers throughout the tissue of social life" (2007, p. 52), while it prompted Boyle (2008) to claim that "as copying costs approach zero, intellectual property rights must approach perfect control" (p. 61). The means of this control takes various forms. Benkler (2006, p. 395) offers a useful five-tiered "institutional ecology" model that shows how control can be exerted over the various layers of digital communication in order to favor the interests of copyright holders. Berry distills the schema to offer the "3 Cs" of control: copyright, code and contract (2008, p. 36). Isin & Ruppert (2015) also signal the importance of the contract as a means of control in the context of exercising digital citizenship (p. 154).

Code

We now segue out of code as IP control into a discussion of code and enclosure as a means of control within informational capitalism, more generally. Deleuze's (1992) notion of the "society of control" has proven a foundational account, while Galloway's (2006) *Protocol: How Control Exists after Decentralization* was an influential corrective to the torrent of claims classifying the internet as an inherent technology of freedom. An important counterpoint to the implied novelty of code as a form of capitalist control is offered by several scholars (e.g., Kiss & Mosco, 2005; Robins & Webster, 1998) who argue in similar fashion that since the advent of industrial capitalism, technology has always been used as a means to control labor; technology has just become more diffuse and extensive. Control is also coded into other forms of information and culture beyond the internet's weave of servers and cables. The integration of digital rights management (DRM) software into the physical media of DVDs and CDs is the focus of Gillespie's *Wired Shut: Copyright and the Shape of Digital Culture* (2007).

Although these physical embodiments of culture may now appear archaic, the essence of Gillespie's argument represents an enduring critique of the way that the architects of informational capitalism control information at the expense of civic agency.

In addition to engineering control into technical architectures through code, web platforms employ political economic means to control lucrative markets through monopoly. According to McChesney (2013), the exploitation of network effects, technical standards, and patent acquisition are the core ways in which digital platforms "control access and the terms of the relationship, not the idea of an internet as open as possible" (p. 135). Apple's "walled garden" of mobile devices tethered to marketplaces of proprietary content is an iconic example of digital enclosure. Coded architecture is complemented by legal constructs, as Cohen argues, that "the combination of scale, asserted contractual control, and technical control enacts enclosure of both data and algorithmic logics as an inexorable reality of twenty-first century networked commercial life (2019, p. 45).

Surveillance

Surveillance as the monitoring of individuals and populations for the purposes of controlling them is carried out in the service of both corporate interests and state power. Campbell and Carlson (2002) characterize surveillance as the "commodification of privacy," a concept previously conceived as a civic right and now traded by citizens as a means of exchange for digital services. One key novelty of online data capture, one which the term "surveillance" does not adequately convey, is the *requirement* of users to divulge their data as a condition of passage for online services (Andrejevic, 2007; Elmer, 2004). The asymmetry of this ubiquitous digital surveillance is one of its fundamental characteristics: while individual citizens become increasingly transparent to the "watchers," the means and extensity of the capture remain stubbornly opaque. This imbalance necessarily engenders control as the impotence of the surveilled is compounded by their ignorance.

Crain (2013) identifies the architects of this digital surveillance infrastructure as the "data-marketing complex," comprising the familiar names of Google, Microsoft, and Facebook, as well as an extensive network of more-obscure data-collection entities. In his thesis, Crain underscores two dynamics of control related to this form of surveillance: one concerns the proprietary, enclosed digital spaces that are built to facilitate data capture, á la Facebook's social network; the other is the ensuing process of individualized commercial targeting, one that increasingly atomizes individuals and results in "the reproduction of social discrimination" (p. 252). The harms of online surveillance in the service of advertising have elsewhere been well chronicled. At the heart of Couldry and Mejias's (2019) critique of data colonialism is that ubiquitous data capture erodes the boundaries of the autonomous self required for society to function effectively, while Zuboff's milestone account of surveillance capitalism defines data capture in part as a process of "digital dispossession" (2019, p. 99).

In terms of the state, history instructs us that the covert collection of information has always been an essential component of maintaining political power, and, certainly, the monitoring of citizens by governments has been standard practice for centuries. As was revealed in exhaustive detail by National Security Agency (NSA) whistleblower Edward Snowden, the digital realm has been subject to far greater scrutiny as the US government worked in partnership with US internet companies to avail itself of their trove of user data (Greenwald, 2015, p. 21). This transfer represents, as Jordan neatly characterizes it, the transition of data "from one enclosure to a nation-state security force's enclosure" (2015, p. 110). In the context of the United States, the relationship between the US military and the nation's communication technology sector could, indeed, be considered symbiotic, with many coinages to label this entwinement that echo McChesney's "Military-Digital Complex" (2013).

Corporate complicity is not essential, however, as the architecture of the internet favors the openness of communication. Governments can exploit this, and efforts at securitization are based on a strategy of total data capture and threat profiling. This is in contrast to the methods primarily employed by authoritarian governments to block, filter, and censor online content that is considered a threat and are well chronicled by the likes of Deibert (2020) and Morozov (2011). If the means of state surveillance are well chronicled, what, though, of its ends? Governments are highly complex entities that require extensive informational inputs in order to function, but in terms of the role of the state within informational capitalism, one notable rationale for surveillance is in securing geopolitical advantage. Spying operations against friends and foes glean the information necessary to conduct diplomatic and military maneuvers as well as gaining economic advantage for corporate flagbearers. Examples of this include the NSA's hacking of the digital communications of Petrobras, Brazil's state oil company (Greenwald, 2015).

In sum, we can argue that control is the handmaiden of commodification, as the multiple means by which it is exerted—IP law, enclosure through code, monopoly, and surveillance—all protect and facilitate modes of private capital accumulation. In all these instances, the fundamental tendency is toward securing control over the circulation of information in order to maximize its profit potential.

The state, as another foundational actor within the system of informational capitalism, demonstrates that the requirement for control is based also on the need to further its geopolitical ambitions and to advantage its economy. The next section examines the dynamics of informational capitalism, or the leading sectors within the system, and the synergies and tensions that characterize their relationships.

Dynamics: Sectors, Synergies, Tensions, Resistance

The preceding section evidences that there is no unified theory or homogenous account of informational capitalism. Whether it is intellectual property or surveillance studies, different theorists suggest particular emphases and perspectives. Similarly, the *system* of informational capitalism is no monolith. The section may have identified commodification and control as its central logics, but this does not negate the tensions and contradictions that also exist within it. Intracapitalist competition remains a defining aspect of capitalism of all vintages, and this most contemporary version is no different.

Within and between the distinct sectors that together constitute the system of informational capitalism, contradictory mechanics to commodify information may be employed. For instance, the commodification of cultural goods through IP law benefits media conglomerates, while search engines generate more profit if those same commodities are freely accessible through the internet so that advertising revenue can be accrued.

Indeed, even within each sector, the drive to capital accumulation, to maximize one's share of finite spoils, ensures antagonism. To provide one very specific example, the Telecommunications Act of 1996 in the United States was a pivotal moment in the deregulation of the industry, one that McChesney characterizes as "a turf war between the regional Bell monopolies and the long-distance carriers" (2013, p. 106); Newman describes the moment as "neoliberalism at war with itself" (2013, p. 56). The tensions that one can observe within sectors of informational capitalism should not negate, however, an overall adherence to the system's core logics.

Moreover, informational capitalism is not a static system. As new technologies, policies, and business practices emerge, tensions between sectors might evolve into synergies, or vice versa. The case of web platforms and telecoms companies being staunchly opposed on the matter of network neutrality in the United States was resolved by a famed agreement between Google and Verizon in 2010 that saw the former concede mobile-network discrimination, creating an improbable synergy between the previous antagonists (Stiegler, 2013, p. 44).

Although many of the principal actors within informational capitalism can be identified in the examination of logics, it is necessary now to understand them in the form of sectors: economic categories defined by shared activities, interests, and business models. It is through an examination of these sectors, the mechanics they employ to impel the system's core logics, and the synergies and tensions among them—as well as sometimes within them—that we can fully appreciate the dynamics that constitute the system of informational capitalism. These dynamics form the texture of informational capitalism and help to illuminate the actions and agendas of those actors that contested the Marco Civil.

Resistance

The logics of informational capitalism do not run unopposed. As French sociologists Boltanski and Chiapello (2007) argue, forces of repression and resistance always exist within capitalism in a form of dialectical tension. Resistance, though, is distinct from the tensions also identified in this section. Those are *endogenous* to the system and represent competing means to impel the system's core logics. Resistance, however, comes from actors external to the system, who contest the logics of control and commodification. These actors include civil society organizations, social movements, activists, hackers, and sometimes legislators.

Their resistance manifests itself in myriad forms but can be usefully categorized across two axes. One is the *form* of resistance: whether it is predominantly *technological* in nature or *political economic*. The other is the *mode* of resistance: whether it seeks to *reject* the logics of informational capitalism by creating an alternative to them or represents an effort to contest or *disrupt* those logics.

The following are just a few examples of resistance that occupy various positions across these axes:

- policy activism that contests restrictions around IP (Sell, 2013) or promotes media reform (Waisbord, 2010)
- the Free Software movement that presents an alternative to the commodification of code (Söderberg, 2008)
- media piracy that challenges the commodity form of culture (G. Mueller, 2019)
- whistleblowers and leaks that reveal the obscure infrastructures of government surveillance (Lyon, 2015)
- platform co-operativism that operates outside of the enclosure and monopoly of web platforms (Scholz, 2016)

- union organizing at technology companies, such as Amazon
  (M. Fuchs et al., 2022); strikes at sites of hardware manufacturing
  that disrupt the exploitation of labor (Dyer-Witheford, 2015)
- encryption of communication flows that obstructs state surveillance
  (Hellegren, 2017)

These forms of resistance operate with varying degrees of efficacy, some constituting a direct challenge to the logics of informational capitalism, while others tinker with its mechanics and are readily co-opted into the system. Indeed, many observers are skeptical of any effective form of resistance being waged using platform technologies. Morozov (2011) argues that distraction and surveillance negate the efficacy of online activism, and Dean (2005) laments that the symbolic overload of communicative capitalism dilutes effective resistance (p. 62). Forms of resistance that make use of the infrastructure of informational capitalism are, indeed, vulnerable to scrutiny and control. Cohen (2019) notes that while platforms can amplify political activity, they "also co-opt the processes and outputs of distributed production in the service of data-driven profit strategies" (p. 250). Finally, as Couldry and Mejias (2019) also contend, even more skeptically, "the thesis that datafication technologies can have democratic potential should be treated with extreme suspicion" (p. 102).

It is not feasible to present an exhaustive account of all the dynamics of informational capitalism because of their scale and complexity. However, by examining one core sector in detail—the web and technology companies—we can appreciate some of these forces at work.

Web and Technology Companies: Synergies, Tensions, Resistance

Web and technology companies are those enterprises that have emerged with and are reliant upon the internet and are dependent upon "an extractive apparatus for data" (Srnicek, 2017, p. 48) for their business operations. These are also referred to colloquially as "Big Tech" or by the shorthand of the GAFAM group consisting of Google (Alphabet), Apple, Facebook (Meta), Amazon, and Microsoft, or more specifically as platform companies.[1] Srnicek (2017) offers a categorization of platforms that is useful here. "Advertising platforms" are those that datafy user behavior and use that information to sell targeted advertisements (e.g., Google and Facebook), "cloud platforms" (e.g., Amazon Web Services) own massive computing infrastructures and sell IT services to other digital businesses, and "lean platforms," like Uber or AirBnB, offer a digital interface and logistical services that leverage individually owned assets. The examples listed here represent the best-known examples of web and technology companies; however, there is a larger ecosystem of advertising networks, on-demand service providers, mobile software developers, and streaming services that are also reliant on information technology (IT) and data and can be encompassed within this sector.

Web and technology companies exist at the vanguard of the system of informational capitalism. This is evidenced by a number of metrics, not least by the size of market capitalization, a list that in recent years has been dominated by Microsoft, Amazon, Alphabet (Google), Apple, and Facebook (Meta) as well as Chinese tech giants, such as Alibaba and Tencent. Several have secured virtual monopolies in search, e-commerce, social networking, operating systems, and digital advertising, leading to huge concentrations of power and wealth. The strategy of these monopolists has been underpinned by core processes of information control: aggressive patent protection to secure software and mobile hardware (Alphabet, Apple) and the creation of enclosed platforms that negate the foundational open vision of the web (Meta, Apple). Moreover, the commodification of personal information within these controlled enclosures also represents a shared logic. Even more, these companies often take the form of platforms and as such constitute the primary scaffold of informational capitalism, one on which billions of users rely for communication and information services and one on which an entire ecosystem of smaller technology companies is based.

The manner in which this dominance is maintained implies synergies and tensions with other key sectors within informational capitalism, notably the security state, telecoms, media, and content production. Finally, we must also consider the forms of resistance that are employed by various actors against web and technology companies in order to contest their logics of commodification and control.

The interoperability of distinct technical systems is widely recognized as being a constitutive feature of the digital economy (Palfrey & Gasser, 2012). Although web and technology companies often seek to create proprietary enclosures of commodified data, those same groups are dependent upon content created by other organizations and users and by third-party applications. For these companies to generate advertising revenue, as well as to effectively surveil their users around the web, an information environment characterized by free flow is essential.

The American state apparatus, part of the core of informational capitalism, exhibits a particular and long-standing synergy with the operational imperatives of web giants, such as Google and Facebook, with regards to free flow. As early as 1869, the American state established the free flow of information and access to foreign markets as essential goals of its foreign policy (Winseck & Pike, 2008, p. 14); the free-flow doctrine was imbued with an ideological dimension during the Cold War (Nordenstreng & Thussu, 2015). The free flow of information has remained a touchstone of American policy to this day, as the state seeks to leverage its national corporate power to impose a global system of economic imperialism in lieu of military expansion. Google and others comprising the GAFAM group simply represent the latest generation of corporate emissaries capable of leading this mission and benefitting from US government initiatives such as the internet freedom doctrine announced in 2010 to the US government's more recent opposition to data localization legislation worldwide (Litt & Monroe-Sheridan, 2022).

More generally, the role of the US Department of Defense in the rise of Silicon Valley has resulted in everyday technologies, such as the global positioning system (GPS), voice-recognition, touchscreens, and the anonymity-enabling software Tor, all owing their existence in part to military funding (A. Taylor, 2014, p. 223). The extent of the military-internet complex does not end there, however, as it constitutes the nexus of US state surveillance. The infamous Prism program and its exposure by Snowden rendered visible a set of relationships characterized by Lyon (2015) as one of "mutual dependence."

Although the congruence around free flow between web platforms and states from informational capitalism's core is clear, the need for other powerful sectors to enclose and control information results in one of the defining tensions within the system. The content-production sector is reliant on a system of information control that protects the commodity form of culture through international IP regimes. Web platforms, exemplified by Google, benefit from the free flow of cultural commodities, from which they generate enormous advertising revenues. The nature of this tension between IP rights holders and web platforms was underscored in the conflict over the proposed Stop Online Piracy Act (SOPA) legislation in the United States, as it pitted one against the other (Anderson, 2013, p. 208).

Although the tension between free flow and copyright might appear to be irreconcilable, there is an important congruence to consider. Haggart and Jablonski (2017) make the case that the "free flow of information creates markets by exposure to intellectual properties, while copyright secures economic benefit to copyright holders from the flow" (p. 103). This potential for complementarity between the two mechanics should ultimately be judged by degree. As they exist in a form of uneasy symbiosis, maximalism on either pole harms the potential for both to be employed in tandem for the advancement of informational capitalism.

We can, however, also observe a clear synergy between web platforms and the content-production sector in terms of the architecture of commercial surveillance online. McChesney (2013) identifies "a synergy of interests between the commercial forces that want to monitor people surreptitiously online to better sell them to advertisers and the copyright holders who want to monitor people online to see who might be using their material without permission" (p. 126).

States in many parts of the world also favor information enclosure for the purposes of domestic political control and/or national security. In China, for instance, web platforms from the core of informational capitalism, most notably Facebook, X (formerly known as Twitter), and Google, are prohibited from operating because their emphasis on information flow undermines the hegemony of the state. Building a national information enclosure allowed Chinese web platforms, such as Alibaba and Bytedance, to dominate their domestic market (while monitoring domestic dissent) and become globally significant (Jin, 2015, p. 86). States that are not reliant on authoritarian control also contest the favored information flow of web platforms, as democratic governments also impose punitive measures against them over the flow of content deemed to incite terrorism or hate crimes, for instance.

The telecoms sector has maintained a long-running and acrimonious rivalry with web platforms over the use of network infrastructure. The chief executive officer of AT&T famously articulated this core tension: "Now what they would like to do is use my pipes free, but I ain't gonna let them do that" (quoted in Stiegler, 2013, p. 86). The conflict over network neutrality regulation in the United States saw web platforms and the telecoms sector take up opposing positions on the issue, as the former group recognized the grave threat that traffic management by carriers represented for the free flow of information. For the telecoms sector, meanwhile, the imposition of network neutrality regulation would signify ceding control over how they could commodify communication, for instance, by favoring proprietary applications through zero-rating models (Hoskins, 2019).

Despite the enormous power and reach of the web platforms, effective resistance to their exploitative mechanics comes in multiple forms. These can be plotted along the axis of form, between political economic and technological. In the former category, for those actors that Srnicek (2017) describes as "lean platforms," "platform co-operativism" has emerged as a potentially potent form of resistance. It represents a political economic mode of organization in which participants attempt to negate the exploitation of platform enterprises by establishing alternatives that are collectively owned and controlled and that employ equitable labor practices

(Scholz, 2016). These co-ops eschew the central logics of commodification and control by operating outside of the enclosure and monopoly of web platforms.

On the technological side, some activists have attempted to hack platform-user interfaces in order to challenge modes of online commercial surveillance, what Galloway calls "counter-protocological attacks" (2006). Forms of encryption and obfuscation, such as the use of the Tor server or the TrackMeNot browser extension, also serve to disrupt the surveillance infrastructure of web and technology companies. Finally, in a mode of resistance that bridges the technological and political economic, alternative architectures for social networking, such as Mastodon, that are not funded by venture-capital firms or based on targeted advertising, offer users a means to experience a form of online sociality that is not thoroughly commodified.

Table 1 gives some of the dynamics of this complex system. This is not an exhaustive survey and, for instance, omits mention of certain sectors that are intrinsically important to the system—such as financial services, pharmaceutical, agribusiness, advertising and/or public relations, and software development—because they are tangential in the case of the Marco Civil.

The next dimension of informational capitalism that must be accounted for is a reckoning with its global nature.

Global Political Economy: Core and Peripheries

Informational capitalism operates as a system of accumulation premised on relationships of exploitation, and as such it is founded upon inequities in power. These inequities so far in this chapter have only been examined in the abstract context of exploited users qua citizens and those system actors that direct the exploitation. A crucial step for this framework now is to transpose the reckoning of the logics and mechanics of informational capitalism onto a global political economy. In so doing we can appreciate the many implications of informational capitalism's inequities on a global scale. This is an essential undertaking because the Marco Civil as a framework of digital rights can only be properly understood within the context of Brazil's status at the periphery of this global economic system.

This is not virgin analytic territory, of course. Much of the heavy lifting in theorizing systemic global inequities has already been performed by scholars working within world systems theory, international political economy, media imperialism, and governmentality studies. The insights gained from this work have not been leveraged for the schema of informational capitalism in any systematic way, and as such, we need to assess how they can be transposed.

TABLE 1. The dynamics of informational capitalism

Sector	Actors	Mechanics	Tensions	Synergies	Resistance
Communication hardware	Apple, Huawei, Samsung,	IP law; datafication	security state	web/tech companies	manufacturing strikes
Content production (cultural industries)	media companies; recording movie and games; studios	IP law	web platforms	legislative state; telecoms	media piracy
Legislative state	trade missions, ministries	law, policy, and regulation	security state	security state	policy activism; civic engagement
Security state	military, intel agencies	surveillance/ securitization	legislative state; comms hardware	web platforms	leaks; encryption
Telecoms	América Movil, AT&T	surveillance; enclosure	web/tech companies	security state; content production	autonomous infrastructure; policy activism
Web/technology companies	Amazon, Facebook, Google	datafication; enclosure	telecoms; content producers	security state	platform cooperatives; hacktivism

In the 1960s and 1970s, theorists of Marxist world systems proposed the notion of a global political economy structured upon a capitalist core concentrated in the West, and a raft of peripheral nations where low-skill labor and resource extraction was exploited for the core's benefit (Wallerstein, 1974). Such an approach was disrupted by the emergence in the 1970s and 1980s of manufacturing zones in east Asia and Latin America, as well as the later rise of the BRICS (Brazil, Russia, India, China, South Africa) nations. Of a similar vintage and intellectual lineage, cultural or media imperialism emerged as a theory to explain the hegemony of the United States through domination of international institutions and media flows (Mirrlees, 2016). It must be noted that media imperialism as a framework also contends that the world comprises centers and peripheries and emphasizes the imbalances in structural power based on economic, military, and media measures (Boyd-Barrett, 2015). Its particular focus on media systems and the political economy of the communication industries means that it does not share the emphasis on information as the primary unit of analysis that defines informational capitalism as a framework. A key distinction, then, is that information-intensive sectors, such as financial services, pharmaceutical, and agribusiness, are subsumed within the former framework as part of the general economic power of imperial centers, whereas they sit at the forefront of an analysis oriented around informational capitalism.

The dissolution of the Soviet empire and the emergence of a multipolar, globalized world inspired a new set of analyses that challenged the continued relevance of cultural imperialism and world-systems theory. Appadurai's (1990) "global cultural economy" and analyses of multidirectional cultural flows and new global media centers, especially in the BRICS nations (Nordenstreng & Thussu, 2015), proved influential. Emerging at a similar time, although inspired by the diffusion of ICTs rather than geopolitical shifts, network theory as expounded by Castells (2000) attempted a global geography based on technosocial networks.

Such varied accounts emphasizing the diffusion of ICTs as well as the dispersal of cultural and political power have proven inadequate, however, to reckon with the rise of neoliberalism as global political economic orthodoxy. In turn, therefore, the pendulum swung away from celebrations of the cultural agency of the global south, toward a new reckoning of their exploitation. Hardt and Negri's (2000) extensive theorization of the postmodern biopolitics of empire was one of the most prominent efforts to engage with the global expansion of neoliberal logics.

Another set of explanations emerged out of critical political economy to account for the globalized nature of neoliberalism, with a common thread emphasizing the notion of coherent capitalist logics alongside local adaptations. Harvey (2005) emphasizes "the complex interplay of internal dynamics and external forces" (p. 117). Freedman (2008), in turn, underscores the notion of "diversity within convergence" in his study of the global neoliberalization of media policy (p. 43), while Schiller (2007) describes how "an omnipresent capitalist logic" and an "overarching congruence . . . do not necessarily generate global uniformities" (p. 121).

How, though, has this broad sweep of efforts to theorize global economic inequities been applied to the more limited project of analyzing informational capitalism? C. Fuchs (2009) and Jin (2015) both advocate for an updating of Lenin's analytical framework to understand the functioning of imperialism in the twenty-first century, one that can be understood as informational or platform imperialism, respectively. Mirrlees (2016) takes Schiller as his muse instead to argue convincingly that cultural imperialism is alive and well in the twenty-first century and is propagated by the United States with an updated suite of tools.

Couldry and Mejias's coinage of "data colonialism" (2019) is also worthy of mention, but data colonialism is not synonymous with informational capitalism. While these accounts affirm the existence of an exploitative core and an exploited periphery, the functioning of informational capitalism can be best appreciated when we cease to imagine it in an abstract sense and attempt to map its global geography, one apportioned into zones based on the directionality of relations of power and exploitation. For the particular cartography of informational capitalism, if we resurrect the spatial metaphor favored by world-systems theorists (Wallenstein, 1974) of the core and periphery, then we may usefully add the category of epicenter.

The epicenter is that configuration of actors—not simply nation-states—in which the economic and political power of informational capitalism is most concentrated, where the technological innovations that drive it are developed, and that in combination are used to orient the relationship with other zones to further consolidate its advantage. In terms of the metrics of informational capitalism, the dominance of the United States is unequivocal, although the rise of China's internet and technology sector and its development of critical infrastructural investments throughout the global south signify that China may be approaching equal billing (Mirrlees, 2023). Accordingly, the epicenter is occupied by a nexus of the security and legislative dimensions of the US and Chinese states, as well as those private-sector actors based within their borders, primarily, the content-production sector and internet and technology companies.

The core is well endowed with power and resources but comparatively less so than the epicenter and is rarely the subject of exploitation. It is made up of state and corporate actors located in other highly developed regions and countries, such as the European Union, Japan, and South Korea, including the likes of Nokia, Samsung, and Axel Springer. The periphery comprises those places where their integration into informational capitalism is primarily as sites of extraction. The level of integration into the system and the degrees of exploitation and resistance implied in these processes of accumulation, in turn, conditions the level of peripherality. These classifications are not static, however, and growing economic power can advance the status of a particular national market.

Moreover, in industries and market sectors that are largely outside of informational capitalism's circuits of accumulation and that comprise capitalist formations of older vintage, some global sites may constitute regional hegemons and bely their peripheral status within informational capitalism. Brazil, according to the analysis of Zibechi (2014), represents a "sub-imperial power" owing to the market power of its multinational enterprises (MNEs) throughout South America. For instance, of Brazil's top twenty MNEs, twelve are from the energy, food manufacturing, or transportation equipment sectors. The remaining eight are based in textiles, mining, metals, and chemicals (Fundação Getulio Vargas, 2015, p. 5). While these industries contain a significant informationalized component—patented manufacturing processes and ICT-based supply chains—they are defined primarily by their close connection to raw commodities.

This zonal system should not be misinterpreted as a structure of *domination*, however, as processes of adaptation and resistance at the periphery are integral to the functioning of informational capitalism as a global system. For example, to the extent that exploitative differential pricing mechanisms and punitive IP law are imposed upon countries in the global south, media piracy operates in a parallel illicit market as a form of resistance. We must also account for local actors in the periphery, such as Globo in Brazil or Televisa in Mexico, which employ the logics of commodification and control, that are capable of exerting regional dominance and while fully integrated into the global system of informational capitalism, cannot of themselves negate the peripheral status of their national base. State actors in the periphery also possess the agency to adapt or reject the imposition of exploitation from the core. In sum, informational capitalism extends itself globally in a fundamentally uneven manner, contingent upon local conditions.

Relationships of exploitation are substantiated through the major mechanics of informational capitalism detailed above. The manner in which these mechanics are calibrated establish zones through the production, consumption, transmission, and storage of information and associated technologies, primarily as sites where value is extracted or where it accumulates.

The zonal classification can, therefore, be judged using particular groups of metrics, such as:

- IP (royalties and patent registrations)
- trade and manufacturing (market dominance in informationalized industry sectors; trade balance in informational assets and high-technology exports)
- infrastructure (internet and telecoms penetration and critical internet infrastructure, such as submarine cables)
- policy and politics (degree of confluence between national policy and the systemic needs of informational capitalism; influence within global policy forums)

In the context of IP, the directionality of the flow of royalties is a clear indicator of the zonal classification of informational capitalism: the greater the derived benefits, the higher the status. Not only do IP royalties constitute an important drain on the limited resources of peripheral societies but they also create a form of knowledge divide that perpetuates their peripherality (Haggart & Jablonski, 2017). The number of patent applications filed by national residents is also correlative with a high degree of information-intensive economic activity and is thus suggestive of a country's zonal status within informational capitalism.

In terms of trade and manufacturing, it should be noted that for orthodox economics, a high proportion of high-tech exports is a positive indicator for a country's upward developmental mobility. Critical political economic research often shows, however, that low-wage manufacturing of high-technology goods—especially electronics—is the product of a relationship of exploitation (Inverardi-Ferri 2022). The case of China, meanwhile, offers a compelling example of the unevenness of informational capitalism, as despite the market capitalization of China's tech giants nearly equaling those of US platform companies, the brutal conditions of the "manufacturing iSlaves" in Chinese factories that assemble Apple's iconic iPhone have been well chronicled (Qiu, 2016).

The flow of cultural and media products also constitutes an important component of trade within informational capitalism. Media conglomerates based in the United States remain some of the globally dominant actors in the content-production sector (Birkinbine et al., 2017). Other analyses have shown that asymmetrically interdependent cultural and media industries exist outside of the United States, particularly in South Africa, Brazil, South Korea, and the like (Nordenstreng & Thussu, 2015).

Such is the dominance of these regional media giants—for instance, Brazilian telenovelas in Mozambique (Pota Pacamutondo, 2014) or Indian movies in Pakistan (Thussu, 2014) that these can be considered as media subimperialisms (Boyd-Barrett, 2015). The global flow of commodified cultural products within informational capitalism tends to follow its zonal structure as the products are exported down through the zones from epicenter to core and core to periphery. Although reception studies (Katz & Liebes, 1990) and theories of cultural hybridity and counterflow (Kraidy, 2002) may challenge the extent to which these media flows constitute a form of *cultural* domination, there is little to dispute the extent to which regional media giants, such as Grupo Globo in Brazil (Straubhaar, 2017) or Naspers in South Africa (Wasserman, 2018), achieve *market* domination in select peripheral markets through trade in their commodified cultural exports.

The mechanics of datafication, surveillance, and enclosure are the principal means by which commercial web services operate and, in so doing, advance the core logics of informational capitalism. Google, Amazon, Apple, Netflix, Microsoft, and Facebook, indeed, collectively lead the world in digital advertising, search, e-commerce, social networking, mobile operating systems, and video streaming services (Mirrlees, 2021). National markets at the periphery offer growth potential that web giants in saturated markets, such as the United States, clearly covet. The continued controversy around Facebook's global connectivity programs—for example, Free Basics—demonstrates the importance that the corporation places on penetrating peripheral markets where a lack of incumbent technology companies eases the path to monopolistic dominance and the continued economic growth demanded by its shareholders (Hoskins, 2019).

Another important dimension of trade is that the global south constitutes a form of terra nullius for data extraction by actors from informational capitalism's core with "multinational corporations scrambling to profile billions of potential new consumers" (Taylor, 2017). The conceptual overlap with earlier patterns of imperial extraction is widely noted. Coleman notes a twenty-first-century scramble for Africa (2018), while Isin and Ruppert (2019) analyze the reach of data's empire from metropole to colony.

In terms of infrastructure, the internet is often conceptualized as a layered system (Zittrain, 2008). There is little doubt, as noted above, that at the upper levels of content and code, internet and technology companies from the United States and, to a lesser extent, China dominate. Below that level, the situation is not radically different. Over 95 percent of all global internet traffic is transported by submarine cables (National Oceanic and Atmospheric Administration, 2020), a global system of fiber optics that was laid in large part during the dot-com boom of the 1990s (Telegeography, 2021). Winseck indicates that a surge of investment in submarine cables since 2008 has not been driven by the United States but predominantly by BRICS countries (2017, p. 241). These are mostly accounted for by four major Asian projects. In all of these, Chinese capital is predominant, with Huawei emerging as a major player in new cable projects, connecting underserved peripheral countries, such as Pakistan and Kenya (Akita, 2019). Moreover, major US web platforms, including Google, Facebook, and Amazon, possess ownership stakes in subsea cable projects, such as the Apricot submarine cable system linking six Asian countries (Roehrich, 2021). The core of informational capitalism is amply represented in this new infrastructure. Even if it was not, preexisting submarine infrastructure—estimated at around four hundred cables worldwide—is overwhelmingly owned by telecommunications companies from the system's core. Over 90 percent of those cables were laid by SubCom based in the United States, NEC from Japan, and France-based ASN (Akita, 2019).

Ownership of content-delivery networks (CDNs) is also extraordinarily concentrated, with the top four companies accounting for 93 percent of all such traffic. Three of those are based in the United States and one in China (Winseck, 2017, p. 242). Ultimately, as Couldry and Mejias (2019) observe, "the Global North still assumes the role of gatekeeper, as it did in the days of the telegraph and the telephone, and data flows continue to replicate the movement of resources from colony to metropolis" (p. 103).

Two other major considerations when assessing the structural disparities in the global political economy of informational capitalism are the role of policy and how presence and influence in important multinational institutions permit some nations to direct flows of power and capital to their advantage and relegate others to the margins. The significance of national policy for informational capitalism is succinctly explained by Powers and Jablonski (2015): "Put simply, the greater congruence between regulatory environments and technical standards, the more able Western corporations are to expand confidently into new markets and turn investments into revenue" (p. 108). Indeed, the manner in which US platform giants shape domestic policy through their massive lobbying efforts is surely reflected on the global stage (Mirrlees, 2021).

The most prominent forums of internet governance, such as Internet Corporation for Assigned Names and Numbers (ICANN), represent key sites of contestation for control of the internet's technical resources and exhibit the global imbalance between core and periphery that is characteristic of informational capitalism. ICANN coordinates policy related to the internet's global system of unique identifiers, such as the domain name system (DNS). ICANN was established by President Bill Clinton's administration in 1998, with the US corporation Verisign designated as the authority over the master root server and owner of the .com and .net top-level domains. One of the consequences of this, as M. Mueller reminds us, is that ICANN is "one of the few globally centralized points of control over the Internet" (2010, p. 61).

Given both its importance and its status as a private corporation beholden to the sovereign power of the United States, it is not surprising that ICANN has been a lightning rod for criticism for those peripheral nations frozen out of the forum. Brazil was one of those countries that in 2012 backed an International Telecommunications Union (ITU) initiative to wrest control away from ICANN and in so doing to align international telecoms systems more closely with the needs of peripheral nations. The tension between this goal and Brazil's commitment to multistakeholder internet governance is explored extensively in chapter 4 of this book.

The global political economy of informational capitalism is enormously complex, but by focusing on a few key metrics, such as IP, trade and manufacturing, infrastructure, and policy, we can capture many of the dimensions of exploitation and resistance that occur between the core and periphery of the system, as well as its uneven nature. As we proceed into the case study of this book, many of the facets of this globalized inequity will become apparent in the way in which the digital rights of Brazil's Marco Civil were contested at the margins of informational capitalism.

Discourses: Legitimation, Power, Digital Rights

The introduction to this book emphasizes that at its heart, this is a study about power and about how fundamental rights are contested in the context of a disputed sociotechnical system and an exploitative and inequitable global political economy. Thus far, the focus has been on the material dimension of power, establishing how we can analyze the systemic functions of informational capitalism with a political economic lens. Next established is how discourse functions as a corollary to material power. More specifically, an appreciation is needed of how discourse legitimates particular socioeconomic arrangements and forecloses alternate possibilities to delimit the cultural horizon (Feenberg, 1995). For the purposes of this study, this is essential because one of the foundational arguments is that the discursive construction of digital rights—one based on the legitimation discourse of informational capitalism (E. Fisher, 2010)—was a decisive factor in shaping the Marco Civil and in producing a framework of digital rights that would ultimately facilitate rather than challenge the exploitative logics of informational capitalism.

This section begins by establishing the approach to studying discourse and justifying its significance, followed by a narrowing of focus to the ways in which discourse works to legitimate capitalism and how it functions specifically in the context of informational capitalism. The work of Eran

Fisher (2010) is drawn upon here to examine what he calls the "digital discourse, that weave of narratives based on the material characteristics of networked ICTs and that responds to the artistic critique of capitalism and serves to legitimate new modes of accumulation and the social atomization of neoliberalism."

Lastly, this section develops Fisher's argument to show how the digital discourse has shaped the dominant conception of digital rights and to demonstrate how informational capitalism's legitimation discourse has produced a commonsense understanding of digital rights that prioritizes individual freedom, creativity, expression, and, ultimately, a set of depoliticized, market-based, technical fixes. This is manifested in a set of first-order rights—network neutrality, digital-data protection, and freedom of online expression—that fail to adequately challenge the systemic logics of informational capitalism in such a way as to secure civic rights of internet users and a medium of genuinely democratic communication.

The Matter of Discourse

Since the advent of the linguistic turn, a plethora of approaches has emerged that focus on the study of linguistics and discourse. Discourse is described by Fisher as an "episteme" or "a body of knowledge that is inextricably intertwined with technological reality, social structures and everyday practices" (2010, p. 15). According to Fairclough (2001), discourses are reproduced within the semiotic realm as "representations of how things are and have been, as well as imaginaries and representations of how things might or could or should be" (p. 231). Finally, from a post-Marxist perspective, a discourse is a "socially contingent, taken-for-granted system of meaning defining a set of concepts, objects and practices" (Dahlberg, 2010, p. 334).

The study of texts, therefore, provides an entry point into discourse as it is made up of language, but it is never reducible to it. Appreciating the dialectical relationship between discourse and social structures of power is, indeed, an essential aspect of this study. Fundamentally, discourse creates the conditions for the way we act; it delimits the boundaries of the possible by establishing what counts as common sense. Such structurings of the semiotic order "sanction and sanctify a particular state of things, an established order" (Bourdieu, 1991, p. 119). This is why the study of discourse is so important: because discourse constitutes an essential mechanism of power and is therefore socially productive. As Foucault put it so succinctly, discourses are "practices that systematically form the objects of which they speak" (1972, p. 49).

The heterogeneous school of critical discourse analysis (CDA) scholars emerged in the early 1990s. As Wodak and Meyer make clear, as well as CDA's defining critical dimension, three concepts loom large in the foreground of any analysis that makes use of CDA: power, history, and ideology (2009). A focus on these elements ensure that CDA researchers avoid the trap of social constructivism and, instead, understand that "discourse is structured by dominance; that every discourse is historically produced and interpreted, that is, it is situated in time and space; and that dominance structures are legitimated by ideologies of powerful groups" (Wodak & Meyer, 2009, p. 3).

Meanwhile, within post-Marxian theory, discourse functions as a mechanism of power by assigning a preferred set of meanings to otherwise empty signifiers and to exclude alternative interpretations (Laclau & Mouffe, 2001). This act of discursive closure becomes ideological because it attempts to create a fixity of meaning around a nodal point, one that legitimizes a particular social order.

A parallel endeavor to marking the preferred boundaries of discursive inclusion is to identify an antagonistic "other" against which the enclosed discourse can further solidify its boundaries (Laclau, 2005). This act of enclosure is never complete, however, and while it attempts to obscure the multiple competing alternatives, these continue to exist and provide the raw material for resistance and possible contestation of dominant discourses.

A final concept within discourse analysis that needs to be considered for this study is that of articulation. Discourse is not a static, settled field: discourses are always in competition with one another, to dominate the conceptualization of big ideas, to imbue key signifiers with meaning. However, as Kimball reminds us, "despite its always transitory nature, discursive construction does come together in particular times at particular sites to suggest a stability and coherence" (2013, p. 35). One of the principal ways that discursive stabilization occurs is through what Hall terms "articulation" (Clarke, 2015). This is the process by which distinct (but related) discourses link together in a stable discursive coalition.

In the context of this study, articulation is a vital concept to grasp because the central legitimation discourse of information capitalism—like the system of informational capitalism itself—does not settle uniformly across the world. It articulates with endogenous discourses to create distinct systems of meaning that can legitimate particular social and political economic conjunctures. For instance, in the case of the Marco Civil, the digital discourse could be observed to articulate with local discourses, such as neodevelopmentalism, sovereignty, and social inequality, to create new discursive articulations that legitimated particular conceptualizations of digital rights in Brazil.

The Legitimation of Capitalism and the Digital Discourse

As a system that relies on consent for it to work, capitalism needs to make itself appear worthy of ordering human affairs, to earn our trust and to legitimate itself in the eyes of those who might seek to replace it. Streeter (2011) offers a pithy description of this phenomenon: "Capitalism may not require pure markets . . . but it does need some kind of legitimacy, some mechanism by which it can be made to *feel* right, or at least worth acquiescing to, among broad swathes of the population" (p. 166). Arguably, one of the most productive frameworks for understanding how capitalism makes itself "feel right" is offered by Boltanski and Chiapello (2007) and their work on what they call the new spirit of capitalism. Capitalism produces a discursive essence that proclaims its capacity to deliver fairness, security, and excitement. One of the main ingredients in this spirit is the incorporation of critique.

It is a mainstay of Western political thought that capitalism has catalyzed two major forms of critique—artistic and social. The former is provoked by alienation and emphasizes "an ideal of liberation and/or of individual autonomy, singularity and authenticity," while the latter addresses material inequalities and is concerned with "inequalities, misery, exploitation and the selfishness of a world that stimulates individualism rather than solidarity" (Boltanski & Chiapello, 2005, p. 176). As the two theorists Boltanski and Chiapello (2005) propose, capitalism *needs* its many critics in order to integrate their quest for justice so as to remain socially legitimate. Indeed, in this quest to maintain legitimacy, capitalism effects transformative change in its "spirit": "the ideology that justifies people's commitment to capitalism, and which renders this commitment attractive" (p. 176).

Boltanski and Chiapello note that this change occurred in the transition from Fordist capitalism to neoliberal late capitalism beginning in the 1970s. The counterculture of the 1960s and 1970s had railed against the alienation generated by Fordism, and, in response, an epochal shift occurred in the spirit of the emergent form of capitalism. This new legitimation discourse focused on the ability of late capitalism to address the many failings of Fordism from a humanist perspective. Most notably, this included the capacity to promote individual fulfilment and creative expression (Boltanski & Chiapello, 2005).

The great theoretical advance E. Fisher offered was to introduce technology into this equation, to show how capitalism legitimates itself discursively using the technological form that underpins it. As many other scholars, like Mosco (2009), Nye (2007), and L. Marx (1997) have shown, technology enjoys a privileged place in society: it is ubiquitous, rational, even sublime. It is intuitive, therefore, that the architects of capitalism would harness the social status of technology to advance their project. Technology provides a material basis for market metaphors (Fisher, 2010).

When Fordist capitalism shifted into a new mode of production, it was informational and networked, and unlike Fordism it was decentralized and flexible, and it demolished the social compact of labor, state, and capital. This liminal capitalism incorporated the dominant artistic critique, as well as the material form of information networks, to produce a new technology legitimation discourse, what Fisher calls the digital discourse. In his words it "translates many of the neoliberal tropes into a digitalistic language" (2010, p. 75). Fisher is buttressed in this claim by Cohen (2019), who asserts that "the dominant forms of governmentality associated with informational capitalism are neoliberal" (p. 7).

The digital discourse is shorthand for the multiple narratives that serve to legitimate informational capitalism (what Fisher calls "networked capitalism") in those encounters between network technologies and various sets of social and economic practices. These narratives translate tenets of neoliberal orthodoxy and its accompanying spirit into a technologistic language that renders them politically neutral, socially legitimate, and grounded in an indisputable material reality.

The digital discourse champions market-led re-regulation, globalization, and precarious employment. And it legitimates these new socioeconomic arrangements by showing how networked ICTs produce autonomous, creative, and expressive individuals. This has become what Fraser calls a "facilitating shell," an enduring metadiscourse that delimits common sense in multiple realms of human existence (2009, p. 118). This is what I understand to constitute the legitimation discourse of informational capitalism, and it provides the foundation we need for understanding the congruence between the rise of informational capitalism and the construction of digital rights.

The Codification of Digital Rights

The origin of digital rights can arguably be traced back to 2003 and the World Summit on the Information Society (WSIS) in Geneva, Switzerland. Although designed by the ITU to establish policies to realize the "information society" on a global scale, it was also supposedly motivated by the desire to channel ICTs and media systems for the public good and, therefore, corresponded closely to a rights-based approach to media and communication. As Isin and Ruppert observe, "the importance of WSIS is that it draws its imaginary force from the [Universal Declaration of Human Rights] UDHR and institutes parallels between those rights and digital rights" (2015, p. 170).

Oriented around a (then innovative) multistakeholder approach, the conceptual terrain centered on internet governance, while the official outcomes were "technocratic and oriented to market-led solutions" (McLaughlin & Pickard, 2005, p. 364). This approach marginalized other more substantive visions for reforming the global media and communication system. For instance, a parallel and independent civil forum in Geneva called WSIS? WeSeize! advocated for communication rights and autonomous and civil society–led media systems (Hintz & Milan, 2011, p. 235).

At WSIS, therefore, a pivotal discursive fork occurred: communication rights—substantive but marginalized—in one direction; digital rights—compromised but dominant—in the other. As Padovani, Musiani, and Pavan (2010) conclude, "the WSIS (2003) has been a turning point in the identification of issues pertaining to human rights in the digital age" (p. 367). And with the change in description from communication to digital, a fundamental shift in the characteristics of these rights occurs. It is this latter path that became the dominant response to the exercise of repressive power on and through the internet and led to the creation of more than fifty statements, manifestos, and charters by 2018 (Pettrachin, 2018).

Padovani, Musiani, and Pavan (2010) identify five core concerns in their discourse analysis of human rights in the digital age: freedom, diversity, inclusion, participation, and a knowledge commons (p. 374).

Researchers at the Berkman Klein Center for Internet & Society examined thirty charters of digital rights and identified seven broad groupings: fundamental freedoms, limits on state power, internet governance, privacy rights and surveillance, access and education, openness and stability of networks, and economic rights and responsibilities (Gill, Redeker, & Gasser, 2015). In Pettrachin's large-scale content analysis of digital-rights declarations from 1997 to 2015, she notes that freedom of expression, privacy, access, and internet governance are the issues included with most frequency (2018, p. 347). As Isin and Ruppert concur in their own work on the emergence of the digital citizen (2015), "three rights—expression, access and privacy—have emerged as the most often debated digital rights. To these, openness and innovation have recently been added. All together, these five rights have come to constitute digital rights in cyberspace" (p. 159).

One of the most valuable frameworks for understanding the tenor rather than simply the composition of digital-rights declarations is provided by Karppinen and Puukko (2020). In their analysis, the researchers identify four principal discourses that comprise the digital-rights movement. These are negative rights, positive rights/state obligations, information justice, and platform affordances.

The negative-rights discourse can be traced back to the genesis of cyberlibertarianism, with the precepts that the liberties and expressive capacities for individual users must be safeguarded, notably from the restrictions of the state. The positive rights/state obligations discourse is largely utilitarian in scope but intersects directly with the human rights tradition, recognizes the citizen as the subject of digital rights, and affords the state a productive role as their guarantor. Information justice, meanwhile, expands the concept of digital rights in depth and breadth as "a vehicle to contest and alter existing mechanisms and relations of power" (Karppinen & Puukko, 2020, p. 317) by recognizing structural inequities within the digital media environment and the need to intersect with broader claims of distributive justice. Finally, the platform affordances discourse is propagated principally by web platforms and sees rights as embedded within technological infrastructure and the subject of those rights as platform users.

Combining Karppinen and Puukko's analysis with the research identified earlier, one can observe that the codification of digital rights most closely corresponds to the negative and positive rights frameworks. There is a clear emphasis on individual rights and freedoms, especially in terms of expression and privacy, realized through technical and market-based solutions, such as network neutrality. Although the state is assigned duties as guarantor of a limited array of rights, the influence of the negative-rights approach sees the state more often framed as a threat to the expressive capacities of individuals, as censor or spy.

Although Karppinen and Puukko do not directly analyze the broader discursive and ideological foundations of their four approaches, they do observe that "rights are not only a neutral tool for the protection of individuals, but also have a more ambivalent function as a form of power, which not only open up possibilities but also circumscribe and channel them" (2020, p. 308). This observation corresponds closely to my central argument that the legitimation discourse of informational capitalism has effectively neutralized the dominant paradigm of digital rights as a form of countervailing power.

The coherence among the tenets of the digital discourse—expression, freedom, participation, openness, and innovation—and the defining features of the digital-rights paradigm are striking.

Fundamentally, informational capitalism's core logics of commodification and control are unchallenged when the subject of rights claims are atomized individuals, and the liberties they safeguard, in fact, serve as fuel for a system of accumulation and exploitation. Newman's (2013) analysis of network-neutrality legislation in the United States encapsulates this paradox: "individual freedoms online exist uncomfortably next to the extant desires of capitalist expansion" (p. 63).

Franklin did not develop her observation that digital rights are "encapsulated by the trope of freedom" (2013, p. 92), but I argue that the "empty signifier" of freedom serves a dual purpose in charters of digital rights. On one hand, it permits the easy conflation of individual rights with the free flow of data essential for informational capitalism to operate. On the other, it forestalls more substantive measures; if we can realize *freedom* through these rights, then why go further?

What is omitted from this dominant digital rights paradigm is just as important as what is included. Conspicuously absent are any connection to broader social justice concerns, any focus on the internet's hypercommercial character, or on public provision of content or services. Although a quantitative approach only provides a partial account, it is telling that in Pettrachin's (2018) detailed content analysis of fifty-eight digital rights charters, the values most closely associated with the social critique of capitalism, such as "justice," "power," "concentration," "public," "discrimination," and "commodity," are not prominent enough to receive mention. As Hintz and Milan (2011) pointedly observe, the fundamental concerns of "netizens" for communications policy are "free and unobstructed activities by individuals" that "overshadows notions of a 'public interest'" (p. 235).

Similarly, Padovani, Musiani, and Pavan (2010) argue in their research on discourses of human rights in the digital age, that "60 years of fundamental rights do not appear to be fully acknowledged in the digital-oriented discourse." The omissions include minority rights, peace, security, and environmental concerns (2010, p. 374). The overlap with Jørgensen's research on human rights in global media discourses from WSIS onward merits mention here as she concludes that "the concrete use of human rights is often limited to either a general framework without specific human rights analysis or referencing the right to freedom of expression and the right to privacy only" (2011, p. 100).

Certainly, the tunnel vision on expression and privacy identified by Jørgensen is quite evident in the dominant digital-rights paradigm. Moreover, in the Charter of Human Rights and Principles for the Internet, Franklin's (2013) account of the development of the Internet Governance Forum (IGF) of the United Nations, she writes that it "would put human rights issues squarely on what had been predominately technocratic and technocentric agendas" (p. 143). I contend that while the general framework of human rights may have been transposed to the digital-rights movement, those technocentric agendas—favoring technical fixes over substantive reforms—remain highly influential.

Other important features of the human rights tradition have influenced the dominant approach to digital rights in a way germane to this study. Following Slaughter's (2018) critique of the Western discourse of human rights, we can observe that its emphasis on the individual over the collective is also much in evidence within digital-rights charters. Isin and Ruppert also note that the figure of the citizen "disappears from the charters claiming digital rights and instead is replaced by the 'human rights' of individuals" (2015, p. 175). Finally, the explicit universalism of human rights is also a core feature of the digital-rights paradigm and corresponds to one of my core arguments regarding the Marco Civil: that it should not be uncritically presented as a global legislative template but, instead, needs to be understood as contingent upon its political economic and sociocultural context.

As Isin and Ruppert (2015) as well as Jørgensen (2011) have documented, digital rights are most often presented as *human*, rather than *civic*, rights. This is a key distinction as the former serves to frame digital rights as "static and universal" as opposed to "historical and situated and arising from social struggles" (Isin & Ruppert, 2015, p. 10). This dominant framing, therefore, often fails to acknowledge how digital rights would intersect with local political economic and sociocultural realities.

Accordingly, it has become commonplace for charters of digital rights to be drafted and advocated for as initiatives with universal scope. Pettrachin (2018) notes that the majority of declarations that she analyzed invoke an explicitly global scale (p. 349). These include the IGF's Charter of Human Rights and Principles for the Internet; the Association of Progressive Communication's Internet Rights Charter, disseminated in twenty languages worldwide; and the Web We Want Foundation's vision of an internet Magna Carta.

The occluded possibilities for digital rights are represented in Karppinen and Puukko's discourse of information justice (2020). The alternative claims therein, which are collectivist, connect to wider social justice agendas, and require systemic change to the online environment, have been articulated in numerous concrete proposals. These include but are not limited to: a data tax (Powers & Jablonski, 2015), government provision of online public journalism (McChesney, 2013; Pickard, 2016), platform co-operativism (Scholz, 2016), municipal and/or community broadband networks (Pickard, 2016), sustainable culture (Taylor, 2014), a "Human Knowledge Project" (Vaidhyanathan, 2013), a distributive digital commons (Jordan, 2015), and data justice (Dencik et al., 2022).

Outside of the academic realm, nongovernment organizations (NGOs), such as the Internet Social Forum (initially proposed in 2015) and the Just Net Coalition, advocate for similarly substantive measures to address the exercise of repressive power on and through the internet. While within the political sphere, Pirate and Green Parties around the world have integrated values of information justice into their platforms, with the goal of "not only protecting existing legal rights, but also the contestation and alteration of hegemonic structures" (Karppinen & Puukko, 2020, p. 319). The connection to the Pirate Party is indeed significant for this study as the Brazilian Pirate Party made proposals for the Marco Civil that corresponded closely to the information justice approach to digital rights. This shows that such ideas were being discussed in Brazil, at the time, by actors closely involved with the Marco Civil process, and they therefore represented a viable path for digital rights in Brazil.

Some may claim that measures within the information justice approach fall outside of the purview of a rights-based framework. However, I argue that if technolegal policy instruments, such as network neutrality, safe-harbor provisions, and data finality measures, are commonplace within digital-rights charters, then why should it be inconceivable to include structural reforms establishing public broadband provision or a data commons?

Turning to Cohen here, note her argument that "in the networked information era, preserving fundamental rights and freedoms for all people requires an institutional foundation that encompasses not only rights to speak, to access information, and so on *but also other structural safeguards—safeguards designed to preserve a well-functioning networked public sphere*" (2019, p. 252, emphasis added).

Moreover, returning to the communication rights approach for a vital corrective to any misapprehension about the proper purview of digital rights, communication rights represent a programmatic attempt to establish a communication environment that promotes both social equity and a substantive democracy. It is an approach that employs a wide-angle lens to encompass systemic reform *alongside* individual rights. Calls from the Communication Rights within the Information Society (CRIS) campaign advocate for freedom of expression and privacy but, vitally, *in conjunction with* calls for a global knowledge commons, media literacy and basic communication skills, pluralism of media sources, and diversity in the systems used for retrieving information. Table 2 does not represent an exhaustive accounting of the differences between digital and communication rights. However, juxtaposing the most-salient values illustrates the divergence between them.

TABLE 2. Rights attributes according to critique of capitalism

Social Critique (communication rights)	Artistic Critique (digital rights)
collectivist	individualist
democratic/public	open
equity	expression
justice	freedom
political	neutral
political economic	humanist
positive	negative
redistributive	technical/legal
systemic change	incremental change

Conclusion

The purpose of this chapter is to establish to the fullest extent possible a schematic for informational capitalism and to be able to assess the form, modes, and scope of the system's power. These, in turn, represent a vital contribution to this study because they enable understanding of the deficiencies of the Marco Civil as a bill of digital rights and of the particularities of its development at the system's periphery.

To do this, some of the most notable accounts that contribute to an understanding of informational capitalism are parsed here. Although these have been drawn from a wide variety of academic literatures—including surveillance, platform, and policy studies—two fields stand out as the most prominent: the political economy of communication and critical discourse analysis. Each is characterized by particular emphases, as well as blind spots, that I have endeavored to account for in this framework.

The political economy of communication shines a light onto the structure and functions of informational capitalism. Schiller (1999; 2007; 2014), Dyer-Witheford (2015), and C. Fuchs (2009; 2011) represent some of the key contributors to this framework, identifying the varied forms of production and accumulation that drive informational capitalism forward. Overlapping accounts from critical legal scholars, such as Cohen (2019) and Berry (2008), that focus on IP and cyber law are also vital for understanding the means of extraction and enclosure that are pivotal to the workings of informational capitalism.

The framework that this chapter has presented also addresses some of the most notable omissions from these literatures. The wide-angle lens employed here captures the broad array of actors that comprise informational capitalism, including the media and telecoms sectors and state actors, thereby evading the narrow focus on web platforms and data extraction that has characterized more-recent accounts (Couldry & Mejias, 2019; Srnicek, 2017; Zuboff, 2019). The global political economy of informational capitalism is similarly a core component of my framework that is largely occluded in the literature.

Although it is widely observed that the global south represents a site of extraction and/or exploitation within analyses of the IP regime (Drahos & Braithwaite, 2002), big-data analytics (Taylor, 2017), global media flows (Mirrlees, 2016), technology supply chains (Qiu, 2016), and others and although mentions of the periphery abound in a somewhat abstract sense, there is a dearth of systematic efforts to conceptualize the zonal geography of informational capitalism, to relate the periphery to the core. I address that omission in this book and, in particular, in this chapter.

Finally, the ideational dimensions of informational capitalism are largely neglected by the political economy of communication. The discourses that legitimate informational capitalism and that are constitutive of the policies, laws, and media framings that, in turn, shape the social and political economic conjunctures of the system are essential to understand. In order to address this blind spot, I have drawn from the wealth of insights provided by scholars of discourse—most notably Fisher (2010), Dahlberg (2010), and Kimball (2013)—to identify the legitimation discourse of informational capitalism and to show how it has indelibly marked the dominant paradigm of digital rights.

Specifically, the framework elaborated in this chapter identifies the core logics of informational capitalism as commodification and control. These are advanced through a series of mechanics that include intellectual property, datafication, surveillance, code, and informationalized production.

Although the logics of informational capitalism are consistent features of the system, it is essential to recognize that the manner in which those logics are advanced implies conflict and contradictions as different sectors compete for advantage. Accordingly, the second major strut of this framework identifies the dynamics of informational capitalism. This involved categorizing the principal sectors—notably, the web technology, content production, telecoms, security state, and so forth—and identifying how their preferred mechanics to commodify and control information create tensions and synergies within the system. Accounting for these interweaving dynamics is essential if one is to understand how the final form of the Marco Civil was shaped by the agendas of competing power blocks within informational capitalism, another analytical dimension that remains obscured if one is to focus myopically on the role of big tech.

The unequal and exploitative global political economy of informational capitalism represents the penultimate strut of this framework. The directionality of power defines the zones of informational capitalism, from the core to the periphery, even while those remain unstable and in constant flux. Foregrounding the importance of the periphery helps us to recognize how local political economic and historical contexts shaped the formation of digital rights in Brazil and the particular ways that the system of informational capitalism manifested itself.

Finally, it is a core conceit of this study that for the exercise of power to be fully understood, we must study it along its material and symbolic dimensions. Accordingly, the final section of this analytical framework examines the discourses of informational capitalism. Tracing their manifestation in the case of the Marco Civil and showing how they articulated with local discourses around democracy, crime, and development—among others—reveals a formative influence on the Marco Civil.

2

Circumscription

The Discursive Delimitation
of Digital Rights

We begin with a prehistory of the bill, examining the civic resistance to a proposed cybercrime law that constituted the Marco Civil's genesis—as well as the stages of public consultation and multistakeholder consultation that shaped the bill as a framework of digital rights. A discourse focus takes priority here in order to understand the narratives that were formative in delimiting the Marco Civil's civic potential from its inception and how discourses that were formative in the construction of digital rights elsewhere in the world (in a manner that facilitated informational capitalism) were also evident in Brazil. These include most notably the neoliberal, technocratic, and cyberlibertarian discourses that are all to some degree constitutive of the digital discourse, as well as its articulations with the local Brazilian discourse of neodevelopmentalism.

It is essential to examine how characteristics of Brazil's contemporary media system, and the legacy of technological dependency and repressed communication rights (characteristic of Brazil's peripheral status within global capitalism) shaped how and why key sets of actors contested elements of the bill. These represent some of the most significant sociocultural and political economic particularities of how digital rights are contested in this specific local and, more generally, peripheral context. In a similar vein, identifying the multiple junctures at which the imaginary of digital rights—informed by the dominant digital discourse—served to circumscribe the civic potential of the Marco Civil is a thread running through this chapter.

To undertake a prehistory of the bill means identifying the factors that created the conditions for the Marco Civil's emergence in Brazil at that time. These can be broadly grouped into three categories: historical, political, and sociotechnical. In the first bracket, a large impetus for the framework of digital rights came from Brazil's historical tendency toward criminalization as its primary legislative impulse: the idea of the Marco Civil was a repudiation of that approach. Also, the punitive cybercrime bill, the Lei Azeredo (the Azeredo law, described in detail in the next section) evoked Brazil's recent history of military dictatorship and civic repression and explains in part the efforts invested in resisting that law and building a civic alternative. Within the political realm, the PT (Partido dos Trabalhadores/Workers' Party) government's neodevelopmentalist agenda implied support for an innovative cyberlaw approach, while its focus on participation as a core political value guided the Marco Civil's early forms of consultation. Finally, in terms of sociotechnical factors, vibrant communities built around free software and the Creative Commons in Brazil meant that the Marco Civil could draw from a wellspring of support from individuals highly engaged in technological issues.

The Centrão, Clientelism, and Corruption

The complex dynamics of Brazil's political culture was an important factor in guiding the Marco Civil's legislative journey. The instability and "inchoate" nature of Brazilian party politics are widely noted (Mainwaring, 1999), and Alfredo Saad-Filho and Lecio Morais trace the roots back to the democratic transition and a political system they describe damningly as "fragile by design." It comprises a "myriad of parties unmoored by ideology or principle, making it virtually impossible for the President to command a majority in Congress without unwieldy coalitions" (2017, p. 45). David Samuels and Kevin Lucas similarly assert that Brazil's "party system lacks the sort of coherence that scholars associate with collective responsiveness and accountability" (2010, p. 42).

One of the most significant implications of this scenario is the pervasive clientelism that exists in Brazilian political culture. The horse trading that is inherent to party politics throughout the world is especially marked in Brazil. The dizzying constellation of political parties in Brazil is popularly described as "acronyms for rent" (Rohter, 2010, p. 257). The political structure in Brasília is also referred to as the *centrão* (the big center): the block of ideologically unmoored politicians who "support any government in exchange for public jobs and official money" (Brazil's triple crisis, 2020). The patronage of the telecoms sector is particularly pronounced within the centrão, and this became a major factor in the passage of the Marco Civil.

One of the consequences of this clientelism is, rather predictably, corruption, with the members of this floating center often implicated in its scandals. Corruption is part of politics, but it exists in varying degrees and with varying levels of visibility in polities around the world. Lamentably, in Brazil corruption is more visible than in many other democracies, to the extent that it represents "virtually a natural phenomenon" (Schwarcz & Starling, 2020, p. 600). The epic corruption scandal known in Brazil as the Lava Jato (Car Wash) is emblematic of the scope of the problem.[1] The fallout from this investigation was largely responsible for the downfall of the Workers' Party government (Saad-Filho & Morais, 2017) and emerges in chapter 4 as it shared some connections with the Marco Civil.

Of course, the incoherence, clientelism, and corruption of the Brazilian political system do not negate the possibility of meaningful policy reforms, demonstrated quite vividly with the passage of the globally acclaimed Bolsa Familia and other progressive legislation by the Lula Inácio da Silva administrations (Ricci, 2013). However, as with the case of the Marco Civil, the complexities of Brazilian political culture leave an indelible mark on even the most well-intentioned pieces of policy.

Setting the Bar: The Lei Azeredo and IP Maximalism

One element of the Marco Civil's prehistory looms largest in the reckoning: PL84/1999, titled O Projeto de Lei dos Cibercrimes (the cybercrime bill). More commonly known as the Lei Azeredo—after senator Eduardo Azeredo, who stickhandled its eventual passage into law—this raft of punitive cybercrime proposals appears to represent the legislative antithesis of the Marco Civil. Although there is a clear juxtaposition between the criminal and civic focus of the two bills, arguably of more significance is that the Lei Azeredo represented an attempt to codify into law IP safeguards to benefit particular sectors of informational capitalism. When these ambitions were denied, they found eventual resolution in the Marco Civil itself.

The civil rights framework of the Marco Civil was conceived in opposition to the criminalization of everyday online activities proposed in the Lei Azeredo. Significantly, this meant that the Marco Civil was the product of a reactive, not a proactive, legislative agenda. As a corrective to the Lei Azeredo, one of the primary goals for the Marco Civil was to limit the regression implied by the cybercrime bill. Not only did this set a low bar for the Marco Civil but it also meant that the measures contained in the Lei Azeredo, as well as the discourses and actors that impelled its passage into law, had a corresponding effect on the initial shape of the Marco Civil and must be examined closely.

In its first incarnation, PL84 appeared in 1999 as the conglomeration of several inchoate pieces of cybercrime legislation into one draft bill (Papp, 2014, p. 21). Not until Azeredo of the conservative Brazilian Social Democracy Party (PSDB) took the helm as rapporteur of the bill in 2006, however, did the proposed legislation become infamous among a diverse coalition of digital activists, free-software enthusiasts, and the technical and academic communities. The issues that galvanized public ire were the amendments that Azeredo introduced to the bill in 2007. These included a compulsory identification and registration of all internet users, mandated data retention for ISPs, and the obligation for ISPs to report illegal activities to a state authority (Solagna, 2015, p. 38).

The Lei Azeredo corresponded to an established tendency within Brazilian politics that sought to criminalize new behaviors as a first resort (Brito, 2015). This is a tendency with deep roots in Brazil. For instance, Brazil established its first criminal code in 1830; the corresponding civil code did not appear until 1916. This tendency, in turn, stems from two important and interrelated characteristics of Brazilian society; both are related to Brazil's historically peripheral status as a Portuguese colony. The first is that Brazil "has always been a country of law and of jurists," one that inherited a Romano-Germanic legal tradition from its Portuguese colonizers and went on to become one of the most prolific nations in the world in terms of the production of legislation (Carvalho, 2013, p. 76). In 2010 research by the Brazilian National Justice Council showed that the country possessed 1,240 law schools (Duran, 2014), while the United States had 199 schools accredited by the American Bar Association (2021).

As of late, this phenomenon has been interpreted by the sociologist Bernardo Sorj in a manner very germane to this book: "The contradiction which presents itself in Brazil is that the *juridification* of society . . . is quite limited, but as a process of *judicialization* of social life, that is, of transference of social conflict to the judiciary, Brazil is, conversely, a very advanced case" (2001, p. 118). This is a valuable insight for understanding the Marco Civil as a bill of digital rights because juridification refers to the introduction of legal norms and mechanisms into different realms of social life. Although this process is understood as a negative development by Jürgen Habermas (1981), among others, its relative absence in the case of Brazil underscores the reality of the extralegal nature of great swathes of social activity. Evading mechanisms of law and bureaucracy is a pervasive fact of life in Brazilian society, referred to as the *jeito*, meaning the "skill required to maneuver around the laws or social conventions that prevent you from achieving an objective" (Rohter, 2010, p. 34). Despite or perhaps because of the indifference displayed toward legal institutions in Brazil, the Marco Civil represents another instance of Sorj's "transference of social conflict to the judiciary" in which digital rights are manifested in legalistic terms that not only negate a substantive civic vision but are also overseen by institutions that are habitually disregarded.

Connected to this extraordinary proclivity for legalism, Brazil is also a country long noted for its entrenched social stratification between the very poor and the very rich. It is a history of division that can be traced back to the enormous number of African slaves transported to Brazil by the Portuguese—over four million—that were violently oppressed by a tiny colonial elite (Rose, 2005, p. 3). Over time, legislation became complementary to violence as a means for the Brazilian political elite to control a vast underclass, first of slaves and later of workers (Holston, 2009; Moura et al., 2014). Members of the conservative PSDB party, one that belies its social-democratic moniker with a neoliberal policy agenda (Guiot, 2010), are more inclined to this instrumental approach to criminalization than the Workers' Party (PT).

Some observers characterized the Lei Azeredo as another instance of a "morality-centred legislative agenda," one that was now increasingly being applied to the internet by the PSDB (Rossini et al., 2015, p. 3). Another line of enquiry would be to observe the powerful economic actors whose interests might be served by the measures contained within the proposed legislation, agents prominent within informational capitalism.

Information Feudalism at the Periphery

The regime of informational feudalism identified by Peter Drahos and John Braithwaite (2002), one premised upon the global expansion of a stringent IP regime in order to control and commodify informational resources, arguably reached its zenith in the late 1990s (Streeter, 2011, p. 166). The agreement, the TRIPS, was signed in 1994. The WIPO Copyright Treaty and the Performances and Phonograms Treaty was adopted by member states two years later. In the United States, the Digital Music Copyright Act (DMCA) was passed in 1998 during the Bill Clinton administration. In 2001 the Council of Europe ratified the Budapest Convention on Cybercrime.

The rationale for this legislative fervor was that "the linking of IP law with international trade enabled IP-exporting countries in the developed world to advance an international trade-based IP regime focused on . . . *the private appropriation of knowledge-based resources at the service of informational capitalism*" (Turcotte, 2016, p. 38, emphasis added). More than simply a set of conventions for states in the core of informational capitalism, TRIPS and the Budapest convention were designed as templates for countries in the developing world to adopt as national legislation in order to harmonize "accumulation by dispossession" from the core to the periphery (Harvey, 2005).

In 2006 Brazil paid out $1.6 billion for the use of registered IP and received $150 million in receipts (World Bank, 2021, Charges . . . payments, and 2021, Charges . . . receipts). The same data source reveals that the United States by contrast paid out $23 billion and received $70 billion. The disparities between the balances of trade in IP-related goods between Brazil and the United States are characteristic of the zonal nature of informational capitalism.

By 2006, when Azeredo introduced the most controversial amendments, IP maximalism was arguably on the wane in a global context. As Thomas Streeter (2011) notes, "after the arrival of the open source movement, the neoliberal assumption that more-property-protection-is-better was no longer unassailable" (p. 160). This did not discourage the senator, however, from attempting to harmonize Brazilian law with those IP templates Europe and the United States devised. His perspective was that this "would be good for global information technology companies, and would therefore promote private investment and technological development in Brazil" (O'Maley, 2015, p. 48). The Lei Azeredo also represented a continuation of the neoliberal informatics policy of the mid-1990s that dismantled earlier protectionist measures and established an open market favoring investment by IT multinationals (Schoonmaker, 2002).

The Lei Azeredo and its provisions were supported by an array of core sectors within informational capitalism, most notably the security state, content production, and the financial services sector. As secretary of legislative affairs of the Ministry of Justice from 2007 to 2010, Pedro Abramovay (2014) explains in a later article that for the proposed law's lobbyists, "the big argument was bank fraud." The director of Febraban (the Brazilian Federation of Banks) did make the extent of their involvement clear in a 2007 interview: "Febraban, as the representative of highly informationalised business, is interested in the bill since its first version . . . and we remain close to all the relators and parliamentarians involved in projects related to digital crime" (UOL Notícias, 2007).

In a research interview, Luiz Moncau, a member of the technology think tank and research center Centro da Tecnologia e Sociedade (CTS, Center of

Technology and Society) at the renowned Fundação Getulio Vargas (FGV; Getulio Vargas Foundation), which would become a founding partner with the Ministry of Justice in creating the Marco Civil, said that the opaque process made it hard to determine who exactly was backing the Marco Civil. However, it was widely understood that "the only one that was clearly mapped was the IP interests because you have the . . . specialty reports that the US releases and they explicitly named the Lei Azeredo as an important bill for protecting IP."

The power and influence of the Lei Azeredo's backers were not reflected in the sophistication of the law itself. Many legal observers noted its incongruous, even naïve, presumptions. Cofounder of the Brazilian Pirate Party, Paulo Santarém noted that "the lexicon of common sense as presupposition, without effective foundation, is significant" (2010, p. 18). Ronaldo Lemos describes the "imprecision" and "limited technical rigour" of the law's articles (2010, p. 3), and in interview, Guilherme Almeida, secretary of legislative affairs of the Ministry of Justice from 2010 to 2013, deemed the law "so obscure, and so totally missing what the internet meant."

Whether these criticisms should be read, however, as a technolegal critique or an ideological clash is a pertinent question. This is because these commentators also formed the cabal of young lawyers who delineated the Marco Civil and whose presumptions about the internet were all guided by the digital discourse. As such, the Lei Azeredo represented a programmatic check on the personal freedoms championed in that discourse. That Abramovay, in his condemnation of the Lei Azeredo in a newspaper interview in 2009, claimed that the "internet is a space of freedom *par excellence*, not a place of fear" underscores this point (Brito, 2015, p. 51).

Certainly, irrespective of the finesse of its legalese, the vision of an internet extensively controlled in the interests of key sectors of informational capitalism—the Brazilian security state and the content production and financial sectors—was met with concerted resistance. This resistance and its influence on the formation of the Marco Civil are the subjects of the next section.

Radical Roots? Blogs, Op-eds, a Presidential Address

The principal opposition to the Lei Azeredo came from three main sources: the Brazilian free-software community, a disparate collection of digital activists and technologists who rallied under the banner of the *Mega Não* (Big No) and of key members of the governing Workers' Party, including even President Lula himself. This was a pivotal phase in the Marco Civil's prehistory because the discourses that percolated through this opposition were decisive in shaping a civic alternative to the punitive Lei Azeredo.

It is not enough, however, to note this opposition; we must pay heed to its form. In tracing the development of the Marco Civil through the accounts of my interviewees, primary media sources, and secondary academic texts, four interventions in the Brazilian public sphere by high-profile figures that constituted key junctures for the bill stand out:

- the blog of an influential freedom of expression advocate and cyberactivist
- an op-ed by one of Brazil's foremost commentators on technology issues
- the blog of a high-profile academic and champion of the free-software movement
- a keynote address at a free-software convention by President Lula da Silva

These key texts served as calls to action in this oppositional period and rendered visible some of the formative discourses of the Marco Civil. Indeed, the importance of the analysis presented here is to show that the discourses drawn upon by these sets of actors, although oppositional to the forms of control proposed in the Lei Azeredo, were shaped to such an extent by the tenets of the digital discourse that they ultimately set the tone for a Marco Civil aligned with the logics of informational capitalism. Moreover, analyzing these discourses reveals another thread essential to this study: that of the *articulation* of the digital discourse with peculiarly Brazilian values and meanings—most notably the country's recent history of military dictatorship—which also had a profound influence on the form that the Marco Civil took.

Cyberlibertarian Bloggers and the Death of the Brazilian Internet

In a November 7, 2006, a post, "The Death of the Brazilian Internet," João Caribé, digital publicist and free-speech advocate based in Rio de Janeiro, started his blog *Xô Censura* to protest an imminent congressional vote on the Lei Azeredo. In this maiden post, Caribé lamented the censorship of "our Internet" that will serve the interests of an unspecified "powerful minority (Caribé, 2006). This blog initially served as a clearinghouse for opposition to the Lei Azeredo and was a precursor to the more organized Mega Não campaign. A critical reading of some of this blog's key posts reveals the discourses that underpinned early opposition to the proposed Lei Azeredo.

Caribé refined the remit of the blog two months later with a short post proclaiming the importance of freedom of expression because the "rancid

. . . practice of censorship" from the dictatorship was still much in evidence (Caribé, 2007 January 9). In May 2007 he updated the "Death of the Brazilian Internet" post as a reaction to the amendments Azeredo added to the bill in April 2007. In this text the passage heralding the internet as "a social amplifier" displays the tenets of the digital discourse most strongly and merits quotation in full here:

> Humanity's greatest conquest of all time was the Internet that democratized communication, gave everyone the option of speaking and being heard, gave everyone the option of relationships without bureaucracy or discrimination, gave everyone F R E E D O M!!! Freedom is what unsettles those dinosaurs habituated to divulging one-way content to a people made imbecile by the mass media. The greatest danger of this freedom, of a free cyberspace is to leave the "King naked," let the king be naked, we are going to reveal the truth, we are going to live freedom, freedom is essential to the development of any nation, and accompanied by deregulation could lead Brazil again to the position of leader of Latin America. (Caribé, 2007 May 4)

In this tract it is easy to hear echoes of what Mosco (2009) describes as the "digital sublime," the recurring conceit that new technologies will usher in a new and unparalleled era of progress. The timing of this post is significant in that regard, as 2006 is identified by Lincoln Dahlberg (2010) as the point at which the discourse he calls "cyber-libertarianism 2.0" emerged in earnest into the public realm. It is a discourse that equates the use of Web 2.0 technologies with the liberation of those users from the shackles of state control, to achieve a new form of democracy through participation and creativity (2010, p. 333).

A curious articulation in Caribé's text, however, deviates from Dahlberg's understanding of cyberlibertarianism par excellence. In what will become a recurring thread in this section, despite decrying bureaucracy, Caribé invokes the values of developmentalism and nationalism to argue that a free cyberspace could promote the national development and regional hegemony of Brazil. Perversely, this prospect is contingent, however, upon deregulation, a core tenet, of course, of the neoliberal discourse. Finally, this passage is characterized by its emphasis on the value of individual freedom, another metasignifier within the digital discourse.

Innovation and Efficiency: The Intellectual Genesis

At the same time as Caribé was attempting to foment grassroots resistance to the Lei Azeredo among Brazilian *internautas* (netizens), another voice emerged to rally the establishment. This time it came from within the academic-technical community in Brazil, and it belonged to high-profile IP lawyer and technology commentator Lemos. His op-ed on the Universo Online (UOL) content platform in May 2007, whose title translated as "The Brazilian internet needs a civic regulatory framework," was a pivotal moment in the history of the Marco Civil. This was the first time that the notion of a civil rights framework or Marco Civil had entered into the public realm. As such, Lemos's text became a touchstone for Brazilian activists and later for the drafters of the Marco Civil, including Lemos himself.

As well as analyzing the discourses present in Lemos's article, it is important to understand the professional trajectory of the man himself to be able to effectively trace those discourses and their origins. The roots of Lemos's rise to prominence can be traced to his decision to leave a career in telecommunications law to pursue a master's degree at Harvard Law School in 2001 (Lemos, 2010, p. 10). At that time Laurence Lessig was teaching at the law school and gaining renown for questioning the legitimacy of IP maximalism online (Streeter, 2011, p. 167). With Lessig as his inspiration, Lemos returned to Brazil and in 2003 alongside two other legal scholars who would become drafters of the Marco Civil—Bruno Magrani and Carlos Affonso Souza—founded the Centro da Tecnologia e Sociedade (CTS) at the Getulio Vargas Foundation law school (Papp, 2014, p. 88).

The initiative that established renown for the center was the 2004 decision to make Brazil the third country in the world to adopt Lessig's Creative Commons (CC) licensing system, a legal framework built on top of the copyright system and designed to better balance creator rights and access to culture (Lemos, 2010, p. 10). Creative Commons in Brazil achieved prominence when newly appointed minister of culture Gilberto Gil—a renowned and prolific musician—championed the project and relicensed much of his own work using CC (Lemos, 2010, p. 11). Lemos adroitly used the public platform offered by CC to become a prominent commentator on technological issues in the Brazilian media.

The Creative Commons project drew plaudits from academics and activists by presenting an alternative to IP maximalism and for "protecting the global sharing of information and resources" (Bowrey & Anderson, 2009, p. 480). However, CC's emphasis on liberal, individual freedoms at the expense of addressing systemic change has also been widely criticized (Berry, 2008; Taylor, 2014).

In charting the conceptual differences between those individuals whom Streeter (2011) dubs the "cyberscholars," Streeter notes Lessig's "obsessive focus on an abstract individual freedom" and his articulation of the idea that "freedom itself is a simple condition, an absence of constraint, the ability of individuals to do what they want, especially to express themselves, to engage their creativity" (p. 164). The coherence is apparent between this description of Lessig's vision for free culture and the tenets of the digital discourse, that is, of expression, creativity, and individual freedom. Moreover, the explicitly libertarian bent within the free-culture movement precluded any vision of systemic reform to overhaul the commodification of knowledge.

Indeed, the values of maximizing individual freedoms and creativity that cohere with the digital discourse are readily apparent not only in Lemos's influential op-ed but moreover in the structure of the Marco Civil itself. Lemos fulfilled a similar role in the context of the Marco Civil, writers such as George Gilder also did so in propagating neoliberal dogma in the United States, according to Harvey's analysis (2005, p. 54) or the various futurists and visionaries Mosco profiles in *The Digital Sublime* (2005). Ultimately, although Lemos gained plaudits for calling for a civil rights framework for the Brazilian internet, the dominant discourses within his text can be characterized as both technocratic and neoliberal.

Although Lemos does once identify the threat posed to "collective and public interests" as well as the incompatibility of some of the bill's provisions with a "democratic state of law," it is in the closing paragraph that Lemos's overriding focus—one that I argue helped to orient the Marco Civil around commercial interests as a proxy for user rights—becomes apparent: "To privilege the criminal regulation of the Internet before its civil regulation has as a consequence an increase in public and private costs, a *disincentive for innovation and above all, inefficiency*" (2007, emphasis added).

In these final lines, Lemos chooses to underscore the dangers of inefficiency and a lack of innovation, not the chilling effects on democratic communication or access to culture and knowledge. *Innovation* and *efficiency* are of course metasignifiers within both the technocratic and neoliberal discourse. As Bernard McKenna and Phillip Graham note, the function of technocratic discourse is to eliminate "dialectical political encounters, and, consequently, the possibility for public debate on important matters of social policy" (2000, p. 224). Accordingly, and implicitly, the real victims of the Lei Azeredo are not citizens but particular sectors of Brazilian business, and by evading a focus on the substantively civic implications of the law, the terms of the debate are steered away from the messy terrain of politics.

A Curious Articulation

As Lemos's proposal for a civil alternative to the Lei Azeredo circulated among the technical, legal, and academic communities in Brazil, activists— of whom Caribé and Sérgio Amadeu, Lula da Silva's confidant, University of São Paulo political science professor, and free-software advocate, became unofficial leaders—developed a more concerted opposition. In July 2008 Amadeu formalized his position on his blog in a manifesto "In Defence of the Freedom and Progress of Knowledge on the Brazilian Internet" cosigned by ninety-five academics and journalists. In collaboration with Caribé, this would go on to become the basis of a viral online petition, one that would bestow legitimacy and public influence on the organizers and help to turn the political tide away from the Lei Azeredo.

Given its significance, the discursive underpinnings of this manifesto merit attention. Moreover, it is an illuminating exercise to set the discourses drawn upon by Amadeu and Lemos side by side. Both were published as calls to arms against the Lei Azeredo, but they represented two quite distinct sources of opposition: one technocratic in tone, written by an IP lawyer concerned with innovation and efficiency, and the other replete with cyberutopian rhetoric, written by a sociologist and self-proclaimed free-software militant, sounding the alarm for blogging and peer-to-peer (P2P) networking.

Ultimately, it was the former that achieved discursive closure around the Marco Civil. Amadeu's rhetoric and support did, however, serve the important function of legitimating the project and, in that important respect, should be seen as complementary to Lemos rather than antagonistic. Also, one reason that Lemos's perspective prevailed is because he was the first to articulate an *alternative to* the Lei Azeredo, as opposed to simply expressing opposition to it.

Amadeu's concern was with the collective construction of knowledge and the forms of creativity and expressive freedoms that the law would curtail. That is reflected in what amounts to the thesis statement of the manifesto: "We defend the necessity to guarantee the freedom of exchange, the growth of creativity and the expansion of knowledge in Brazil" (2008).

Akin to Caribé, Amadeu repeatedly invokes the trope of freedom in his manifesto and presents it as an inherent characteristic of the internet. In this regard, one can readily identify the cyberutopian discourse that he draws upon for this manifesto. The idea that the internet is ushering in a new dawn of human achievement is at the crux of cyberutopian and information-society rhetoric and can be observed here: "The Internet reclassifies collaboration, reunifies the arts and the sciences, overcoming a division erected in the mechanical world of the industrial era. The Internet represents, although always potentially, the newest expression of human freedom" (2008).

As well as these utopian themes, the discourse of developmentalism is also present in Amadeu's manifesto. This is perhaps not surprising given his association with the Brazilian free-software community. As Shaw (2011) shows, free/libre/open–source software (FLOSS) in Brazil began as a potent expression of resistance and as an alternative to information dependency on the global north. This theme is evident in Amadeu's claim, "The Internet offers an unrivalled opportunity to peripheral and emerging countries in the new information society" (2008).

The early influence of Amadeu on the formation of the Marco Civil does appear contradictory. On one hand, his was a radical vision for the internet in Brazil: staunchly opposed to the control leveraged by the content-production sector and cohering instead with the neodevelopmentalism of the free-software movement in Brazil. However, Amadeu's cyberutopianism also aligns clearly with the legitimation discourse of informational capitalism that established the boundaries of common sense around the Marco Civil. Ultimately, despite this seeming incoherence, Amadeu proved to be a pivotal figure in the resistance against the Lei Azeredo.

Echoes of Repression

Another one of the most significant discursive interventions against the Lei Azeredo also involved Amadeu. This act engineered an important articulation between the discourse of resistance to the bill and popular memory of the oppression of the Brazilian military regime. The Ato-Institucional 5 (AI-5; Institutional Act 5) was enacted in 1968 under the regime of President Costa e Silva and enforced the complete suspension of civil rights in Brazil. When Amadeu referred to the Lei Azeredo in an interview in January 2009 as the "AI-5 digital" (Santarém, 2010, p. 86), he was deliberately drawing parallels between the infringements of liberty implied by the Lei Azeredo and one of the most acute moments of civil oppression in Brazilian history. The gambit was effective and served as an effective rallying cry for collective opposition, as well as demystifying the more arcane aspects of the legislative process for potential participants.

As per the analysis of Santarém, "as a result of the denomination 'AI-5 Digital,' the project became better known and . . . there was a shift in focus, that receded from the specific provisions, and on to the associated ideas" (2010, p. 82). Although Lemos's op-ed is often interpreted as the conceptual genesis for the Marco Civil, it was Amadeu's intervention that was decisive in garnering the public support and political will necessary to consider a framework of digital rights in Brazil, even though it was Lemos's technocratic focus that ultimately oriented the project.

Later the same year, the activist Caribé formed the Mega Não, initially a blog but that would go on to become a loose social movement opposed to the Lei Azeredo. The digital and street protests under the banner of the

Mega Não, the continual *blogagem políticas* (political bloggings) Caribé and Amadeu organized, the online petition initiated by Caribé that garnered over three hundred thousand signatories, as well as the public hearings organized by sympathetic members of congress, cumulatively influenced a change in tack by the PT government in relation to the cybercrime bill (Caribé, interview, 2015; Abramovay, 2017, p. 59). It shifted from a stance of tacit acceptance to explicit opposition. The Lei Azeredo was stripped of its most extreme provisions related to data retention and the obligation for ISPs to report illicit acts (Santarém, 2010, p. 93). It was this much-denuded bill that was passed into law in 2012.

Although the opposition described here accounts for the partial defeat of the Lei Azeredo as a legislative project designed to control the Brazilian internet in favor of the financial-services industry and IP lobby, the birth of the Marco Civil required one last inducement. This came in the unexpected form of a keynote speech given by President Lula at the 2009 Fórum Internacional de Software Livre (FISL; International Free Software Forum) in Porto Alegre. It was in this charismatic and free-wheeling address that Lula gave the presidential seal of approval to the concept of a framework of civil rights for the Brazilian internet.

Free Software and Lula's Launch

The FISL had been organized as an annual event in Porto Alegre since 2000 by the Associação de Software Livre (ASL; Free Software Association) and had served as an important gathering point for the burgeoning free-software community in Brazil. Free software emerged as a reaction to informational capitalism's sweeping logics of commodification and control, particularly, as manifested in proprietary software in the 1980s (Söderberg, 2008). Although an apolitical libertarianism became the dominant ethos among programmers in the United States, by contrast, FLOSS was notably politicized in Brazil.

This politicization occurred by association with a number of factors: the country's recent history of civic repression and media control; the trade-union movement, particularly, the current of *novo sindicalismo* (new trade unionism), the PT government's agenda of national development, and the genesis of the community in Porto Alegre where participatory democratic experiments had characterized municipal politics since the late 1980s (Baiocchi, 2017, p. 38–39; Shaw, 2011). Accompanying all of these factors was the perception among many free-software advocates in Brazil that this mode of technology production would permit Brazil to transcend the constraints of its peripheral status within global capitalism.

As Affonso Souza of the CTS opined to me, "to talk about technology is increasingly essential for your everyday political agenda." That Lula described digital inclusion as the "sexiest word in government" in his FISL keynote is, in this regard, a telling claim (Tiemann, 2009). Ultimately, given that in 2009 the PT were already positioning themselves for the 2010 presidential election and that the promotion of free culture and free software constituted some of the most acclaimed aspects of Lula's second term in office, it should perhaps not be surprising that Lula opted to make a landmark announcement at the FISL.

Alongside the electoral calculations, there was a personal dimension that played a large part in Lula declaring his support for the Marco Civil that also emanated from the politicized free-software community. It came most prominently in the form of Amadeu. A measure of Lula's confidence in Amadeu can be gleaned from the fact that Lula recruited him in 2003 to head the federal agency Instituto Nacional de Tecnologia de Informação (ITI) in charge of state encryption tools (O'Maley, 2015, p. 50). Amadeu's influence on the president was understood to have been key to Lula's decision to publicly pronounce against the Lei Azeredo and in favor of a Marco Civil (Pedro Paranaguá, interview, 2015).

The discourses in President Lula's address were the political genesis of the Marco Civil. They played a large part in establishing the boundaries within which the Marco Civil would be constructed, most notably for the drafters of the bill in the Ministry of Justice who cited Lula's address as providing them with the seal of approval they needed to begin work on the project. As both a political champion of free software and digital inclusion and as head of a neodevelopmentalist state project, President Lula draws upon a particular fusion of cyberutopian and developmentalist discourses in his speech. Both of these discourses were pivotal in shaping the legislative project of the Marco Civil itself.

The Presidential Framing of Freedom and Development

In his characteristically folksy style, Lula began by likening the difference between free and proprietary software as the difference between preparing a dish themselves with "a Brazilian flavor to the food" or simply "eating whatever Microsoft wanted to sell us" (Tiemann, 2009). It is in the next lines, however, that the tenets of the digital discourse are revealed.

In the competition between the dishes, "what prevailed, simply, was freedom." Elaborating on this idea, Lula claims that FLOSS "valorizes people's individuality" and that "there is nothing more that guarantees freedom than if you guarantee individual freedom and that people allow their creativity to flourish." Moreover, Lula uses the closing line of his address to claim, "Finally, this country is getting a taste for freedom of information" (Tiemann, 2009). The signifiers of individual freedom, creativity, and the free flow of information are key tenets of the legitimation discourse of informational capitalism.

The discourse of cyberutopianism is also apparent in Lula's speech as he proceeds to eulogize the internet as a transformative technology. It is also one into which he articulates themes from Brazilian history, as evidenced here: "I think that we are living through a revolutionary moment for humanity in which the press now does not have the power that it had a few years ago, information is no longer a selective thing that the holders can use for a coup d'état."[2] Evoking "a revolution for humanity" as a consequence of the internet's diffusion is a recurring conceit of cyberutopianism. The use of the term "coup d'état," meanwhile, refers to the information control imposed by the military dictatorship and its media apparatus. This reference also connects implicitly to Amadeu's coinage of the AI-5 Digital. The connection between the Lei Azeredo and Brazil's history of media control is made more explicit when Lula addresses the topic of the controversial bill directly. He claims that the Lei Azeredo "does not seek to address abuses of the Internet. It, in truth, seeks to create *censorship*" (Tiemann, 2009, emphasis added). According to Santarém's analysis, censorship was the "magic word," because it made the Lei Azeredo "publicly indefensible" (2010, p. 93).

To be clear, the central charge of censorship is only one of many that Lula could have chosen to make against the Lei Azeredo. He might also have drawn attention to the intended political economic effects of the bill: to minimize the risk exposure of Brazilian financial entities,[3] to surveil users on behalf of the IP lobby and security state, and to protect the central commodity form of IP rights holders from unauthorized circulation. Reference to any of these aspects of the Lei Azeredo's provisions might have signaled to the drafters of the Marco Civil that the legislative project should consider the relationship between online civil rights and the structural inequities of informational capitalism in a concerted way.

Instead of any of the above dimensions of the Lei Azeredo, however, Lula opted to sound the alarm of censorship. By doing so he was able to associate himself with the popular activism focused against the AI-5 Digital, a term coined by his confidant and colleague Amadeu, that invoked the specter of the military dictatorship. Moreover, censorship represents the antithesis of the creative freedom enabled by FLOSS, in particular, and the internet, in general. Not only is creative freedom a metasignifier within the digital discourse but by invoking it in his speech, Lula also allied himself with the free-software community in a resonant way. It was, in some respects, a strategic alliance as the government would need a supportive constituency for this project. As Affonso Souza of the CTS explained to me, "if there was some group that we thought that could easily be plugged in to the whole idea of the Marco Civil, it was at the time the community around free software."

Another core discourse in Lula's address is that of developmentalism. For instance, one of the PT government's core digital inclusion programs was Computador para Tudos, which aimed to make the desktop computer "arrive at the country's periphery" (Tiemann, 2009). Indeed, in the context of recounting various initiatives of the PT government focused on digital inclusion, Lula states, "This country is still finding itself, because for centuries we were treated like third-class citizens, we had to ask permission to do things, we could only do the things that the United States or Europe let us do." The notion of Brazil existing at the periphery of the global economic system is explicit in Lula's statement here and is one that is key to understanding the significance of the Marco Civil within a global system of informational capitalism.

Lula's FISL address marked the political genesis of the Marco Civil. One important reaction came from Guilherme Almeida, at the time an adviser within the Ministry of Justice's Secretaria de Assuntos Legislativos (SAL; Secretariat of Legislative Affairs): "It was the carte blanche SAL needed to be able to touch the issue" (Brito, 2015, p. 52). The manner in which Almeida and his colleagues addressed the issue of the Marco Civil is the focus of the next section. This is the phase in which the horizon of possibility for the Marco Civil was, in theory, opened up by the decision to undertake an online public consultation but in fact underwent rapid constriction.

Institutionalization: IP Hipsters and Brazil's "Ten Commandments"

In order to understand how the Marco Civil reached its eventual form and how alternative visions were occluded in the process, the exercise of power needs to be approached in a multifaceted way: not only material *or* discursive but their myriad combinations. One of the most significant ways in which discursive and material power are combined in practice is in establishing the boundaries of debate for a contentious topic. After all, following Michel Foucault: power is not simply oppressive; it is productive (1972). The title of this chapter—circumscription—indeed underscores the importance of that dimension of power.

Danish researcher Mikkel Flyverbom's exploration of how objects and actors are ordered within global internet governance shows how "power and authority are not only about hard government, decisions and clear-cut victories, but also about the ability to foster and steer dialogue, to make issues visible" (2011, p. 160). In examining the network-neutrality debates in the United States, Newman (2019) arrives at a similar conclusion, arguing that the regulatory authorities and the corporate stakeholders succeeded in consolidating "a form of 'processing bias': the arguments themselves, in their processing by all players involved, needed to hew to a particular set of terms in order to *matter* as an actor where decisions were made" (p. 26). This reasoning was not lost on the protagonists in the Marco Civil. A senior figure at a US web company commented to me about the online consultation, "If there's something that's biased about these tools from the get-go, it's that they invite comments on the draft, *and there could be plenty of things that are not on the draft*" (2015, emphasis added).

The focus for the next section settles on the process of institutionalization that occurred as the Marco Civil transformed from an aspirational concern into a concrete legislative project. As a nucleus of young IP and technology lawyers took the reins, I argue that the digital discourse became a dominant force in shaping the contours of the Marco Civil and the digital rights therein. Some of the decisive factors in this process were the decision to use a document drafted by the Brazilian Internet Steering Committee called the Ten Principles, or *Decálogo*, as a template for the Marco Civil's rights framework; the partnership forged between the Ministry of Justice's SAL and the Vargas Foundation's CTS, a partnership that precluded the inclusion of more-radical voices in the project's formation and heralded the creation of what Streeter (1996) terms an "interpretive community," one that can designate which positions are open for debate and which are beyond the pale.

The Formation of a (Miniature) Interpretive Community

In his pivotal FISL keynote speech, President Lula commissioned Tarso Genro, the minister of justice, to establish the Marco Civil. In the process of bureaucratic delegation, the task fell to the SAL, which operates within the Ministry of Justice. The role of the secretariat is to develop frameworks for new laws and stickhandle their passage through the relevant organs of state. In 2009 SAL was occupied by two key figures: Abramovay, secretary of SAL from 2007 until 2010 (when he became the youngest secretary of justice in Brazilian history), and Guilherme Almeida, adviser to the secretary from 2009 until 2010 (when he was promoted to chief of staff). Both men were in their mid-twenties and formed a nucleus around which the SAL was populated with young lawyers committed to the democratization of the legislative process (Abramovay, 2017, p. 67). Moreover, both Almeida and Abramovay—alongside Lemos, who wrote the pivotal op-ed analyzed in the previous section—were classmates in law school at the Universidade de São Paulo during the late 1990s. These three men would become the architects of the Marco Civil.

The impetus generated by the president's speech catalyzed the formation of two external partnerships with SAL. One provided the technical capacity and was struck with a program in the Brazilian Ministry of Culture called the Fórum da Cultura Digital Brasileira. This permitted SAL to use an open-source digital platform, culturadigital.br, which the ministry had created to facilitate debate around public policy (Santarém, 2010, p. 96). The other partnership was institutional and connected SAL to CTS, It is the latter partnership that constituted the interpretive community that delimited the civic potential of the Marco Civil.

Lemos, the lead researcher and cofounder of the CTS team, had already become the de facto public face of the campaign for a civil regulatory framework for the Brazilian internet. More than that, Santarém explained to me, Lemos's public profile was "incomparable with any other figure like him. . . . He transcends the question of law, he is more about entrepreneurialism, technology." This profile translated into the vision of a Marco Civil outlined in his influential op-ed, one focused on the protection of innovation and efficiency that, in turn, became an orienting framework for the nascent bill.

Rather than adding a greater variety of perspectives to the SAL team, arguably the partnership with CTS served to further distill the ideology of the group, to undergird the creation of an interpretive community. The tongue-in-cheek appraisal by Affonso Souza, a senior researcher and cofounder of CTS, is instructive in this regard; he describes the CTS as made up of "IP and Internet regulation hipsters" (Papp, 2014, p. 40). Nearly all young men, they were trained in IP law and/or technology law. In our interview he also lauded the uniformity of opinion that reigned within the partnership: "They had the very same view that we had for the Marco Civil as a whole. So, in terms of substance, of content, there was no major discussion or different opinions from the team of the Ministry of Justice and our team" (2015).

Streeter's description of an "interpretive community" refers to the entire communications policy apparatus in Washington, DC (1996, p. 117). It is for this reason that I characterize the CTS-SAL group—comprising less than a dozen core members—as an interpretive community *in miniature*. I argue that the remarkable ideational harmony that Affonso Souza describes was derived from their shared professional vocation and worldview. It resulted in certain principles of the Marco Civil—examined later—being embraced as commonsensical, while others were dismissed as inconceivable. This constitutes the real essence of Streeter's "interpretive community."

The centrist legitimacy of the CTS as a development partner for the Marco Civil was instrumental in discrediting claims that it was the project of "communists" or "anarchists." The label of communism remains a charged political term in Brazil—a legacy of the military dictatorship—and was a rhetorical device frequently used against the Marco Civil by its political opponents. Although Almeida dismissed the viability of codeveloping the Marco Civil project with, for instance, the ASL, it is hard to dismiss the idea that the partnership with CTS-FGV served to marginalize actors with a distinct vision for what the Marco Civil could become; one that might be much further removed from the logics of informational capitalism and its legitimation discourse. The Partido Pirata (Brazilian Pirate Party) represented one such actor.[4]

The Partido Pirata had been prominent in the opposition against the Lei Azeredo (Papp, 2014, p. 29; Santarém, 2010, p. 91). The proposed cybercrime bill was antithetical to the pirate movement's core values of eliminating government surveillance and reforming IP (Beyer & McKelvey, 2015). Accordingly, the Partido Pirata and CTS became unlikely allies, united in their opposition to the Lei Azeredo. The prospect, however, of the IP hipsters of the CTS's technocratic vision of digital rights aligning with that held by the Pirates was negligible. This is underscored when Moncau characterized the Marco Civil to me as a "process of the community understanding that maybe that declaration of 'Freedom of Cyberspace,' maybe it's not so true" (2015).[5]

The Pirate Party overcame an innate suspicion of government regulation of the internet to voice initial support for the Marco Civil. Out of pragmatism rather than conviction, the Partido Pirata would continue to support the bill through its congressional phase, until the concessions demanded by the powerbrokers of informational capitalism dragged the Marco Civil into direct conflict with the values of the party.

The Empty Signifier of Participation

One of the facets of the Marco Civil's development that marked it for international acclaim was its preliminary phases of open public debate (*Net closes*, 2014; Web We Want Foundation, 2014). The limitations and peculiarities of this public consultation derived in part from Brazil's status at the periphery of informational capitalism. It suffices at this stage to focus on a different dimension of the consultation phase, one that also challenges the notion that the Marco Civil represented a blueprint for digital rights simply by virtue of having conducted a public consultation. Rather than allow the fact of the consultation to obscure its substance, we need to understand not only the rationale for conducting this process but also how the parameters of the debate were constricted from the outset.

It would be misguided to present the decision to conduct a public consultation as a cynical exercise, one frequently observed where the state's agenda is obscured by a veneer of democratic legitimacy. The intentions of the drafters to stretch the sinews of social participation in the legislative process, as far as one can discern reliably from the outside, were sincere. Affonso Souza related in interview that it was an effort to "create the best and most diverse and most transparent bill of law that Brazil ever saw. . . . It was a process to radicalize the democratic component of the legislative process" (2015).

This idealism was necessarily buttressed by pragmatism, an understanding that a law that was legitimated through the input of Brazilian society might better withstand the forces of realpolitik exerted within the Brazilian congress. Santarém, the manager of the online consultation, affirmed to me, "We were looking to present to the Congress a project that had the weight of social legitimation" (2015). Undergirding this rationale, however, were the precepts of the digital discourse and their crystallization within the SAL-CTS team as common sense. This served to heighten the value of participation within the group to the extent that the *fact* of the consultation they facilitated may have blinded them to its *nature*.

Participation is a metasignifier within the digital discourse, one used to legitimate the workings of informational capitalism. According to this discourse, participation in networked communication technologies allows users to overcome the limitations of traditional hierarchies and to enjoy the rewards of "democratization and decentralization" (Fisher, 2010, p. 111). The framing of participation in the digital discourse promotes a form of shallow engagement that occludes the power inequities between platforms and users. As Mejias (2013) argues, "the participatory culture of the digital network has more in common with the society of control" (p. 25). Participation as signifier also serves a dual function in terms of what it co-constitutes: a social atomization conducive to the workings of the market and a mode of activity that "feeds" many of the main business models that drive informational capitalism.

The following statement by Daniel Arbix, SAL's then chief of staff (2008–9), reveals the influence of participation in this regard. He describes how "for everyone in this moment there was a great belief that *participation is a value in itself and must be maximized*" (Brito, 2015, p. 54, emphasis added).

In a general sense, the PT government under Lula had gained renown for its efforts to extend participation in the democratic process (Avritzer & Anastasia, 2006), although its initially radical nature had been hollowed out by the end of Lula's second mandate. As per Baiocchi (2017):

> Today, the version of participation that dominates both governmental discourse in Brazil and discourse among international traffickers of participatory blueprints incorporates elements of the radical-democratic and revolutionary councils, which emphasize equivalence and inclusion, *even if they have given up ideas of social transformation and popular empowerment.* (p. 43, emphasis added)

In a similar vein, Abramovay, secretary of SAL, declared that he was actively trying to create a "Wiki-culture" within the legislative process (Abramovay, 2017, p. 69). A precursor to the Marco Civil created in 2007 between the Italian government and the Brazilian Ministry of Culture under Gilberto Gil also merits mention here. Sociologists Engin Isin and Evelyn Ruppert (2015) cite the bill's architects as arguing that "the Internet constitutes a world without borders and will require a new cultural model of making digital rights claims from the bottom up" (p. 173). Or, that as the process was ongoing, Brazilian internet activists referred to the consultation as a "hacking of the state" (Solagna, 2015, p. 80). Given the quite modest nature of these experiments, it brings to mind the caustic observation by Alessandro Delfanti and Johan Söderberg (2015) in their analysis of hacking that "the very idea that tinkering offers a way to subvert the agendas of the powers-that-be has become a foundational myth of contemporary capitalism" (p. 461).

Perhaps the most convincing evidence that the digital discourse was a formative influence in the decision to undertake a public consultation can be discerned in the rhetoric Abramovay used at the opening ceremony of the Marco Civil in October 2009. He declared, "We knew that new technologies give us infinite possibilities to rethink democracy. . . . Today it is possible to place everyone in a public square" (O'Maley, 2015, p. 71). The ideas that ICTs offer the potential to redesign our democracy and that a return to the Athenian Agora is possible correspond to the discourses of cyberutopianism (Dahlberg, 2010) and the "digital sublime" (Mosco, 2005).

The significance of underscoring the constitutive force of the digital discourse here is to show that the fact *there was open participation* at the inception of the Marco Civil obscured for many observers and participants, including arguably the drafters themselves, both the shortcomings of that participation and *what they were being asked to participate in.* This latter deficiency demands attention and is what the remainder of this section focuses on.

WSIS to the Marco Civil (via the Decálogo)

Almeida of the SAL, faced with the daunting prospect of a blank canvas at the launch of the drafting process, explained to me:

> We have this problem that we have to make our institutions, which are national, which are local and sovereign, dialogue with the internet, which is like global, constantly evolving, and so forth. And how can we merge them both? And we tried to bring in from two different origins. One was the ten commandments of the internet in Brazil, which was how can we perceive internet from our lead entity that is legitimate to do this, and the second was the Brazilian Constitution. (2018)

The ten commandments, or decálogo, is a set of principles published in 2009 for the governance of the Brazilian internet by the Brazilian Internet Steering Committee (CGI.br), the product of a multistakeholder development process (CGI.br, 2009). The foundational role of this document is what allows us to draw a line connecting the genealogy of digital rights detailed in the last chapter to the development of the Marco Civil.

The decálogo was devised over the course of two years by the twenty-one members of the CGI's standing committee (Virgilio Almeida, interview, 2015). The impetus to produce this document was generated by the manifold threats to what many committee members considered to be the founding principles of the internet's operations and structure. These threats included the proposed Lei Azeredo but also several judicial decisions in Brazil in the mid-2000s. One notorious example was the 2007 decision by a lower-court judge to block the video-sharing website YouTube for all Brazilian users because of Google's refusal to remove a contentious video (YouTube, 2007).

The fact that the development of the decálogo began around 2007 is significant. The World Summit on the Information Society (WSIS) events occurred in 2003 and 2005 and set the paradigm for digital rights, one based upon technocratic, market-friendly, and individualist fixes. The decálogo emerged as one of the first post-WSIS digital rights charters and, I argue, was molded in its image. Although published with the subtitle "principles for the governance and use of the internet," the decálogo was also explicitly created as a set of digital rights. As the early internet pioneer and CGI.br member, Carlos Afonso (popularly known as Caf) explained to me: "The point of view of civil society is always supposed to be the point of view of rights. The right to communicate, et cetera. . . . So that is why in 2007 . . . we created those famous Ten Principles" (2015).

Specifically, the ten commandments comprised: freedom, privacy, and human rights; democratic and collaborative governance; universality; diversity; innovation; network neutrality; limited third-party liability; functionality, stability, and security; standardization and interoperability; and legal and regulatory environments (CGI.br, 2009). Each of these rights or principles is accompanied by a short explanatory text. A critical analysis of these helps to reveal the discourses that oriented the charter.

For instance, alongside the first principle, freedom, privacy, and human rights: "The use of the internet must be driven by the principles of freedom of expression, individual privacy, and the respect for human rights, recognizing them as essential to the preservation of a fair and democratic society." The promotion of freedom of expression within the digital-rights paradigm is presented as a negative right that obfuscates the structural conditions in which communication occurs. This, I argue, is the result of the celebration of the expressive capacities of netizens within the digital discourse. Moreover, the emphasis on human rights serves to individualize, universalize, and depoliticize digital rights (Slaughter, 2018), while demonstrating a shallow engagement with freedom of expression and privacy but neglecting other substantive parts of the paradigm. The explicit reference to individual privacy is another characteristic of the digital-rights paradigm. As surveillance and legal scholars remind us, privacy is too often presented as hyperindividualist and legalistic and fails to adequately confront the surveillance regime that it purports to rebuff (Gilliom, 2011; Renieris, 2023).

The second principle of democratic and collaborative governance declares, "Internet governance must be exercised in a transparent, multilateral, and democratic manner, with the participation of the various sectors of society." Multistakeholder policy development for the internet is another core tenet of the post-WSIS paradigm. It serves to depoliticize the entrenched power relationships within informational capitalism, covering it instead with a veil of consensus-based decision making (Gurstein, 2014).

The principle of innovation is also a key signifier within both the digital and the neoliberal discourses, one that gives "technological clothing" (Fisher, 2010, p. 74) to the flexibility of market-based policies. The principles of network neutrality and limited third-party liability are both shallow proxies for user rights that favor a particular sector (such as, web companies) within informational capitalism.

The only stipulation for the legal and regulatory environment is that it "must preserve the dynamics of the Internet as a space for *collaboration*" (emphasis added). The elevation of collaboration to the foremost principle of the internet's function should not be dismissed as happenstance. Collaborative production is vaunted within the digital discourse as a means to achieve user empowerment as well as decentralization and democracy (Fisher, 2010, p. 109). Collaboration as a signifier is also used to obscure the value of collaborative activities online as a mode of accumulation within informational capitalism. And as the Brazilian legal scholar Marcelo Thompson points out in his critique of the Marco Civil, lauding the value of collaboration is part of a worldview that technologizes society, one that understands people "being operatively assimilated by multitudinous networks rather than the other way around" (2010, p. 9). Finally, and most important, a zealous focus on collaboration forecloses many other possibilities for legal and regulatory measures that could safeguard the internet for democracy.

Ultimately, any connection to wider social-justice agendas, any reference to collectivist principles, or the hypercommercialism of the internet is obscured in this reckoning of digital rights and principles. The decálogo draws heavily upon the digital discourse whose tenets privilege individual autonomy, creativity, and expression that, in turn, serve to legitimize the functions of informational capitalism. That the resultant text was eulogized by one of the founding members of the CGI.br as embodying "the spirit of the internet" (Getschko, 2009) and that the principles were depicted in the 2013 edition of the annual CGI.br magazine, Revista.br, as stone tablets presented by God (CGI.br, 2013), suggest the degree to which the CGI.br presents its decálogo as dogma, obscuring alternative priorities for the network.

Neoliberal Roots of Multistakeholderism

We must also contend with the history and composition of the CGI.br in order to understand how its actions align with, rather than challenge, the logics of informational capitalism. The CGI.br was founded in 1995 as part of the neoliberal reforms and privatizations undertaken in Brazil by the administrations of Fernando Collor de Mello (1990–92) and Fernando Henrique Cardoso (1995–2003). Caf and his colleagues successfully lobbied Sérgio Motta, minister of communications, to separate the internet from telecommunications as objects of regulation and to ensure that there was no state monopoly over provision of internet services (Knight, 2014, p. 31). They also convinced him to create the Internet Steering Committee (CGI. br) as the main actor with legal authority over the internet in Brazil. The committee was explicitly multistakeholder as it comprised members of the appropriate ministries, two appointees from business, and one each from academia and civil society (M. Carvalho, 2006, p. 142; O'Maley, 2015, p. 100–102).

Although it might appear that multistakeholderism in Brazil was born of a genuinely pluralistic effort to further the public interest, I argue that the committee bears the foundational imprint of neoliberalism. More widely, I concur with the critique of Canadian researcher and policy adviser Michael Gurstein (2014) that multistakeholderism is the mode of governance par excellence of neoliberalism: it negates democratic accountability, disguises established power imbalances, champions technical over public-interest concerns, and veils the maintenance of a promarket status quo with the rhetoric of participation. We would also be well served to heed Streeter's (1996) observation:

> If there is going to be government intervention on the industry's behalf, it must be done in a way that at least suggests the presence of neutral principles and expert decision-making. . . . Even corporations have an interest—an ambivalent one—in fostering institutions that are not mechanically tied to corporate designs, institutions that demonstrate some autonomy. (p. 120)

As Gurstein (2014) argues, multistakeholderism may well be an effective and legitimate means to manage the technical minutiae of the internet's functions. However, when multistakeholderism is permitted to transcend that limited remit to become the default governance mode for all matters pertaining to the internet—especially given the internet's foundational role in sustaining informational capitalism—this demands a skeptical analysis of its rapid ascent.

In the case of the CGI.br, Sérgio Motta, the communications minister responsible for its founding, was one of the earliest champions of market-based reform in Brazil (Font, 2003, p. 172). Motta's agenda was, however, also congruous with the Brazilian internet pioneers' vision for the network. It is well established that the internet pioneers in Brazil were leftist exiles who abhorred the oppressive potential of a media system centralized under the state (O'Maley, 2015). Neoliberalism, therefore, offered a means to wrest control of the internet away from the state telecoms monopoly, Telebras. The fact that decentralization of the internet's governance was accompanied by an outsize role for market actors was part of the trade-off.

As was clear in my interviews, CGI.br members display their multistakeholderism as a badge of honor (Carlos Afonso and Virgilio Almeida, 2015). Multistakeholderism is often promoted within the internet-governance community as a value in itself, that is, an end and not the means (Raymond & DeNardis, 2015). This is particularly true post-WSIS, after efforts by developing state actors to wrest critical internet resources from US control were placated through the creation of new multistakeholder fora for discussing internet governance (McLaughlin & Pickard, 2005). The role of the digital discourse in promoting the value of participation should also be accounted for. In the case of the decálogo and its virtually unchallenged legitimacy, the *fact* of multistakeholderism obscures its nature in much the same way as the public consultation does in the case of the Marco Civil.

Indeed, the multistakeholder form of the CGI.br should not be conflated with democratic legitimacy. Although the CGI.br was extensively reformed in 2003 by the Lula administration to permit a greater diversity of representation—in keeping with the PT's emphasis on participatory government—the effectiveness of these measures is questionable.[6] The presence of long-term members casts doubt on the degree to which the committee is truly open to new and diverse voices. Carlos Afonso also conceded to me the "imperfections," as very few eligible NGOs participate in the electoral process, and the business representatives are nominated in a "prearranged" fashion. Awareness of these imperfections was manifest in the Pirate Party campaign launched in 2012 to reform a CGI.br they describe as "insufficiently democratic, minimally representative, and obscurely transparent" (Partido Pirata, 2016).

Having analyzed how the early blueprint for the Marco Civil was formed within the dominant paradigm of digital rights, the focus moves now to the two phases of public consultation that defined this first phase of the Marco Civil's development within the context of Brazil's status at the periphery of informational capitalism.

Legitimation: Public Consultation at the Periphery

On October 29, 2009, on a summer afternoon in FGV's headquarters in Rio de Janeiro, Tarso Genro, Brazilian minister of justice, flanked by Lemos, Abramovay, senior executives from the FGV, and three members of congress, announced to the assembled press that the first phase of an online consultation for the Marco Civil da Internet would begin (Abramovay, 2017, p. 80). Brazilian citizens qua internet users were directed to the culturadigital.br site hosted by the Ministry of Culture, where citizens had forty-five days to offer their suggestions on the provisional framework drafted by the SAL-CTS team. This constituted the start of the first phase of public consultation on the draft bill.

Phase 1

The initial blueprint for the Marco Civil legislation that Brazilian citizens were invited to comment upon was based on a framework that did not disguise its origins in the CGI.br's decálogo. It was divided into three main axes: individual and collective rights, private-sector obligations, and government directives. Each axis contained a number of more clearly defined principles, hyperlinked on the website (Ministério da Justiça, 2009). Every one of those, when clicked, revealed a short description of the principle, the rationale for its inclusion, and an explanation of its treatment in existing Brazilian law—particularly, the constitution and the Código da Defesa do Consumidor (the Consumer Defense Code)—as well as relevant international equivalents.

Each principle contained a link that opened a blog page on which site users could leave a comment. The initial framework was divided as follows:

1. individual and collective rights (axis 1)
    1.1. privacy
        1.1.1.   intimacy, privacy, and fundamental rights
        1.1.2.   inviolability of correspondence and communications
        1.1.3.   log storage
        1.1.4.   how to guarantee privacy
    1.2. freedom of expression
        1.2.1.   federal constitution and Universal Declaration of Human Rights
        1.2.2.   conflicts with other fundamental rights: Anonymity
        1.2.3.   freedom of expression on the internet
        1.2.4.   the right to receive and access information
        1.2.5.   anonymous access
    1.3. right to access
        1.3.1.   connections to freedom of expression
        1.3.2.   access to internet and social development
        1.3.3.   means of access
2. private-sector obligations (axis 2)
    2.1. clear definition of intermediary liability
        2.1.1.   absence of specific legislation
        2.1.2.   a liability regime compatible with the dynamic nature of the internet
        2.1.3.   administrative processes and extrajudicial precedents
    2.2. nondiscrimination of content (neutrality)
        2.2.1.   the end-to-end principle
        2.2.2.   unwarranted filtering
3. government directives (axis 3)
    3.1. openness
        3.1.1.   full interoperability
        3.1.2.   standards and open formats

3.1.3. access to public data and information
3.2. infrastructure
    3.2.1. connectivity
    3.2.2. broadband diffusion and digital inclusion
3.3. capacity building
    3.3.1. digital culture for social development
    3.3.2. public and private initiatives

During this first round of consultation, a total of 686 comments were registered on the blog. The principles that attracted by far the most comments were: anonymity (139); intimacy, privacy, and fundamental rights (76); and log storage (75) (Ministério da Justiça, 2009). The remaining principles attracted less than half of those comment tallies. This fact suggests that an inclination to participate in the consultation was driven by the public opposition to the Lei Azeredo. Anonymity, privacy, and log storage were, after all, the highest-profile elements of the notorious cybercrime bill. It is noteworthy that as the Marco Civil progressed through the legislative process and gained a new tripartite structure based on data protection, network neutrality, and limited third-party liability, the latter two of those three pillars enjoyed limited salience at this stage. If we compare this to the public furor in the United States when network-neutrality rules were in play (Newman, 2019), the contrast is stark. This underscores the limited public awareness of such technical issues, a fact indicative of Brazil's peripheral status within informational capitalism and one examined later in this section.

Although none of the principles selected by the drafters explicitly addressed the political economic underpinnings of the internet, many of them could have opened up discussion on issues related to mass surveillance, datafication, an advertising-driven online economy, and public ownership of data and platforms. The reality, however, revealed by a close reading of comments registered under the three principles identified above shows that participants were predominantly following a libertarian agenda or were debating the merits of particular technical dimensions of internet functionality, such as the adoption of the IPv6 protocol.

Certainly, my reading of these comments aligned with the interpretation of Latin American researchers Rachel Bragatto, Raphael Sampaio, and Maria Nicolás (2015, Inovadora) of the first phase consultation as a whole. According to those authors, libertarianism was the main position the participants espoused. This entails the "non-regulation of the online environment or in the creation of rules that maximize freedom in cyberspace, looking to guarantee anonymity, to oppose log storage and favorable to absolute freedom of expression online" (Bragatto et al., 2015).

THE PIRATES' LONE DISSENT   One user that deviated notably from these trends was the Brazilian Pirate Party. The Pirates envisioned a digital-rights framework based on quite different principles to the SAL-CTS team and expressed this vision through fifteen comments in this round of public consultation. As outliers to the general trends exhibited in the consultation, these demand closer inspection.

For instance, one comment logged under "how to guarantee privacy" makes explicit reference to the "exchange and sale" of user data and advocates for its complete prohibition (Ministério da Justiça, 2009). This is noteworthy because the overriding concern among other commentators was the role of the state in accessing user data, not the practices of market actors. Another comment registered under "freedom of expression on the Internet" states that freedom of expression (FoE) was impossible unless all protocols, standards, and formats were open and prohibited from being proprietary and closed. This position identified the structure and ownership of communication as intrinsic to FoE. This runs against the grain of the predominant understanding of freedom of expression articulated by other commentators: that FoE can be effectively safeguarded so long as the state is constrained from acting as censor.

In "internet access and social development," the Pirate Party warned that "one must pay attention to not permit the great holders of the means of mass communication to suffocate the independent and distributed production on the Internet . . . with the goal of maintaining their communicative hegemony." This clearly refers to the control of media giants in Brazil, such as Globo, and is a warning that such market concentration should be guarded against online.[7] In "a liability regime compatible with the dynamic nature of the internet," meanwhile, the Pirates note that the "importance of the framework is to separate the service from the content" (Ministério da Justiça, 2009). This notion of a structural separation framework between telecoms service providers and content platforms is flagged by Newman in the US network-neutrality debates as a mechanism of great democratic value that is obfuscated by focusing on the technical minutiae of network neutrality (2019).

In "broadband diffusion and digital inclusion," the Pirates demand that the state regulate private telecoms monopolies in order to facilitate broadband diffusion. Building upon that comment, later in the same section the Pirates advocate for publicly owned telecoms infrastructure as the only viable way to universalize internet access throughout Brazil. Perhaps, the most radical departure from the prevailing views expressed in this consultation comes in the penultimate section on "digital culture for social development." Here the Partido Pirata proposes revision of IP law and the creation of state-owned digital platforms to disseminate the work of small content producers. Furthermore, "the state could intervene directly in network infrastructure to provide services to citizens. Not only of access, but also the production of content and the infrastructure to do so" (Ministério da Justiça, 2009). The notion of publicly owned content platforms corresponds quite precisely to the digital-rights attributes of a social critique of capitalism. *It is political, collectivist, and public and founded upon state intervention and systemic change.*

That the Partido Pirata was ploughing a lone furrow in its conceptualization of digital rights offers two important considerations. The first is that, as per Flyverbom's (2011) notion of the exercise of power within internet policymaking, the drafters' consultative framework was extremely effective in circumscribing the scope of debate within the intended limits. As Dolber (2013) also notes, "policy reform activists must be in conversation with the values and norms of the dominant institutions in order to be taken seriously" (p. 149). Another explanation points to the constitutive force of the digital discourse in constricting consideration of issues by Brazilian citizens qua internet users outside of the digital-rights paradigm; that is, expression, freedom, and individualism as opposed to social justice, equality, and collectivism.

"ARTISANAL" OR "HORRIBLE"? A total of 130 registered participants logged a comment in this first phase. As the analysis by Bragatto, Sampaio, and Nicolás damningly reveals, the concentration of participation was even greater given that 67 percent of the comments were posted by thirteen individuals (2015, Inovadora, p. 150). This shows that despite the high-profile activism that accompanied the Lei Azeredo, the first phase of online consultation for the Marco Civil attracted a level of participation that was vanishingly small. Even in the context of Brazil's internet population, the disparity is stark: internet diffusion in 2009 stood at around 40 percent, equaling approximately eighty million people (Internet Live Stats, 2009). Moreover, the participants were nearly all lawyers, programmers, researchers, and IT professionals (Papp, 2014, p. 54), a tiny technical elite whose work tightly orbited the issues under discussion.

The drafters were at pains to note that the limited uptake did not undermine their vision of the process, one founded on a collaborative rather than a participatory ethos. The former values openness, whereas the latter emphasizes the volume of input (Guilherme Almeida, interview, 2015). The low number of comments allowed the small SAL-CTS team to assess and discuss each in a manner repeatedly described as "artisanal" (Affonso Souza, interview, 2015). The careful and qualified deliberation implied by this scenario is not uncontested, however. As per the scathing assessment conveyed to me by a senior executive at a US web company, the participation was comparable to "YouTube comments, I am afraid to say. . . . Ninety-nine percent of things were really horrible, and one percent were actually salvageable" (2015).

Without doubt, though, that all contributions were read and considered speaks not only to the good faith of the drafters but also to the fact that methodologically, the Marco Civil team was operating at the vanguard of established practice in terms of generating a federal law in this manner. Indeed, such was the improvisational nature of the process that if the consultation had "run to like sixty thousand comments," it would have been rendered unviable (Guilherme Almeida, research interview). Lemos later described the process as "crowdsourced" (Affonso Souza et al., 2017, p. 3). I contend that this characterization is misleading. It simultaneously overstates the level of public participation and underplays the framing role of the drafters. It is also indicative of the rhetoric that permitted the innovative nature of the experiment to overshadow the limitations of both the consultative process and the provisions of the resulting draft law.

The first phase of consultation closed on December 17, 2009, and over the course of the next month, the SAL team presented a first draft of the law to all relevant ministries and offices (Papp, 2014, p. 57).

Phase 2

This first draft of the bill, which was made available for a second round of online consultation on April 8, 2010, retained the tripartite structure of the previous framework based upon user rights, private-actor obligations, and state directives (Ministério da Justiça, 2010):

Chapter 1. Preliminary provisions
Chapter 2. The rights and guarantees of users
Chapter 3. The provision of connection and internet services
    Section 1. General provisions
    Section 2. Internet traffic
    Section 3. Data logs
        Subsection 1. The storage of connection logs
        Subsection 2. The storage of access and internet service logs
        Subsection 3. Protecting the secrecy of internet communication
    Section 4. Content removal
    Section 5. The judicial requisition of logs
Chapter 4. The role of the state
Chapter 5. Final provisions

From both a quantitative and qualitative perspective, the second round of consultation raised the low bar set by its predecessor. Aided by an upgrade in discussion tools, the higher public profile of the project, the engagement of civil and private organizations (albeit, often in a shallow and instrumental way), and the benefit of an actual draft law to analyze, the second round of public consultation received 1,141 comments (Bragatto et al., 2015, A segunda fase, p. 241). More significant than the volume of participation, this latter phase of debate was widely heralded as more qualified, technical, and substantive than the first consultation. It was once again highly concentrated, however, with 63 percent of the comments posted by just fifteen users in the three most commented sections (article 2 outlining the main principles of the law, article 14 on connection logs, and article 20 detailing the mechanisms for lawful content removal) (Ministério da Justiça, 2010).

The activist Caribé suggested to me that although the debate required either a technical understanding of the internet or legal knowledge in order to participate fully (2015), it was still not elitist. I contend the opposite. Despite Brazil's noted proclivity for legalism (or perhaps because of it), those requirements of legal and technical knowledge did succeed in establishing a bar for participation that kept out all but a handful of Brazil's eighty million internet users. Moreover, this was not at all infelicitous for the drafters, who strove for quality over quantity, knowing that the perception of democratic legitimacy would be bestowed upon the process however limited it was in practice.

Another significant recurring theme was the characterization of the positions advocated by commentators. According to the same analysts—and as signaled by Caribé—the commentators could be broadly grouped into two camps: those associated with the IT sector and those with a legal background (Bragatto et al., 2015, A segunda fase, p. 248). More significant, it was quite straightforward to identify the discourses propagated by individuals within these groups. Those who worked in IT tended to espouse libertarian views "prioritizing creative freedoms and rejecting any central control" while legalists were technocratic, concerned with "detailed and thorough regulation." These are, according to my analysis, the discourses that constituted the ideational foundation of the Marco Civil, and to identify their predominance at this formative stage of the Marco Civil's development shows how tightly the civic potential of the bill was constrained.

PLACATING THE PLATFORMS In terms of the manner in which the business practices of content and service providers would be addressed, once again the measures in the first draft of the bill failed to confront the systemic logics of informational capitalism, promising, instead, to tinker with its mechanics. Although some of these provisions—most notably related to network neutrality and data collection—would prove to be the object of bitter dispute between sectors of informational capitalism, it is my contention that these represented struggles over profit maximization, rather than warding off existential threats. It is necessary to inspect some of those provisions to understand why.

Articles 9 and 14 refer to the obligation for ISPs to maintain connection logs for a maximum of six months—so as to meet the needs of possible criminal investigations—although they would be prohibited from maintaining records of user navigation history. This latter stipulation was designed as a privacy safeguard for users, as the Lei Azeredo had demanded a storage duration of two years. This is one of many examples of the impact that the repressive provisions of the Lei Azeredo had in tempering the civic ambition of the Marco Civil.

Article 10 highlights another recurring feature of the Marco Civil: the invocation of the security state as a privacy threat, while ignoring the repressive potential of commercial data collection. This can also be observed in subsection 3, protecting the secrecy of internet communication, of article 18. As examined later, in a more concerted fashion, it suffices now to underline that Brazil's history of military tyranny caused the security state to gain an outsized role as a privacy bogeyman, while platforms—whose business models are legitimated through the digital discourse—largely escaped scrutiny.

Article 12 outlines the requirements for ISPs to treat all data equally, irrespective of source or destination, which is the basis of network neutrality. Although this would later become the object of most public attention, defined as the "heart of the bill" (Alessandro Molon, interview, 2015) and the subject of a bitter dispute between key sectors of informational capitalism, the topic at this stage enjoyed very limited salience, attracting only seventeen comments. This low profile was, I argue, a product of Brazil's status at the periphery of informational capitalism.

In 2010 the term "network neutrality" had not even appeared in *Capes*, the principal directory of Brazilian academic research (Ramos, 2014, p. 16). There were no Wu's or Yu's contesting the concept and raising its profile in the academic realm.[8] Prior to the Marco Civil, the national telecoms regulator Anatel only once, in 2005, established a position on the issue in relation to internet telephony, and there was no mention of the topic in congressional records (Ramos, 2014, p. 73). In contrast to the United States' high degree of concern about net neutrality, including the infamous case of Comcast's discrimination against BitTorrent in 2007 (Van Schewick, 2016), and although anecdotal evidence of Brazilian ISP throttling peer-to-peer traffic certainly existed (Mizukami, et al., 2014), Brazil lacked any such high-profile cases.

In subsection 2, the storage of access and internet service logs, article 16, represents a significant instance where the drafters of the Marco Civil did intend to place limits on practices of data commodification. Here, the proposed provisions mandated "free and informed prior consent from the user" for the "treatment, distribution to third parties or publication" of data pertaining to access logs. Moreover, data that could be used to identify individual users could only be shared upon issuance of a judicial order.

At first glance, article 16 appears to represent a meaningful attempt to protect users from the loss of privacy associated with the commodification of their data by web companies. It would provide users with the means to be aware of and reject a platform's privacy policy. The reality, however, of the power imbalance between user and platform should lead us to be more circumspect. Communication policy researcher Jonathan Obar refers to this as the "fallacy of information self-management" (2015). This asymmetry between user and platform implies that the notion that reams of dense legalese might constitute the free and informed consent of the average user is more theoretical than real. These views are buttressed also by legal scholar Julie Cohen (2019), who charts how "consent to data extraction is being sublimated into the coded environment, and along the way . . . becomes a form of Kabuki theater that distracts both users and regulators from what is really going on (pp. 58–59). Informed by these judgements, article 16 represented little more than business as usual for web companies, a fact underscored by my interviewee at a US platform who informed me that article 16 did not even feature on their lobbying agenda for the Marco Civil.

What did appear at the top of that list, the item that was "really the thing to get" was limited third-party liability, or safe harbors (US web platform executive, interview, 2015). This duly appeared in the Marco Civil as article 19, section 4, content removal. This mandated that web platforms would only be held legally liable for third-party content if they ignored a court order to remove content and it appeared to secure an improbable triple win: for media conglomerates, web platforms, *and* the millions of Brazilian social media users uploading content daily.

Media companies possessed the economic resources to easily obtain court orders to remove infringing content. They also avoided the messy potential for posters to effectively dispute and reinstate content. Web platforms secured the coveted judicial assurance that protected their business models from excessive liability. And for Brazilian internet users, content removal by court order protected them from the arbitrary infringements on their freedom of expression that led to Brazil becoming the global leader in state-generated content-removal requests in 2009 (O'Brien, 2010).

At the heart of this apparently harmonious arrangement, however, lies a paradox. An individual's expressive rights cannot be truly protected by using the limited liability of platforms as their proxy. In other words, protecting individual freedom of expression is only a secondary effect of securing the invulnerability of web platforms. The true beneficiaries of these arrangements are web platforms, and they exploit that benefit by perpetuating a surveillance-based business model that exploits users, even as those users gain access to a speech platform to express their ideas. This is the safe-harbor paradox.

The Pirates' Proposal

The final section of the first draft of the bill focuses on the role of the state. These final five articles listed the obligations and duties of the state with regard to the internet in Brazil. Most of these focused on technical issues, such as promoting interoperability, open standards, accessible e-government services, and open-data policies. Other more profound proposals included the commitment to "promote digital inclusion of the entire population, especially for those on low income" (*Ministério da Justiça*, 2010).

Few of these principles attracted more than a handful of posts in the online consultation, many receiving Web 2.0's most dreaded outcome: "no comments." This would prove to be a recurring theme through the Marco Civil's development: that the private-sector obligations monopolized the attention of activists as well as the media and formed the basis of the most-protracted conflicts. This was occurring even when the state was being held liable for a goal as ambitious as connecting the entire country to the internet. This low profile, I believe, can be attributed to two factors. On one hand is the skepticism exhibited by much of Brazil's citizenry to its representatives. As Brazilian legal scholar Marcelo Thompson, indicates in his critique of the Marco Civil, "Brazil much prefers its courts to its lawmakers" (2010, p. 5). I believe that this is a characteristic born of centuries of a state that is corrupt, repressive, and/or ineffective. So, when the state presents lofty goals for itself, the civic tendency is to shrug rather than applaud.

The other factor is even more germane to this study and refers to the role of the state within the dominant digital-rights paradigm. In this reckoning, the state is not so much marginalized as assigned pariah status. Only private-sector actors, lauded within the digital discourse as the champions of innovation, connection, and participation, can facilitate the expressive rights of users qua citizens. To the state is assigned only the presumptive role of rights infringer. The best that can be hoped for is that the state recognizes its own innate malevolence and shackles itself with the necessary constraints.

Other than the multistakeholder input (discussed below), the last reference we need to make to this second round of public discussion focuses on a contribution that sets the rest of the debate into relief. This was not a celebrated moment in the consultation and stood in discord with the general tone. Although, overall, the proliferation of arguments would seem to suggest vigorous debate, this participation really only served to validate a limited range of positions: libertarians offered a semblance of radicalism, railing against any regulation under the banner of freedom, while legal experts debated the minutiae of the provisions with a legitimating gusto. Only the Pirate Party offered an entirely different conception of what digital rights could mean.

The Brazilian Pirate Party had produced an alternative draft of the entire bill, dubbed the Marco Pirata v1.1 (*Ministério da Justiça*, 2010). It was the product of internal debate and was published on both the party's own website and the Cultura Digital site and embodied a curious paradox of libertarian and socialist positions.

As would be supposed from the Pirates' political agenda, several of the provisions are designed to protect user privacy and freedom of expression and would do so with an almost extremist vigor. For instance, the Pirates proposed that no access whatsoever to log data would be admissible in criminal proceedings. Users would also enjoy a complete freedom to publish or access online material of "any nature." Other provisions extended the safeguards already featured in the Marco Civil, such as eliminating *any* legal liability on the part of those actors responsible for publishing content online.

As with their contributions in phase I, some of the most radical proposals resulted when libertarian sentiments were set aside, and the Pirates reimagined the role of the state in providing public online services. There is no specific provision for network neutrality in the Marco Pirata because the Pirates imagined a content-and-access infrastructure provided by a state committed to complete freedom of information. Article 9 reads, "The state must facilitate the free exchange of content and opinions on the internet, providing isonomic infrastructure to all citizens." Further to that, "the state should provide a network of software and content repositories, . . . a public network of access points, . . . content servers administrated by users."

Fundamentally, what is proposed here are the physical and content layers of the internet as noncommercial operations. This is why there is no specific safeguard for network neutrality or any prohibitions upon the "treatment, distribution to third parties or publication" of data as outlined in article 16 of the original Marco Civil. There is no need for such safeguards because the Pirates envision this data only being used for "public service" requirements. Effectively, these arrangements would negate the commodification of data, surveillance infrastructure, and ubiquitous advertising that the original Marco Civil at worst ignores or, at best, tinkers with. As such, we can observe in the Marco Pirata a conceptualization of digital rights that shatters the dominant paradigm, one that envisions systemic reform premised on collectivist principles. *This is the exception that proves the rule.*

Low-Stakes Holderism: Demands Not Deliberation

Multistakeholderism is one of the tenets of the post-WSIS digital-rights paradigm (its critique elaborated earlier). Rather than simply reasserting that argument, here I question the validity of the term as applied to this last precongressional phase of the Marco Civil, which presented the appearance of open, consensus-based, *horizontal* decision making among a diverse set of actors, when the reality was a long way from that ideal. The reality was of the unidirectional presentation of instrumental demands by the most powerful sectors of informational capitalism.

This phase of the Marco Civil is important to examine because it allows observation of how battle lines were being drawn up around the bill by powerful economic interests. In many cases these concerns defined the form that the law took in its final reckoning.

Despite the best intentions of the SAL-CTS team to facilitate an open debate, industry bodies invariably presented their contributions at the eleventh hour, shortly before the consultation closed. This was done with the clear intention of circumventing, not facilitating debate. As per Almeida: "Even though we were trying to create a dialogue, people were still speaking unidirectionally to the government, even if it was in public" (interview 2018). Moreover, these association statements arrived in the form of letters or PDF attachments addressed directly to the Ministry of Justice, not as part of the comments section where individual participants could engage with and critique them. Only 4 percent of all comments emanated from entities or organizations, rather than individual citizens (Bragatto et al., 2015, A segunda fase, p. 243). The scenario described here clearly diverges a great deal from the consensus-based ideal of multistakeholderism.

To the drafters' credit, whenever such sealed contributions arrived, the SAL-CTS team insisted on publishing them on the website so that they were at least exposed to public attention. In addition, as a tactical tweak the team set the end of each public consultation period for a Sunday night. They did so knowing that corporate legal departments would not work over the weekend, meaning that any late contributions would arrive on a Friday afternoon, allowing any civically minded participants at least two days to respond to the statements (Almeida, interview, 2018). The critique of the Internet Governance Forum (IGF) Flyverbom (2011) presented is germane here, however. He questions the idea that simply because the transcripts of its meetings are published online that this equates to the democratic ideal of transparency. Effectively, if no one can parse the voluminous proceedings, they are not rendered transparent but invisible (p. 150). In the case of the Marco Civil, could one reasonably expect any substantive interrogation of the legalistic and lengthy contributions of private-sector actors, by individual citizens over the course of a weekend?

Synergies and Tensions

Twenty-two Brazilian organizations took the opportunity to show their hands in this second round of public consultation. These included economic, civil society, and state actors. In addition, six international associations of IP rights holders presented contributions to the process. Only the largest of them, International Federation of the Phonographic Industry (IFPI), is referenced here, as all of the associations' demands are almost identical. Through an analysis of these contributions, one can identify the tensions and synergies that existed among these sectors of informational capitalism.

The most prominent claim was for greater IP protections to be included in the Marco Civil. This took the drafters by surprise. One of the CTS researchers commented, "We knew that there would be some reaction by IP holders, but we didn't know that they would be so organized" (Moncau, interview, 2015). These claims were advanced by associations representing the content-production sector, particularly, of music, software, and film. The proposals they made were intended to promote IP protections that, in turn, would secure the logic of control over the flow of commodified immaterial resources. The form that their proposals took reveals two important things. The first is that in spite of the shrill dissent of content producers, their proposed amendments nearly all constituted *additions* to the Marco Civil, rather than *modifications*. This suggests that the existing provisions of the Marco Civil represented only a minor threat to the operations of the content-production sector. The second aspect revealed by these proposals are the synergies and tensions that existed with another key sector of informational capitalism, namely, the telecoms sector.

The first recurring claim worthy of interrogation was that the rights of IP holders should attain the same status as the other fundamental rights and principles enshrined in the Marco Civil. As Streeter reveals, the use-of-rights language was first harnessed by content producers and distributors in the 1980s (2011, p. 79). Cohen (2019) similarly notes the "entrepreneurial appropriation of discourses about fundamental human rights to describe the rights and privileges of corporate entities" (p. 257).

Although neither Cohen nor Streeter describes it in these terms, this appropriation of rights claims was an attempt to legitimate informational capitalism's logics of control and commodification. Here we see the same ploy in an updated form: the drive to legitimate the mechanic of IP law by including it within the framework of *digital* rights. This also speaks to the function of the dominant paradigm of digital rights, generally; it is worth striving to achieve inclusion within it because it offers an effective means to legitimate the systemic functions of informational capitalism.

The other recurring claims centered on the obligations of the telecoms sector with regards to the protection of IP. In terms of their respective sectorial interests, this represented both a synergy and tension. The tension equated mostly to content producers wanting ISPs to share the burden of identifying, notifying, and possibly even penalizing IP violators using their networks. This would constitute a quite onerous demand on ISPs, without any obvious upside in terms of the business interests of the ISP. Indeed, in its submission, the telco Embratel supported the proposal that ISPs should only be obligated to share user data if mandated by a court order. Seemingly, they, too, recognized the encumbrance that disclosing user information to IP rights associations would represent.

The evident synergies between the demands of the content-production and telecoms sectors were more numerous and more significant. On the topic of network management, the content producers shared a concern with ISPs for loosening the possible restrictions that network neutrality would imply. Content producers sought the freedom for ISPs to be able to not only monitor internet traffic to detect IP violations but also to throttle or block it if necessary. This was clearly congruent with the stated desire of the telecoms sector to be able to manage internet traffic, although under the guise of maintaining security and efficiency, rather than policing IP violations.

It was also in the interests of content producers to create network-neutrality provisions flexible enough to leave room for the development of new business models, as suggested by the Motion Picture Association of Brazil (*Ministério da Justiça*, 2010, Contribuições recebidas). It is possible to imagine scenarios in which content producers without their own platforms might seek to develop consumer distribution channels that compromised the principle of network neutrality. Once again, this corresponded to the vested interests of the telecoms sector to be able to discount strict network neutrality in pursuit of potentially lucrative new business models. Indeed, the telecoms sector made the demand for the freedom of business models, a recurring motif for the Marco Civil once it reached congress.

As a last mention of the contributions from the telecoms sector, the proposal by the telecoms provider Claro, that as per article 16, further restrictions need to be applied to the ability of web companies to commercialize user data. It may seem curious that a telecoms company would use its finite political capital to make a proposal that could only stymie the business interests of another sector, rather than to try and advance their own. This view, however, misunderstands the degree of hostility exhibited by the telecoms sector toward web companies. The antipathy of the telecoms sector for over-the-top (OTT) services is well documented, and this dynamic of informational capitalism was as evident in Brazil as in the United States. The proposal by Claro represented only a warning shot for what would become a barrage of hostile fire.

We should also recognize the importance of a competing claim made by another actor within the content-production sector, in this case a broadcaster, and the only one that broke ranks to make a contribution to the Marco Civil. In contrast to the associations representing IP rights holders, the broadcasting conglomerate Bandeirantes sought a strengthening of net neutrality provisions that would explicitly prohibit traffic prioritization by ISPs for economic purposes. The rationale for this was that broadcasting groups in Brazil feared the prospect of having their digital assets held for ransom by ISPs exploiting net neutrality loopholes. In the context of informational capitalism, this equated to a tension between competing visions of control over data flows. This also represented the early demarcation of a battle line that would become more entrenched as the Marco Civil process ground on: broadcasters versus web companies for control over data networks. Once Globo joined the fray, the defenders of network neutrality would gain a decisive new ally.

The security state was the other main sector of informational capitalism involved in trying to shape the Marco Civil according to its interests. The Federal Police of Brazil (PF) presented a demand that would reverberate later: that all web-content providers be subject to Brazilian law, regardless of their national location or ownership. This stemmed from the frustration experienced by Brazilian law-enforcement authorities seeking user data from web companies based in the United States. Recourse to mutual legal assistance treaty (MLAT) agreements was often deemed insufficient.

This frustration would manifest itself several years later under the guise of a contentious data-localization provision added to the bill at the behest of the security services.

In terms of the civil-society contributions, only two entities opted to make contributions at this stage, both of them consumer-advocacy groups: IDEC (Brazilian Institute of Consumer Protection) and Proteste. That only consumer-rights groups saw fit to participate underscores the nature of the digital rights preliminarily embodied by the Marco Civil: a series of technical, market-based fixes. The nature of the proposals these organizations presented for the Marco Civil reveals a limited set of ambitions born of their status as consumer-rights groups. Although some claims went further than others—such as making network-neutrality violations a criminal offence—none of them fundamentally challenged the inequities of the internet's political economy under informational capitalism.

In sum, we can observe from the above description of the Marco Civil's multistakeholder phase that it did not correspond, in reality, to the ideals of multistakeholderism. This was a process marked by the issuance of demands from powerful economic interests, with little or no interest in dialogue or compromise with other stakeholders. As stated in the introduction to this section, this is a critique worth elaborating because the label of multistakeholderism was attached to the Marco Civil as a marker of its democratic legitimacy. Akin to the larger process of public consultation, this meant that the actual form that this multistakeholder process took largely escaped scrutiny; the kudos associated with the term was sufficient to blind most observers to its substance. Peel away the hype, and actually scrutinize the proceedings, and it becomes evident that powerful sectors of informational capitalism were not inclined to observe the dialogic niceties of a multistakeholder process and, instead, stood ready to impose their demands on the Marco Civil.

Going further still, the characteristics exhibited by this process of private-sector involvement can be explained in part by the coordinating role of a peripheral state. At this early stage of the Marco Civil's development, the Ministry of Justice served simply as a clearinghouse for demands, not a facilitator of dialogue. This inability (or unwillingness) of the Brazilian state to effectively mediate conflict with and among elites would manifest itself more acutely when the powerbrokers of informational capitalism really rallied their strength once the bill reached congress.

Perhaps, the most important reason to analyze this phase of the Marco Civil in detail is because it allows one to identify the territory staked out by some of the key sectors of informational capitalism. The tensions and synergies one can observe between some of the system's sectors, as well as the provisions of the Marco Civil that proved most contentious, would take on an outsized form once the Marco Civil entered its next crucial phase and became the object of intense political conflict.

The bill's prehistory featured numerous factors that help to explain how and why the Marco Civil emerged in Brazil at this time. These included: the fervor of a politicized free-software community creating a bastion of support for the concept of the Marco Civil; the legacy of Brazil's military dictatorship sensitizing activists to the repression of communication rights implied by the Lei Azeredo; the historical tendency toward criminalization as a first resort, imbuing a bill of digital *civil* rights with greater urgency; and the impetus to harmonize Brazilian law with IP frameworks from the core of informational capitalism characteristic of the periphery as a site of extraction. All of these factors bely the perceived universality of digital rights and, instead, emphasize the many social, cultural, and political economic contingencies that create the conditions for their emergence.

Using a discourse analysis lens, some key texts were examined that revealed discourses that were formative for the initial conceptualization of the Marco Civil: cyberutopian, neoliberal, technocratic, and neodevelop-mentalist. These had an enduring impact on the Marco Civil and help to explain some of its emphases and blind spots. I argue, in particular, that the neoliberal and technocratic tenor of the op-ed written by Brazilian technology commentator Ronaldo Lemos—widely recognized as the intellectual genesis of the Marco Civil—negated the possibility of any confrontation with informational capitalism.

The role of the digital discourse remained a pivotal factor later in the Marco Civil's development, shaping the contours of the digital rights therein. The Brazilian Internet Steering Committee's Ten Principles for the internet, which served as a template for the Marco Civil's rights frame-work, constituted a direct link between the Marco Civil and the dominant digital-rights paradigm established post-WSIS. Moreover, by probing the neoliberal origins of the steering committee itself, this chapter revealed the roots of the Marco Civil's alignment with the logics of informational capitalism. The initial discursive circumscription of the Marco Civil was also evident in the interpretive community of the bill's drafters who shared a common sense for the Marco Civil that precluded the inclusion of more radical voices in the project's formation.

By discounting much of the celebratory rhetoric around the two phases of public consultation, this chapter critically analyzed the democratic deficien-cies of these processes to show how they legitimated the narrow remit of the Marco Civil and thus enabled a hollowed conceptualization of digital rights. Rather than allow the fact of the consultation to obscure its substance, we need to understand how the parameters of the debate were constricted from the outset.

One of the most significant aspects of the public consultation was the contributions of the Brazilian Pirate Party. The Pirates' vision for the Marco Civil showed that a substantive conceptualization of digital rights—one closely aligned with the discourse of information justice (Karpinnen & Puukko, 2020)—premised upon systemic reform of the internet's infrastructure and political economy was conceivable for the Marco Civil. The Pirates represented the outlier in a consultation process that otherwise served to validate a very limited range of positions.

Through detailed analysis of the provisions in the first drafts of the bill, this chapter demonstrates how, from the outset, the digital rights of the Marco Civil aligned with the operational logics of informational capitalism, rather than challenging them. The manner in which the practices of content and service providers were addressed in the bill was based primarily on consumer protections and promised only to tinker with the mechanics of informational capitalism. Moreover, these technolegal measures occupied the policy space that could have been used to advance structural reform. Finally, the multistakeholder contributions to the Marco Civil showed how they corresponded to the synergies and tensions that exist between core sectors of informational capitalism. This revealed not only the dubious democratic credentials of multistakeholderism but also some of the core dynamics that became acutely evident later in the Marco Civil's development.

The significance of the Marco Civil entering the congressional arena is the focus of the following chapter.

3

Contestation

Power Plays and Debate Pollution

What the telcos expected is that whatever
the bill of law that these people will propose,
we'll handle it when it enters Congress, we
can pay the politicians, and that was the
hard part, that was really a hard part.
—Carlos Afonso

Certain sectors of informational capitalism exerted material power to shape the Marco Civil according to their own agendas as it reached the Brazilian Congress. The mechanics and dynamics described in chapter 1 are operationalized here to show how the telecoms sector, web platforms, and content-production sector were alternately forming alliances of convenience or engaging in bitter rivalries. These dynamics were decisive in curtailing the civic value of the bill, creating, instead, a framework of digital rights conducive to the functioning of informational capitalism. This chapter focuses, particularly, on the disputes around the core digital rights of network neutrality and limited third-party liability (or safe harbors).

In the case of net neutrality, the telecoms sector was determined to resist the measure in order to protect future business models. These included, most notably, the offer of zero-rating mobile plans—now ubiquitous in the global south. Also revealed is the surprising ambivalence of the web-company sector in securing a neutral internet. This derived from Brazil's status at the periphery, as US web companies were keen not to rouse dormant antagonisms from the core and were also constrained to act in public by their American origins. I contend that a paradox of network neutrality is that the more fiercely the telcos resisted the measure, the more civil society groups were convinced it was a core civil right and occluded more substantive alternatives.

The contestation of safe harbors and the way in which one of the Marco Civil's architects covertly introduced a highly controversial IP carve-out in order to win the support of the Globo Group is charted in the following pages. This event further reveals the coherence between the Marco Civil and the systemic logics of informational capitalism and resulted in an even-greater dilution of the already limited civic value of the safe harbor provisions. Finally, a discursive focus reveals the local significance of digital rights in the context of Brazilian discourses of social inequality, the politicization of consumption rights, and the historic fear of communism.

Shifting Sands: Political Appointments, Corporate Maneuvers

By August 2010 the draft bill had received a rubber stamp from all the ministries with some stake in the project. The political upheaval implied by a presidential election and the transition of power from the Lula to the Rousseff administrations, however, delayed its introduction to Congress by one year. On August 24, 2011, the Marco Civil did make its grand entrance to the Brazilian Congress, bearing the docket number PL 2.126/2011. This bland identifier did little to suggest that it would soon occupy the center of a power vortex.

The most obvious political change that would bear upon the development of the Marco Civil was the transition in the Brazilian presidency from Lula da Silva to Dilma Rousseff. Although they were close allies and both members of the Workers' Party, the political trajectories, personal characteristics, and policy priorities of the two leaders were quite distinct, and these differences would directly influence how the Marco Civil would now be treated as part of the government agenda. The personal journey of Lula from illiterate son of northeastern workers immigrated to São Paulo contributed heavily to his man-of-the-people appeal and to his comfort and effectiveness consulting and communicating with the Brazilian people (Schwarcz & Starling, 2018). By contrast, Rousseff was a technician rather than an orator, with a late conversion to the Workers' Party in 2000, and no particular connection to the free-software community in Brazil.

Pivotal to the fate of the Marco Civil was the fact that the transition from one PT administration to another was not limited to a rotation in the presidency. The change at the top was accompanied by a raft of new ministerial appointments, several of which would signal new configurations of power, aligning certain policy directions of the new PT government more closely with the systemic logics of informational capitalism. More specifically, some of these can be interpreted as the early strategic moves of powerful economic sectors seeking to influence the direction of the Marco Civil. These developments, in turn, need to be understood within the complex political dynamics that accompanied the election victory of Rousseff in 2011.

According to the judgment of Saad Filho and Morais (2017), the policy platform of Rousseff made her the most left-wing president of Brazil since João Goulart in the 1960s (p. 108), as she sought to further expand programs of social assistance. Additionally, the PT's majority in both houses was staked on a fragile coalition of ten parties, of which only one-third of the seats were held by parties of the left (p. 107). The combination of having to retain the faith of the markets for a left-wing policy platform and having to secure the allegiance of numerous right-wing coalition partners meant that Rousseff needed to be able to offer political sops in the form of ministerial appointments.

One of the most notable exits was that of Juca Ferreira, minister of culture. Promoted from within by Lula, Ferreira had been appointed to the ministry initially by the self-proclaimed "Ministro hacker" Gilberto Gil. Ferreira had been heavily involved in Gil's efforts to support an early forerunner of the Marco Civil in the form of a bilateral bill of digital rights with the Italian government in 2007 (Carlos Afonso, interview, 2015). Ferreira also strove to establish a more equitable system of IP regulation in Brazil. He had worked with Gil in creating the widely acclaimed Pontos de Cultura national network of cultural hubs. Ana de Hollanda, his successor, demobilized all of this in 2011.

Despite being another musician and the sister moreover of the fabled Chico Buarque, de Hollanda shared none of Gil's reformist instincts. One of her first acts in office was to remove the Creative Commons logo from the ministry website and later replace it with corporate versions, such as YouTube's (Silveira et al., 2013, p. 560). Indeed, her direction of cultural policy overall was characterized as a "backward march" by the same authors. Widely known to be a supporter of more-stringent IP protections, the appointment of de Hollanda meant that not only had the Marco Civil lost an important ally but also that more broadly the Rousseff administration would be more accommodating to the demands of the powerful content-production sector. This perception would be reinforced by other developments.

Within the Ministry of Communications, Paulo Bernardo was appointed by the incoming administration. Bernardo was well-known for his connections to the telecoms sector, to the extent that he was lauded with the honorific of Telecoms Man of the Year in 2012 by a telecoms trade association (Telebrasil, 2012) and was criticized for refusing to countenance mass-media reform (Ekman, 2013). The consequences of this corporate allegiance would become more overt as the Marco Civil underwent its fraught journey through Congress.

Other significant blurring of state and corporate lines occurred in 2011. As well as consolidating the influence of the telecoms sector within the Rousseff administration, the connections between the new government and major web platforms were no less conspicuous. Within the executive office, Ivo Correa moved from head of public policy at Google Brazil to become vice head of legal affairs within the civil service. In the opposite direction, Bruno Magrani, a core member of the SAL-CTS research team working on the Marco Civil, became head of public policy at Facebook Brazil. Although these may have only represented the fulfillment of individual ambitions, these moves hinted at a significant congruence between major web platforms and the Brazilian government vis-à-vis the Marco Civil.

Meanwhile within the telecoms sector, its industry association, Sinditel-ebrasil, was reinvigorated in 2010. Although founded in 2003, the association had existed "only on paper until April 2010 when the companies resolved to make it work," in the words of Eduardo Levy, the man elected to its presidency in 2011 (Abramovay, 2017, p. 111). That moment, not coincidentally, aligned with the launch of the second phase of public consultation of the Marco Civil. The conspicuously low profile of the telecoms sector during the consultations can be ascribed to the fact that its industry association effectively lay dormant. The association's reinvigoration as an entity with physical presence in Brasília, meanwhile, should be understood as a collective response to the perceived threat potential of the Marco Civil project.

Another major event related to the telecoms sector that occurred in the period since the consultation closed was a regulatory shift for cable television that placed the telcos into direct competition with the media sector, especially Grupo Globo. The Lei do SeAC, or Pay TV Law, passed in 2011, introduced a raft of changes for the pay TV sector, including quotas for Brazilian content and an end to limits on the investment of foreign capital. However, the tectonic shift implied by the Lei do SeAC was that for the first time, telecoms companies would be able to offer subscription services through cable, having previously been limited to provision via satellite systems (Miranda, 2011). This head-to-head competition between the content-production sector—led by Globo—and the telecoms sector would have a crucial impact on the eventual formation of the Marco Civil.

According to congressional norms, every law needs to have a congress-person individually responsible for its passage through the house. Alessandro Molon, a new congressman from Rio de Janeiro, volunteered and was accepted for the role. His first major act was to present to Congress on July 4, 2012, the first of what would be five amended versions of the bill (*substitutivos* in Portuguese), each the subject of fierce controversy. Substitutivo 1 included a number of changes, mostly minor, but also a few that signaled the most important points of future contestation.

By far the most important changes pertained to article 9 on network neutrality. Here, Molon opted to strengthen the language to minimize the loopholes available to skirt the intended protections. Net neutrality was, after all, the element of the Marco Civil that Molon had identified as the "heart" of the bill that would benefit Brazil's "80 million netizens" (UOL, 2013).

The first attempt to vote the Marco Civil into law was scheduled for July 10, 2012. The vote was abandoned due to a failure to achieve quorum. This scenario repeated itself on July 11. Although the influence of the telecoms sector on these events was never made explicit, many of my interviewees with insight into the congressional process were unequivocal about the pressure this sector applied to prevent a vote. The nature of this influence, the manner in which it was exerted and resisted, and the rationale for doing so are the focus of the ensuing section. Indeed, examining the pressure exerted by the telecoms sector casts a bright light on how one of the foremost powerholders within informational capitalism in Brazil used discursive and material power to shape digital rights at the periphery.

Nothing Neutral about the Net

The total revenues for the telecoms sector in Brazil in 2013 were equivalent to 4.5 percent of gross domestic product (GDP) in Brazil and accounted for nearly half a million jobs (Telebrasil, 2018). By 2010 the total market capitalization of telecoms companies on the Brazilian stock market was US$73 billion (Moreira, 2016, p. 4). Finally, as a percentage of GDP, the Brazilian telecoms sector surpassed any of their equivalents in the Organisation for Economic Co-operation and Development (OECD) in the same year (OECD, 2013). Although its economic significance is evident, the political influence of this sector was yet more formidable.

Obstruction, Obfuscation, and the Telco Rasputin

In 2012 one individual provided the key to understanding the political reach of the Brazilian telecoms sector. Before Congressman Eduardo

Cunha's dizzying fall from grace culminated in a fifteen-year prison sentence in 2017 on corruption charges, he represented a Rasputin-like figure in Brazilian politics. A contemporary analogue would be the fictional character Frank Underwood from the Netflix political thriller *House of Cards*. This comparison was spectacularly made by the current affairs magazine *ISTOÉ* in a front cover in March 2014 that portrayed Cunha in the famous Underwood throne pose from the show, under the headline "Saboteur of the Republic." This turned out to be a watershed moment for public awareness of the corporate hostility to the Marco Civil.

In 2013 Cunha was voted leader of the conservative PMDB (Brazilian Democratic Movement), a party that while nominally part of the governing coalition with the PT, under his leadership became the principal bulwark against the government agenda. Later, in 2015, Cunha would go on to become the house leader. He also represented the conduit through which the demands of the telecoms sector were manifested in the legislative arena. Cunha's connections to the telecoms sector date back to the 1990s when he was appointed president of the Rio de Janeiro state telecoms company, Telerj, during the infamous Collor administration (Solagna, 2015, p. 100). He oversaw its privatization and eventual takeover by the company Telemar, that in turn became Oi, one of the largest telecoms companies in Brazil (until its takeover in 2022).

As well as constituting a key figure in the neoliberal reform of the telecoms sector, Cunha represented a formidable lobbyist and fundraiser for the PMDB, leveraging his connections to channel funds and influence from the telecoms, energy, and construction sectors into Congress. His sphere of influence was commensurate with this role: the parliamentary arithmetic revealed to me in interview by a special adviser for the PT was that of the 513 seats in the Chamber of Deputies, Cunha funneled financial contributions to 167 and could count on the support of a total of 250 to 300. Based on all of this, Cunha was evidently the point man for the telecoms sector to impel their agenda for the Marco Civil. The *means* by which Cunha initially sought to impose that agenda could be characterized as alternately obstructionist and obfuscatory, employing material and discursive power, respectively, to try and shape the development of the Marco Civil to the telcos' desired ends.

(Mis)understanding Network Neutrality

The fact is that explaining complex technical issues such as those contained within the Marco Civil to Brazilian deputies and senators was extremely difficult. The challenges involved in elucidating the details of network neutrality to these elected officials was expressed to me, both by Molon—who described the task as "very difficult. . . . I had to explain it to them hundreds of times"—and civil society organizer Bia Barbosa. Barbosa represented the communication rights group Intervozes, one of the only civil society groups based in Brasília championing the Marco Civil. As such, Barbosa maintained a near-permanent presence in the Congress and described how "100 percent of my time was spent working in the Congress to explain to parliamentarians . . . because there were very few who understood what the Marco Civil was" (interview, 2015). Even the director of Sinditelebrasil disclosed in interview that they struggled with the level of understanding of the Brazilian deputies: "For lay people, the same as Parliamentarians in the Congress, it was difficult to explain what network neutrality was."

I contend that the nature of this ignorance among Brazilian representatives should be understood within a peripheral frame. That is not to say that politicians in the global north possess a robust understanding of the intricacies of network neutrality. One congressman in the United States memorably displayed during a congressional debate that this was far from the case when he declared that the internet was "a series of tubes" (Kimball, 2013, p. 41). Moreover, according to an interview researcher Des Freedman conducted with a US media-policy lobbyist, "Most members of Congress haven't got any idea about communications policy. They get beyond the surface-level discussion of the issues and they are completely lost" (2008, p. 913). It is not even as though expertise is a prerequisite for legislation. Governments habitually issue laws pertaining to such complex phenomena as aviation, pharmaceuticals, and biotechnology. What *is* an important distinction between the United States and Brazil on a highly technical topic, such as network neutrality, is that the advanced technological development of the former in contrast to the latter is manifested in the relevance of such issues in the public policy realm, as well as the interest and understanding of the electorate. These factors, in turn, compel a greater degree of qualified engagement from elected representatives on the issue.

As described in the previous chapter, this lack of public awareness can be observed in the very low levels of participation in the consultations for the Marco Civil. In a country riven by egregious economic inequality and high rates of crime, we might do well to consider this as a variation on Bertolt Brecht's maxim, "Grub first, then ethics." This was a reality that several of my interviewees also reflected upon. As Molon revealed to me, "to explain what it is and its importance to people's lives, that was the greatest obstacle . . . to explain why this changes their life." Or as Carlos Afonso explained, "There is and continues to be a task of sensitizing people to the relevance of the issue, one that is far from trivial. There are people who think that because everybody uses it, everyone is concerned with the future of the internet, but it is not like that" (Papp, 2014, p. 54).

These dynamics are exacerbated moreover by the opacity of network neutrality, as Pedro Ramos, lawyer and prominent Brazilian neutrality expert, explained to me in an interview. Unlike content removal, which is highly conspicuous, the fact that traffic management practices exist under the hood makes it very difficult for consumers to be aware that their rights may be infringed; an Achilles heel of the individualist approach to digital rights, generally.

A significant corollary to the lack of technical knowledge and concern among the Brazilian deputies was that it rendered them more pliant for the telecoms lobbyists, who were so prominent in Congress. As a member of the CTS team related to me, this resulted in "this deputy or this senator bringing out . . . an argument that you could expect from a lawyer from a telco to bring to the table" (Affonso Souza, interview, 2015). An example of this observation was made vividly by a parliamentarian, Ricardo Izar, who claimed in 2012 that, according to the telecoms sector, the cost of creating a 100 percent neutral network would be a mammoth 250 billion reals, a cost that would all be passed on to the consumer (Guerlanda & Decat, 2012).

The lobbying by the telecoms sector was so intense, it was often described in bellicose terms by my interviewees: "an information war" by Molon and "white terrorism" by civil society lawyer Flávia Lefevre. What, though, was the agenda that the telecoms sector sought to advance through this intense lobbying? What elements of the Marco Civil were perceived as a threat to their business interests? There are two dimensions to this agenda, both defensive and offensive.

The Telco Agenda and One More Paradox

Before exploring those dimensions, reconsider one fundamental point: for the foremost sectors within informational capitalism, the digital rights of the Marco Civil did not represent an existential threat. Although the disputes that enveloped the bill and the energies invested in disrupting its progress were significant, these were undertaken as an inherent part of intra-capitalist competition: the Marco Civil offered core sectors of informational capitalism an opportunity to secure legal assurances that could optimize revenue generation through the internet vis-à-vis competing sectors. There is a clear parallel here with US media scholar Russell Newman's description of the US Telecommunications Act of 1996 as "neoliberalism at war with itself as capital formations struggled for dominance" (2019, p. 25).

Ultimately, the digital rights contained within the bill did not confront the systemic logics of informational capitalism, instead attempting to modify their mechanics. As such, although the Marco Civil was worthy of dispute, these disputes should not be considered a mortal struggle. The most important lesson to be drawn from this point is that the *fact of* the telcos' fevered resistance to network neutrality served to consolidate the misapprehension that it represented a core digital right. This anomaly could be added to Newman's "paradoxes of net neutrality" (2019): the greater the resolve against net neutrality displayed by the telecoms sector, the more civil society groups and their political allies became convinced it was fundamental to their own interests, and the less they would consider more substantive alternatives.

In terms of the defensive dimension of the telecoms agenda, the principal focus was to avoid restrictions to the creation of future business models. Stepping back and considering this in terms of the logics of informational capitalism, the telcos' primary concern was to permit themselves as much leeway as possible to commodify data packets and to surveil their users. My interviewee at a web platform reported that during a closed-door meeting of representatives of his company and the telecoms sector, he had asked, "Why exactly are you guys so up in arms against network neutrality? If you claim you already do all of these things, what are you so concerned with? What exactly is that going to change in your business practice?" He was told, "We are concerned that we won't be able to have new business models, it's not what we are doing right now."

Indeed, it was not a coincidence that the telecoms sector largely ignored the Marco Civil during the consultation phase, when network neutrality was included as a *general* principle, and this sector took concerted aim at the bill once *specific* legal criteria were introduced. Essentially, while net neutrality was broad and ambiguous in its definition, the telecoms companies could introduce new network-management practices and then argue that they remained in compliance with the law. Once the noose of legalese started to tighten around the concept, the telecoms sector sensed that certain—potentially or actually lucrative—business models would become untenable. Essentially, the telcos had not yet arrived at a firm conclusion as to which mechanics of commodification would generate most profit, and that uncertainty, coupled with potentially looming restrictions in the Marco Civil, generated great unease.

This contradicts what I was told by Sinditelebrasil executive Alex Castro, who explained, "We wanted [network neutrality] adjusted so that it became clear and avoided five hundred different interpretations, and we had a torrent of judicial actions." Many of my interviewees did, indeed, advise me that in their estimation, despite the staunch opposition of the telcos to the bill, the judicial certainty implied by the Marco Civil was a boon for the sector in terms of encouraging investment. For instance, one senior adviser in the state telecoms regulator, Anatel, advised me that "a well-defined set of rules is the foundation for continued investment in the sector." A senior executive at Embratel underscored to me in vivid terms that Embratel's telecoms infrastructure, an investment by its parent company, América Móvil, could not be ripped out and returned to Mexico. As such, a secure regulatory environment was imperative for the sector. With all that said, it appears that the telecoms sector wanted "clarity" on its own terms.

Positive Discrimination: Choice and Freedom

One of the principal vehicles the sector used to articulate its opposition for the Marco Civil was through Sinditelebrasil, which published a glossy brochure in 2014 to belatedly intervene in public discussions on the Marco Civil, with the headline,

"Are telecommunications providers favourable to network neutrality?" in large font. The response was clearly intended to reassure:

> The answer is yes! Whoever states the opposite is wrong! In truth, the discussion about network neutrality is already settled! The telecoms sector defends the guarantee of a free and open internet, preserving fundamental user rights, including transparency, freedom of communication, accessibility, nondiscriminatory treatment, and your right to choice and privacy. (2014, p. 5)

Later, the brochure outlined what the sector concluded that network neutrality should *not* do: "Restrict free initiative and competition; delimit business plans for access providers; restrict the offer of differentiated services; restrict network management techniques for access and connection providers" (2014, p. 5). There is much worthy of analysis in these statements.

We can identify once more the metasignifiers of the digital discourse that were so formative in the early stages of the Marco Civil process. That the internet should be kept "free and open" signified that it should remain permeable to market-led development. "Transparency" is used as a signifier for both the market economy and democracy, with the opacity of state bureaucracy backgrounded as the implicit and antagonistic other (Springer, 2012). Freedom and choice, meanwhile, are some of the principal virtues of a market economy.

In essence, the telcos felt compelled to come out and disavow negative discrimination: the "nasty" side of network management. Blocking websites and throttling traffic conflates easily with the specter of censorship and defiles the sacred cow of expression. It is, in any event, less lucrative than its "positive" counterpart. What the telcos were desperate to secure was the discursive territory around choice and freedom, where the various practices of positive discrimination—making certain sites and content are *more available* than others—would be allowed to prevail.

This strategy was evident in a parliamentary debate on the Marco Civil in 2013, when Cunha was forthright in condemning the ills of negative discrimination: "We all agree that we need neutrality, that nobody should be prevented from transmitting their content . . . that no one is privileged, that nobody filters, that nobody monitors, that we have privacy controls. This receives applause from all of us. We are all in favor of neutrality of content" (Câmara dos Deputados, 2013).

Beyond expressing such pieties for the sake of public appearances, there was also an economic rationale behind the stand against negative discrimi-nation, one that derives from Brazil's peripheral status within informational capitalism. According to a group of Princeton University researchers, 84 percent of all internet paths originating within Brazil route via the United States (Edmundson et al., 2018). This occurs even when a user might be accessing the website of a Brazilian newspaper, for instance, and is based on internet-routing protocols that send data via the fastest path. Given such a heavy reliance on the infrastructure of US telecoms companies, the neutral nature of those systems becomes paramount to Brazilian telecoms companies. Castro explained to me, "If [an American telco] prioritizes the traffic of my competitor here in Brazil or discriminates against mine, what is going to happen to me? My clients are going to migrate to my competi-tor, right?"

Moreover, the instances where the telcos outline the presumed negative potentials of network neutrality in the Sinditelebrasil brochure are where we can read the economic interests of the telecoms sector and the specific goals of permitting positive discrimination. The capacity to develop new business models represented the ultimate goal of the telecoms sector. What were those business plans that they did not want to obstruct?

Ground Zero for Zero-Rating

One such potential business plan is outlined in the telecoms brochure: the offer of differentiated services (Sinditelebrasil, 2014). This refers to the desire of the telecoms companies to be able to offer stratified access to the internet, for both the core and the edge of the network. For the core, "What we wanted effectively was paid prioritization. We wanted that possible"

(Castro, interview, 2015). This would mean that application and content providers could pay the telecoms companies a fee to be able to offer their users a fast track to access. Castro justified this to me as analogous to the sale of different classes of seat on an airplane: "Why can't I do this? Just because there is an executive class on the plane, the fact that the guy travels economy class does not mean that he's going to have awful service." However, an Anatel report in 2013 declares that its minimum standards for mobile broadband were not being met by any major operator in twenty-three of the twenty-seven states of the country (Amato, 2013).

For the network's edge, meanwhile, differentiated services could be constituted in various ways. For instance, one obvious possibility would be to offer an internet "light" package, where open web surfing was permitted, but video streaming was available only in a degraded form. Or, perhaps, the telecoms companies might partner with Facebook where access to the social network is free, the practice known as "zero-rating" (Hoskins, 2019). Indeed, at a telecoms industry trade show called Futurecom in 2013, Mario Girasole, a vice president of the telecoms giant TIM, stripped bare the rhetoric and declared that in the Marco Civil, "We are not talking about freedom but about good old money, about business models" (Grossman, 2013).

The other element within the Marco Civil that had the telecoms sector fighting a rearguard action was clause 3 of article 9 that stipulated that "in the provision of Internet access . . . it is prohibited to block, monitor, filter, analyze, or inspect the content of data packets, save for the situations permitted in the legislation." That these prohibitions were included in the article dealing with network neutrality shows that the intention of Molon was to safeguard neutral network from the discriminatory intentions of the telecoms operators. The interpretation of the telecoms sector was quite different: "one more example of an unparalleled intervention that the law makes in the operations of the telecoms providers" (Sinditelebrasil, 2014, p. 8).

At a parliamentary meeting, Castro even lamented, "There isn't anywhere in the world with this reality" (Telesíntese, 2013), and he may well have been right. While these prohibitions certainly strengthened protections for Brazilian users and would impinge upon some legitimate network-management practices, there was still more to their protestations than appears on the surface. In a research interview with me, Virgilio Almeida, the national secretary for information technology policies for the Brazilian government (2011–15), speculated about the commercial intentions of the telecoms sector: "I perceive that the telcos want to go up. . . . It's no longer only the data packet. They're interested in the user, in consumer behavior. So, the telcos also now see that below, the commercial possibilities might be more restricted than above." If this reckoning was correct, it added another dimension to the righteous indignation of the telecoms sector. The telcos might, indeed, have perceived that greater profits beckoned from beyond the pipes. This possibility not only bolsters the argument that, in fact, the telcos' apparent desperation around network neutrality was more perceived than real but also feeds into my next point around the offensive aspect of their agenda and a heated competition to exploit lucrative user data.

Contesting the "Law of Facebook"

The telco agenda was more than just defensive. As well as seeking to safeguard certain network-management practices, the telecoms sector had a rival in their crosshairs that potentially stood to gain the most from the provisions in the Marco Civil: the web platforms. This hostility represents one of the core tensions within the dynamics of informational capitalism and both Castro and another telecoms executive I interviewed made clear their resentment at what they considered a parasitic, underregulated industry existing "on top" of their infrastructure. Castro went to lengths to detail the inequity:

> They only obey the laws of California, no? The telecoms sector generates five hundred thousand jobs. And there, the guy comes from away, he has five thousand employees there, no? The infrastructure, the platforms are offshore, they're not here. . . . We invest 29 billion reals per year, no? Google invested half a billion in five or six years, you understand? It's that disproportional. (2015)

This position was clarified in public at the aforementioned Futurecom event where the president of Telecomp, João Moura, declared, "The question is who appropriates the value generated and who incurs the cost. What we fear is that we continue to see what we could call an irrational use of the network without being able to monetize it in some way" (Grossman, 2013). It would be irrational, indeed, from the operators' perspective, to manage infrastructure from which untrammeled profit could not be rendered. At the same event, and returning once more to Girasole, he was equally categorical: "We can't have a Marco Civil that carries a free rider. . . . The operators cannot be treated like pipes" (Grossman, 2013).

We should return also to the Sinditelebrasil brochure that formalized the sector's position on the Marco Civil (2014). In the introduction, the text describes application providers as "big global companies that operate in Brazil in a nearly virtual way, *providing the most minimal social and economic contribution* for the high revenues they generate from local users" (p.

3, emphasis added). Finally, Cunha sang from the same hymn sheet as he decried the Marco Civil in a parliament: "If I vote for this here, I'm going to vote for Google's law, the law of Facebook. I am not going to vote for a law for those who are not investing in our country" (Câmara dos Deputados, 2013).

The redress the telcos sought through the Marco Civil was to lobby for more onerous commitments to apply to the "free-riding" web companies, as the telcos sought that the regulatory gap between the two sectors vying for primacy within informational capitalism be narrowed in favor of the telcos.

Polluting the Debate: The Telcos' Discursive Strategy

Another important aspect of the telcos' offensive agenda was to make programmatic interventions in the discursive realm, to sow discord and confusion, and to propagate discourses about the Marco Civil that would legitimate their agenda in the Brazilian public sphere. As mentioned previously, a core part of these efforts was to lobby Brazilian congresspeople and exploit their ignorance of the technical realities of the internet and the likely impacts of the provisions in the Marco Civil.

As one of the senior researchers at CTS explained to me in vivid terms, the telecoms sector "went the public route, but instead of putting the debate on the table, they were kind of disturbing the debate, polluting, creating noise, trying to confuse the issue. . . . There are excellent arguments if you look at the debate in the US. . . . They were not brought to Brazil." These claims were mirrored by Lefevre who described how she and the other civil society–organization representatives in Brasília would try and explain the precepts of the Marco Civil to parliamentarians. The challenge, she said, was that the telcos were "waging a strong campaign of disinformation. . . . You won't be able to do this or that, it's going to be a form of government of the internet, businesses won't have freedom to develop business models, and they painted a dark picture of what would emerge if they passed the Marco Civil" (interview, 2015). Once again, I argue that the strategy of disturbing the debate, rather than engaging directly with opposing arguments, should be understood through the frame of digital rights being contested at the periphery.

In his analysis of the US network-neutrality policy process, Russell Newman describes at length the sprawling and arcane debate that occurred between legal experts around network engineering or "of arguments over pricing, double-sided markets, and consumer surplus foregone or gained" (2016, p. 5970). In the United States, a glut of expertise on the technical and legal dimensions of telecoms network management meant that both critics and advocates of network neutrality were able to elaborate policy proposals and counterproposals (2016, p. 5976).

The nature of the debate signified more than just the United States' remarkable level of technological development, and the related fact that public discussion of an otherwise arcane policy issue could be imbued with such technical rigor. According to Newman, the debate was carefully circumscribed by the telecoms and cable giants in order to legitimate the limited terms on which the issue of net neutrality could be considered, thus forestalling other more substantive visions for the internet (2016; 2019). Des Freedman makes a similar case in the United Kingdom:

> By reducing it to mere "traffic management issues," policy makers have sought to limit what should be a discussion about how best we should organise and facilitate the circulation online of information, media and culture to a much narrower pre-occupation with ill-defined notions of transparency, competition and "openness." (2012, p. 109)

The critiques thus elaborated describe a very distinct reality to the one observable in Brazil around the Marco Civil. As the preceding chapter outlines, the concept of network neutrality enjoyed very limited prominence in academic, policy, or economic spheres. As such, technical arguments were not, in the word of Luiz Moncau, a key CTS team member, "brought to Brazil," essentially because they were not needed (interview, 2015). There was no discursive foundation on which to build a rational, technolegal debate around network neutrality in Brazil. That is not to say, however, that the telecoms sector did not wish to limit the terms of discussion in the same way that their counterparts in the United States did. It is simply that in Brazil they elected to pursue a different discursive strategy, one in which the ideological component was much more clearly foregrounded, and disinformation more blatant.

In terms of the latter component, one medium that the telecoms sector tried to mobilize in their favor was social media and, in particular, YouTube. Once again, rather than attempting to engage directly with the arguments presented by proponents of network neutrality (most notably, consumer-welfare arguments premised on cost but also social justice arguments based on economic equality), the proxies of the telecoms sector aimed to propagate confusion and antipathy toward the Marco Civil. Prominent YouTubers spoke out on the platform against the Marco Civil. These included the famous Brazilian comedian and writer Danilo Gentili, who posted a recording in conversation with two collaborators roundly criticizing the Marco Civil. In the video, the three figures repeat a familiar claim that the Marco

Civil would result in a regime of censorship and that it was a policy similar to those implemented in Venezuela and Cuba (Rede Livre, 2014).

Online free-speech activist João Caribé considered the arguments proposed by these commentators to be "completely insane." He was under no illusions as to the origin of these claims:

> They represented other interests. . . . The smoke screen worked a bit . . . because they were really positive players and they reached a lay audience that didn't know the Marco Civil. . . . So they created opposition to the project . . . and then we realized for certain that this articulation represented the telecoms sector. (interview, 2015)

It should be noted that the telecoms sector perceived that the flow of disinformation around the Marco Civil was not unidirectional. Castro decried an "enormous politicization of the debate" with "ideologies prevailing in the discussions" (interview, 2015). He was particularly animated about a video produced by some of the bill's civil society backers showing a user of a non-neutral internet being forced to choose a bespoke content package in order to go online. It was "an exaggerated discourse, of antagonism . . . so we started to discuss, to want to enter into their games." He also invoked comparisons with the US debate that the telecoms sector was "demonized," along with the "dissemination of fear and alarmism." Accordingly, the telecoms sector opted to fight fire with fire, by foregrounding an ideological component in their opposition to the Marco Civil.

The Venezuelization of the Brazilian Internet

What proved to be an enduring tactic was to try and engineer a discursive articulation between the historical specter of communism and the legislative project of the Marco Civil. The receptivity of the traditional media to "red scare" rhetoric in Brazil made this a viable tactic.

The mainstream commercial media in Brazil was shaped by the military regime as part of a far-reaching plan of nation building and social control (Fox, 1995; Mastrini & Becerra, 2002; Pait & Straubhaar, 2018). A core part of the media's function in this system was to showcase the achievements of the regime and to denigrate any opposition that emerged from within Brazilian society. Given that the dictatorship (1964–85) was in place during the height of the Cold War (1947–90), the prospect of communist insurrection was considered an acute threat to the regime (Schwarcz & Starling, 2020). And as Marinoni (2015) notes, "the few individuals and groups selected by the dictatorship, or that already existed and passed through the ideological filter of National Security, basically conformed to the broadcast bourgeoise that dominates the sector until today" (p. 15). As such, the commercial media in Brazil retained a strong institutional aversion to any political project associated with communism.

It needs to also be noted that the intense social stratification in Brazil, with a numerically tiny elite class seeking to maintain hegemonic dominance over an enormous and impoverished subaltern class results in communism acquiring the mantle of the bogeyman (Ribeiro, 1995). This explains the strategic importance for the telecoms sector of connecting the Marco Civil with communism. The combination of the historical relationship between the media and communism, as well as elite fears of redistribution, are essential peripheral dimensions to consider when analyzing how digital rights were contested in Brazil.

The Brazilian Congress was one of the primary venues in which the telecoms representatives, usually through their parliamentary proxies, promoted red-scare rhetoric around the Marco Civil. Solagna (2015) notes how the debate "acquired ideological contours" with the values of freedom and equality juxtaposed along political dividing lines (p. 107). He goes on to cite the speech of one congressperson, Fábio Ricardo Trad, as emblematic of this discourse. On November 11, 2013, Trad claimed that "because the left embraces equality emotionally, this has a strong appeal. We are going to have to sustain the basic principles of free initiative, to defend the notion that who uses more, pays more. . . . It's inequality in the name of equality" (p. 107). In another speech made in Congress, this time made by the telcos' chief proxy Eduardo Cunha, the articulation with communism was made explicit. In a lengthy diatribe, Cunha pronounced, "Yes, we are socializing, communizing the internet. This is what we are going to end up doing!" (Câmara dos Deputados, 2013).

According to Intervozes campaigner Barbosa, the basis for these claims connected to a prevalent ideology within the Brazilian Congress. She described this position to me as "neoliberal, extreme . . . that any regulation is prejudicial to the market. And the service providers strengthen this discourse saying that . . . Dilma wants to transform Brazil into Venezuela."

The next section assesses how the telco agenda around network neutrality intersected with the competing agendas of other sectors within informational capitalism, as well as those civil society organizations that championed the bill.

The Contours of a Turf War

Owing in part to the kind of claims detailed above, the telecoms sector acquired an outsized status by virtue of its "bombastic declarations" in public (web-platform executive, interview, 2015) and the sector's more obscure efforts to impede the bill in private. Certainly, for civil society organizations, the telecoms sector became the villain of the Marco Civil narrative, owing to its staunch opposition to network neutrality. It was not, however, the only interest group with a vested concern in whether and how network neutrality would be legislated.

The prospect of enshrining network neutrality in law did, of course, impinge upon other powerful sectors within informational capitalism, impacting their favored mechanics of revenue generation. Net neutrality had also been elevated to the centerpiece digital right by Molon and his supporters in civil society, analogous to the civic values of freedom of expression and access to knowledge. As such, the focus of this subsection is on the multiple contestations that evolved around network neutrality, the discourses that accompanied them, and how these represent some of the key tensions within the dynamics of informational capitalism.

As mentioned in this chapter's introduction, informational capitalism in Brazil observed the advent of a powerful new rivalry in the form of Globo Group versus the telcos. This was due to the passage in 2011 of the Lei do SeAC (Pay TV Law) that permitted the telecoms sector access into a national cable-TV market, which was highly lucrative for the Globo media group. It meant that for the first time, Globo, with US$5.7 billion revenue, was cast into direct competition with the two Latin American communications conglomerates with the highest revenues: Telefónica with US$65 billion and América Móvil with US$50 billion (Mastrini & Becerra, 2017, p. 259).

The development of the Lei do SeAC could be interpreted as a dress rehearsal for the power dynamics observed during the Marco Civil. The former was the object of major dispute for more than three years before it was eventually passed. The struggle also pitted the core sectors within informational capitalism against one another in an effort to secure the optimal legislative environment for their business models.

The eventual compromise solution saw Globo's needs largely addressed, with legislators ignoring its near-monopoly control over content production, while international players were mollified by the abolition on foreign capital caps in distribution enterprises, and the telecoms sector gained access to a lucrative new market. The most compelling parallel is that the end product was the result of various sectorial agendas being blended together in a grand political bargain, while sold as a public interest victory and mediated by a state that was ill-equipped or unwilling to impose its own priorities (Lima, 2015, p. 37).

These developments likely informed Globo's agenda for the Marco Civil, one that included securing network neutrality near the top of its wish list.

This is because of the nature of Globo's participation in the subscription-TV market in Brazil. Although Globo dominated the content side—either through domestic production or its formidable bundle of exclusive licensing agreements with US studios—it relied on partnerships, rather than ownership of the distribution companies. With the introduction of the telecoms sector into the cable-TV market, a raft of actors capable not only of funding content (up to a 30 percent ownership stake in any event) (Wiziack, 2013) but also distributing content through its own infrastructure, it became imperative that Globo secure network neutrality in order to avoid finding itself at the sharp end of positive discrimination. As Brazilian researcher Sonia Moreira (2016) observes, the Lei do SeAC "benefited the four dominant groups operating in Brazil: Spain's Telefónica, Mexico's América Móvil, Telecom Italia (Italy), and Brazil's Telemar with Portugal Telecom" (p. 27).

In 2012, content production and/or programming represented 25 percent of the Globo Group's total revenues. This was divided between paid TV channels and online distribution (Possebon, 2013). Although the lion's share of the group's revenues at this time, 71 percent, still came from the sale of advertising on its open and paid TV channels, content production and/or programming was the single-largest growth area, as its revenues increased 34 percent from the previous year. This was clearly a golden egg worth protecting from the threat of the telcos. Indeed, just four years later, in 2016, its satellite division Globosat would represent the second-largest source of revenue for the Globo Group after its open TV stations (Feltrin, 2016).

In 2012, Globo was thus on the defensive with regard to the restrictions imposed upon it by the Pay TV Law. Although its domination of content production within the paid TV market was unaffected, stipulations regarding cross-ownership of content production *and* distribution enterprises meant that Globo was being compelled to make significant changes in its economic holdings.

Specifically, in 2012 Anatel demanded that Globo sell the stake it retained in NET/Embratel—recently acquired by Carlos Slim's América Móvil—in order to comply with the Lei do SeAC cross-ownership rules (Tavares, 2012). NET/Embratel at that time dominated 38 percent of the pay TV market, with nearly double the number of subscribers of its nearest rival, SKY/DirecTV (Tavares, 2012). Moreover, shortly afterwards, América Móvil consolidated its power in the Brazilian media market by assuming majority control of NET/Embratel and thus "strengthened the ever-growing presence of Carlos Slim, the Mexican media tycoon, in Brazilian telecoms" (Moreira, 2016, p. 23). As Globo processed this new threat, it "turned its focus towards the production rather than distribution of stations" (Mastrini & Becerra,

2017, p. 262), in the process becoming even more vulnerable to the possibilities that the newly entered telcos would discriminate against Globo's content. A legislative assurance of network neutrality offered a powerful hedge against this risk.

At the outset of the Marco Civil's journey through Congress, Globo opted to maintain a low public profile. Indeed, a keyword search of the Factiva database reveals that in 2012 the only occasions that the Marco Civil was mentioned in Globo's flagship newspaper, *O Globo*, were in two op-eds only tangentially related to the bill. The group was likely keen to observe the initial skirmishes from the sidelines, to see how network neutrality and IP—its two major concerns in the Marco Civil—would be affected.

Globo's "Doctrine" of Neutrality

Tonet Camargo, Globo Group's public policy director, assured me that network neutrality was a foundational concern for the organization: "It is a doctrinal base, an axiomatic base, from which everything else is built." He went on to develop this perspective:

> [Without network neutrality] I am not going to have the internet that it is today, a space that is naturally free. *Naturally free*. . . . Because if everyone had the same opportunity for the traffic of their data through the internet, it is going to continue to be a free medium. And when I say a free medium, I am not saying that we don't have to have tax regulations or, indeed, internet businesses that charge fees, that we don't have safeguards for property rights, or any of that. I am talking about the flow of data and the flow of contents on the internet. (interview, 2015)

Camargo was evidently at pains to define what he meant by the internet as a free medium and how that related to network neutrality. It is a perspective that is reminiscent of the US free-flow doctrine, in which freedom is narrowly construed to justify a media system in which the most powerful content producers were able to distribute their material without restrictions (Nordenstreng, 2011). It is a form of freedom that, conversely, does not preclude all manner of *control over* the user, in the form of taxes, fees, and IP restrictions.

This tract offers a valuable insight into the tension at the heart of network neutrality as a first-order digital right. At the same time as it offers internet users the possibility to access information, it constitutes a form of freedom that favors the powerful content producers and distributors that dominate the internet, and as such network neutrality facilitates a core mechanic of informational capitalism.

Meanwhile, the tension implied by this doctrinal commitment to network neutrality and by Globo's relationship with the telecoms sector was also made explicit by Camargo:

> The position of Globo in relation to net neutrality was the same from the start to the end. Does this generate tension with the telecoms companies? It does, it did, because they are clients of ours and we are clients of theirs. . . . But these things remained well separated, no? The discussion was one of a political nature. (interview, 2015)

The "political" nature of these discussions refers most likely to the capacity of these entities to set aside their commercial interdependence in the interests of pursuing their preferred ends for network neutrality with a winner-takes-all mindset. This manifested itself in the way Globo used its full media arsenal to publicly lobby for network neutrality (B. Rosa, 2014) at the expense of the telcos after it had privately secured its other main target: notice and takedown for copyright violations. As well as ensuring a head-on confrontation with the telecoms sector, Globo's position on network neutrality implied an important synergy with the positions of other important actors in the development of the Marco Civil: its civil society and state backers and the web platforms.

In the case of web platforms, although there was an obvious alignment with Globo in terms of support for network neutrality, the two sectors of informational capitalism were at loggerheads on the issue of copyright. This was vividly illustrated in the dispute over third-party liability in the bill—examined at length later in this chapter—but earlier episodes demonstrate that this was not an isolated incident. For instance, in 2011, Brazil's National Association of Newspapers (ANJ) (of which Grupo Globo is the most prominent member), recommended to its 154 members that they leave Google News because it offered no remuneration for republishing its copyrighted content. This dispute unsurprisingly received prominent coverage in Globo's own newspaper (G1, 2012).

Moreover, in 2012, Globo adopted an internal policy that prohibited the sharing of links to Globo content through the official Facebook pages of Globo media products, such as *G1* and *O Globo*. The stated rationale for this "declaration of war" was because Globo executives were displeased with the ratio of Globo content that appeared in the newsfeeds of Facebook users and because they were concerned about the amount of information that Facebook gleaned about Globo's own audience, as well as their capacity to advertise directly to them (Mizukami et al., 2014, p. 123). We can observe here a core dynamic within informational capitalism: the tension between information flow and control. On the topic of network neutrality, however, Globo and Google were broadly aligned.

The Curious Ambivalence of Google

Google and other web giants had taken a vanguard role in the US net neutrality debates in the mid to late 2000s. They made common cause with public interest groups like Free Press to pressure the US Federal Communications Commission (FCC) to enact safeguards for a neutral network (Kimball, 2013). In so doing, the web platforms successfully aligned their own economic interests in preserving an open internet with the civic goals of access to information and freedom of expression. As well as trading on their history of advocacy in the United States in support of network neutrality, the web platforms adroitly associated themselves with key signifiers in the digital discourse, particularly, "open," "neutral," "transparent," and "free" (Golumbia, 2013). In the case of Brazil, web platforms were thus positioned as natural allies of the Marco Civil.

The Marco Civil's civil society and government supporters might have anticipated that the internet companies would represent a steadfast and powerful ally in the battle to achieve network neutrality protections. The reality fell well short. Although curiously, the *perception* among civil society groups and the telecoms companies was that the US net neutrality alliance had been replicated in Brazil. What could account for this disparity between reality and perception?

According to my web company interviewee, the companies that made up the sector

> were not really engaging in network neutrality at all. They were just looking out to see. Do any of these things actually limit our practice? No, they don't. Is this a positive thing to have? Yes. But should we advocate strongly for it? No. The rationale for this strategic judgment takes us back to the hostile relationship observed in the United States, because they didn't want to anger the telcos more than we already had worldwide. (2015)

Once again, we can observe that Brazil's place at the periphery of informational capitalism influenced the manner in which digital rights were contested and constituted. In this instance, my interviewee is referencing the net neutrality disputes in the United States, described above, that pitted internet companies against the telecoms sector. That hostility was reconciled in part through the infamous gentlemen's agreement between Verizon and Google in 2010 (Dolber, 2013, p. 148). It is likely then that the web platforms did not wish to revisit the antagonism between the two sectors that had reached such heights in informational capitalism's core and preferred to pursue a more discreet tack at the periphery. Moreover, this strategy would make particular sense in a country like Brazil.

Data in 2011 showed that Brazil's web traffic was dominated overwhelmingly by US corporations, including Google, Facebook, Microsoft, and Twitter (now X) (Comscore, 2012). This paucity of Brazilian national flag-bearers had a significant bearing on the ability of internet companies to legitimately intervene in public debate. While the country may boast one of the world's largest Facebook user populations, their status as American companies, in a country famously sensitive to American interference in its national affairs (Rohter, 2002), means that it is prudent for internet and technology companies to keep a low profile in matters of national import. Moreover, it is widely understood that innovation and free speech are lofty ideals in American society, and web platforms were able to position themselves on network neutrality in order to appropriate those connotations. These currents in Brazil, by contrast, do not enjoy the same degree of salience.

Also needed is a focus on the web platforms' guiding principle of "Do any of these things actually limit our practice?" with regard to network neutrality. Within a strategic calculus, any desire not to antagonize the telecoms sector would surely be set aside if the platforms perceived that network-neutrality provisions in the Marco Civil could bestow significant economic advantage. That the telcos only sought protections for future business models implies that there was no immediate threat for the web platforms. As chapter 1 explored, infrastructure is a key dimension in the constitution of the zones of informational capitalism, and as Winseck (2017) astutely reminds us, Google's lower profile on network neutrality policy disputes coincided with a massive increase in internet infrastructure investment; in effect, if Google owned its own pipes, then the telcos could manage theirs however they wished. In 2016, Google announced the construction of a submarine cable linking Rio de Janeiro to São Paulo (BNAmericas, 2016), a project that may well have formed part of Google's strategic considerations. In any event, the major US platforms had formidable resources to pay their way through to the user in a non-neutral network environment. And finally, if the term "future business models" implied zero-rating and its variations, then those same platforms would be the favored content providers in those arrangements with the telcos (Hoskins, 2019).

As regards civil society's perception of the internet companies' role in promoting net neutrality, my interviewee was again quite clear: "Maybe they didn't realize that we were never actually engaging on that. But, yes, for them, we were all on the same side. . . . *For civil society* we were as strong supporters of net neutrality as they were" (2015, emphasis added). We should compare that bald self-assessment of the web platforms' ambivalence with the perception of one of the leading civil society organizers. Lefevre, who is also a CGI board member: "So the big content providers ended up on the side of neutrality: Google, Globo, et cetera. So, this was an important thing for us in the fight for network neutrality" (interview, 2015). Other interviewees from civil society and the SAL-CTS teams also identified what they imagined to be a significant marriage of convenience between civil society organizers and the web platforms (interviews: Almeida, 2018; Affonso Souza, 2015; Moncau, 2015). Even the telcos were drawn into the illusion, as my web-platform interviewee reveals:

> The activists were already so up in arms defending neutrality that the telcos thought wrongly—which was very funny—that we were the ones fueling the fire. They thought that the web companies are the ones controlling and are behind the scenes of the activists because why would a regular person care about net neutrality is what they were saying. . . . We actually let them think that even though it wasn't true at all. I didn't have even one-tenth of the leverage that they thought that we did. (interview, 2015)

For the web platforms, network neutrality appeared to constitute little more than an agreeable bonus from the Marco Civil. As the previous chapter discusses, safe harbors were "really the thing to get" (web platform executive, interview, 2015). One exception to the general strategy of discrete lobbying by the platforms was a letter of support for the Marco Civil, cosigned by Facebook, Google, and the Brazilian e-commerce site Mercado Livre, issued in September 2012.

As per the strategic goals of the sector, in the two pages of this letter, network neutrality did not receive a single mention. Instead, the web companies harnessed the digital discourse to promote the economic and societal benefits of safe harbors:

> Online platforms transform the political and social scenario, facilitating communication and access to government and creating new possibilities for interaction, organization and social mobilization. . . . The recent political reform and the end of totalitarian regimes in various countries around the world, facilitated in part by the use of online tools, shows the democratic potential of the Internet. (Facebook, Google, and Mercado Livre, electronic document, in author's possession, September 18, 2012)

In sum, we can see that in the case of the Marco Civil, the contestation around network neutrality lays bare some of the dynamics of informational capitalism and is defined in part by Brazil's status at the system's periphery. The telecoms sector resisted network neutrality in order to safeguard future business models, most likely including the practice of zero-rating that has become ubiquitous as a mode of offering mobile internet access in the global south. Globo, meanwhile, sought to retain its dominance as a content conduit over the telecoms sector by securing network neutrality. Finally, the web companies defied public perception and sought not to further inflame its tensions with the telecoms sector by remaining passive on net neutrality. One group of actors decidedly non-neutral about network neutrality, examined in the next section, was the informal consortium of civil society actors supporting the Marco Civil.

Civil Society, Consumption, and the Favela Online

Although the principal civil society organizations that championed the Marco Civil—Intervozes, IDEC, Proteste, Partido Pirata, Movimento Mega Não, Artigo 19, and FNDC (National Forum for the Democratization of Communication)—had displayed their support from the inception of the project, it was not until the bill reached Congress that many of the groups really began to amplify their advocacy work. This was partly in response to the interventions of the telecoms and content-production sectors and, once the bill entered Congress, the security state. Also, an obvious political opportunity structure was implied by the Snowden revelations in 2013.

TABLE 3. Civil society organizations (CSOs) engaged in the development of the Marco Civil

CSO	Remit	Year Founded
Artigo 19	communication	2007
FNDC	communication	1991
IDEC	consumption	1987
Intervozes	communication	2003
Movimento Mega Não	communication	2009
Partido Pirata	communication	2012
Proteste	consumption	2001

Much of this advocacy work was focused upon and motivated by the fate of network neutrality in the bill. As my web-platform interviewee explained: "A couple of activists and especially consumer groups were really strong in defense of network neutrality. I would say that if it wasn't for them, then that might have gone away" (2015). Given that this dogged support from a small band of CSOs was critical for keeping the issue on the government agenda, what requires examination at this stage, therefore, is *why* concerns for network neutrality were foundational to so much of this work. In so doing, what comes into focus is a bundle of discursive articulations connecting the concept of network neutrality with national sociohistorical narratives. These show how Brazil's social inequality and its checkered history of media democracy, when associated discursively with the concept of network neutrality, garnered strong support from civil society groups for a technolegal policy measure otherwise unheralded at the outset of the Marco Civil's development. In turn, this observation helps to address one of the core questions animating this book: Why were the Marco Civil's civic ambitions so modest?

Insurgent Citizenship: Civil Society in Democratic Brazil

At this juncture, a more in-depth examination of the composition and history of the civil society sector in Brazil is necessary in order to understand how the commitment displayed by a core of CSOs—so vital for the bill's eventual passage into law—was connected to Brazil's history of media democracy and its status at the periphery of global capitalism.

One important dimension of civil society's character in Brazil lies in the force of the urban poor seeking civil, social, and political rights through collective action. Brazil experienced a massive process of urbanization during the 1960s and 1970s as millions of poor rural inhabitants were encouraged by the state to move to the city in an effort to drive modernization and economic growth. The newly constructed urban peripheries, unserved by a neglectful state and the subject of an "unjust and exclusionary citizenship" (Saad Filho & Morais, 2017), organized themselves to acquire the necessities of life and in so doing enact a form of "insurgent citizenship" (Holston, 2009). Moreover, the order in which Brazil established its classes of rights (first social, then political, and then civil) also contributed to the emphasis on securing civil rights in Brazil (J. M. Carvalho, 2013, p. 17). This history of rights claiming, although rooted partly in an urban underclass unconnected from those CSOs supporting the Marco Civil, did produce an influential legacy that helps to explain why digital rights were enacted in Brazil in the explicit form of a *civil* rights framework.

A further related aspect lies in the process of democratization that occurred in Brazil after the 1985 transition. President José Sarney (1985–90) established a National Constituent Assembly in 1985 that permitted popular amendments. This facilitated the participation of CSOs that sought provisions on health and urban issues (Avritzer, 2017, p. 54), as well as communication rights (Fórum Nacional, n.d.). As a result of these processes, a certain path dependency was created in terms of the willingness of the state and civil society to cooperate on the topic of civil rights. Indeed, as Brazilian sociologist Gianpaolo Baiocchi (2017) opines, "unlike, perhaps, civil society organizations in 'liberal' societies that have a stronger claim at 'separateness' if not 'autonomy,' civil society in Brazil has often had ties with the state" (p. 43). This legacy was manifested in the close coordination between Congressman Molon and the CSOs during the parliamentary phase of the Marco Civil, as well as that between the Ministry of Justice and the CSOs in the foundational phase. Finally, there is, however, an important ambiguity in this dimension of civil society's relationship to the state in Brazil: the abuses of the military dictatorship also led to an attraction to the internet as a tool for disintermediating society *from* the communicative control of the state.

The specific characters of the relevant CSOs deserve further scrutiny now, as civil society is often mischaracterized as a homogenous block. Indeed, in the case of the Marco Civil, it was composed of a group whose organizational emphases could be broadly divided between consumer and communication rights. The distinct remits of these two sets of CSOs were a significant contributing factor to the nature of the digital rights that constitute the Marco Civil.

A Bulwark: Net Neutrality and the Generals

Much of the basis of the staunch support of CSOs for network neutrality in the Marco Civil can be connected to Brazil's history of military dictatorship. Not only were civil and political rights severely repressed during the regime's twenty-year rule (1964–85) but the emergence of the mass media also was managed carefully by the generals in order to serve their socioeconomic goals for the nation. The legacy of the media's servitude to dictatorship is an enduring one in Brazil and is manifested within the civil society sector both in the broad mistrust of the main media groups (especially Globo) and, conversely, by the faith placed in the internet as a last redoubt of potential media democracy.

For the communication rights–focused CSOs, the fundamental rights contained in the Marco Civil were deserving of their support because these rights offered safeguards for freedom of expression that had always been under grave threat in Brazil. I argue that recognition of this historic vulnerability resulted in the readiness of many of these communication rights–focused CSOs to accept and support a weak conceptualization of digital rights as framed in the Marco Civil. Moreover, as argued at the outset of this chapter, the perceived legitimacy and urgency of the bill were greatly increased by the resistance of the broadcast, content-production, and telecoms sectors. In essence, the fact of this opposition served to reinforce the perception of the Marco Civil's worth among its civil society backers, despite its profound shortcomings as a guarantor of civil rights.

According to the Movimento Mega Não cofounder Caribé, the provisions in the Marco Civil protecting freedom of expression were important to "counteract a conservative, monopolist, and controlling media." Caribé also noted how previous efforts to check the media power of the broadcast sector in Brazil had been abandoned. The Marco Civil, in this context, offered a new opportunity to "create conditions in which we have a communication channel that is freer on social media." Neutrality, in his reckoning, was fundamental for this, "guaranteeing that our voices are heard equally" (interview, 2015).

Moncau raised a similar point in interview. He claimed that in order to understand the significance of the Marco Civil in the context of Brazil, one needed to appraise the current and historical state of media concentration:

> There is one thing that is very important, which is concerns about media democracy and diversity, pluralism, et cetera. So network neutrality gains a higher profile because of this. I think countries such as Germany that have a better environment for media maybe don't understand how deep the question is when you have only certain types of discourse circulating. (2015)

Other Brazilian academics have similarly recognized the exalted status of the internet for Brazilian activists, for the same reason expressed by Moncau and Caribé. Political scientist Rosemary Segurado asserts that the context in which TV licenses are distributed in Brazil as a means of "political currency" means that "the concern for netizens is to prevent that the Internet under the command of the state privileges political groups and limits individual and collective freedom" (2011, p. 13). Also, legal scholar Marcelo Thompson, in his polemic published during the consultation phase of the Marco Civil, describes how the Brazilian public sought judicial rather than political oversight of the internet because of its perceived status as "a virgin, holy, pious territory" (2010, p. 5).

An Existential Concern: Consumption at the Periphery

Beyond the issue of media democracy, the other side of the equation also connected to Brazil's historically peripheral status pertains to consumption rights, the groups that championed them, and the egregious social inequality in Brazil that makes this advocacy work such a pressing concern.

In order to appreciate this dimension of the Marco Civil, one must first take a step back to consider the broader question of what consumption means in Brazil and other societies in the economic periphery of the global south. Sorj (2003) describes the central characteristic of consumption in contemporary society not in terms of its role as a marker of social status but as "chances for social participation." He adds, "For the poorest populations of the planet, globalization is not the expectation of eating at McDonald's or wearing Nike, *it is access to food, water, electricity*, appliances, radio, television, telephone, Internet, antibiotics" (2003, p. 23, emphasis added). Fundamentally, for societies at the periphery, unlike the global north, consumption rights pertain to access to essential service and goods, to the existential question of the right to life, as opposed to the economic rationality of the right to fair treatment in the marketplace.

As has been widely documented, in Brazil in the 1990s, the stabilization of the economy and the end of hyperinflation through the Real plan catalyzed an increase in the minimum wage, mass access to consumer credit, and an overall increase in welfare for the salaried poor (Barbosa & Wilkinson, 2017, p. 150). Consumption behavior among the urban poor changed radically as a result and the emergence of a "new middle class" was widely championed (Barbosa & Wilkinson, 2017). Social inequality and wealth concentration continued, however, to be defining markers of Brazilian society (J. M. Carvalho, 2013; Holston, 2009). As Sorj argues in his milestone book *A Nova Sociedade Brasileira* (The New Brazilian Society), consumption rights became a new mode of citizenship (2001).

The politicization of consumption rights in Brazil was also closely connected to the transition to democracy and the participatory processes that accompanied the construction of the country's new constitution. The new democratic constitution did, indeed, enshrine consumer rights, and two years after its promulgation, the government enacted into law a consumer protection code. It was an advanced piece of legislation that was partly the product of "popular movements advocating greater equity between groups and classes" and went on to become "a model for consumer protection laws" throughout Latin America (Vaughn, 1993, p. 284).

One needs to also consider the fact that consumer groups in Brazil—notably, IDEC and Proteste—were heavily involved in efforts to universalize access to telecoms infrastructure in Brazil prior to the Marco Civil. This question of the right to internet access contained in the Marco Civil thus represented one of the principal footholds for consumer-advocacy groups. As Veridiana Alimonti—a lawyer for the IDEC group and interviewed for this study—explained, the emphasis on broadband diffusion was due to its potential to "strengthen rights like education, culture, freedom of speech, and access to information" (2016). Similarly, Lefevre from Proteste explained:

> When you speak of public services, like access to the internet, then we're not talking about something contractual, specific, it's talking about the right to access, and the Marco Civil made this very clear. . . . There is a reinforcement between what we at Proteste see as the right to consumption and the rights of the citizen. (interview, 2015)

Advocating for broadband access as a means to strengthen civil rights also permeated the consumer groups' approach to network neutrality. Moncau explained these connections between a developing world view of consumption, the social inequality in Brazil, and the issue of network neutrality:

> Consumption is not just what you pay, et cetera, but how to include the whole portion of people that doesn't have access to the market, that don't have . . . access to education, basic services like energy and water, these are deeply linked to human rights, to what in our constitution is called the *dignidade* [dignity] of the human being. . . . There is this strong perspective of creating an environment of equality. Network neutrality is related to that . . . related to [the fact that] Brazil is one of the most unequal countries in the world. (interview, 2015)

Through these observations, I contend that we can detect an important paradox in the influence of consumption rights on the Marco Civil. On the one hand, in Brazil consumption is politicized to a much-greater degree than one would expect in societies in the global north, given the histories of state-led agendas of exclusion and the present and profound social inequalities. On the other, however, I argue that the high profile and social importance of consumption rights in relation to the Marco Civil actually served to further *depoliticize* the bill; the conflation of digital rights with the kind of individualist, technical fixes that inhere in the realm of consumption was, to a significant degree, legitimated by the exhaustive advocacy work of these consumer rights–focused CSOs.

Brazilian scholar Marcos Dantas's observations (2013) regarding the involvement of civil society groups in the neoliberal restructuring of the telecoms sector in Brazil and the parallels with the Marco Civil are stark and offer a fitting conclusion here:

> There expanded an idea of a "civil society" constituted by multitudes of particularist, communitarian, identity-focused movements in search of "rights" that were *exclusive* and *excluding*, little disposed to any hierarchy of priorities, for which *systemic questions*, especially those directly related to capital, were not intellectually attractive or politically mobilizing. (p. 195, emphasis added)

Uploading the Favela

The goal of the telecoms sector to introduce differentiated services proved to be the glue that bound together civil society concerns around social inequality and support for network neutrality provisions in the Marco Civil. Pedro Ramos, a young lawyer and academic researcher, became one of the most prominent independent voices articulating the importance of network neutrality during the Marco Civil process. Ramos invoked, in what became a widely cited comparison, the phenomenon of Brazil's urban favela communities to make a strong case against the telcos' plans:

> With the charging of differentiated services, the same social separation will be reproduced that occurs within Brazilian cities today: peripheries with limited access . . . and rings of wealth around which barriers of social stratification will be built with the objective of preventing the passage of the periphery. (2014, p. 13)

A similar case was introduced at a public audience hosted in the Brazilian Parliament to debate the Marco Civil by Sérgio Amadeu. He cited research by CGI.br showing that of the poorest 15 percent of Brazilian internet users, 72 percent used social networks, and 52 percent used YouTube. The prospect of charging differentiated access to multimedia content would, therefore, unduly penalize the most marginalized sectors of Brazilian society, in an argument that he described as "fatal" to the presented rationale of Eduardo Cunha and the telecoms sector (quoted in Solagna, 2015, p. 107).

Barbosa articulated similar concerns with regard to the potential for differentiated services to create a two-tiered internet that would follow

Brazil's fractured socioeconomic lines: "If people didn't have net neutrality, this inequality would increase even more. So, to use this argument in public debate was important because, in reality, 40 percent of the Brazilian population don't have access to the internet" (interview, 2015).

These arguments did not, of course, go uncontested by the telcos. Indeed, the claim that network neutrality was a bulwark against the favela-ization of the Brazilian internet was turned on its head by representatives of the sector. Castro highlighted to me in our interview the argument that differentiated services in the form of zero-rating and the related infringement of network neutrality would aid the freedom of expression of "forty million Brazilians who don't have money to pay for the service . . . and won't be able to exercise, at least partially, their role as citizen."

This concern for the speech rights of the most economically excluded in Brazil was also explained in connection to the 1,670 municipalities in Brazil that are not served by broadband connections owing to their economic and geographic marginalization. According to Castro, the provision of zero-rated mobile web services could allow telecoms operators to provide at least partial internet access to regions where it was otherwise not economically viable for them. For the inhabitant of those areas, "when you don't have service that you can't pay for, or you don't have infrastructure, when do you have freedom of expression? You don't. You cannot speak, you don't have the means" (interview, 2015).

This appropriation of social justice arguments *against* network neutrality by the telecoms sector was also evident in the US neutrality debates. Dolber (2013, p. 157) explains how telecoms companies courted African American community organizations to make the case for how enacting neutrality would imperil possibilities of increasing access for marginalized communities.

Thus, an important discursive articulation occurred between the discourses critical of social inequality in Brazil and those advocating for the defense of network neutrality. In this articulation, network neutrality was defended as a fundamental facet of the Marco Civil by virtue of its capacity to prevent Brazil's favelas from becoming manifest online. As such, social divisions characteristic of Brazil's peripheral status became central to the contestation of network neutrality by key protagonists in the Marco Civil. The discourse of social inequality buttressed the other—sometimes contradictory—dimensions of civil society advocacy for the Marco Civil that are characteristic of the periphery: the beleaguered state of media democracy, the politicization of consumption, the urgency of civil rights claims, and the interrelationship between state and civil society.

Any Port in a Storm: Safe Harbors and "Free" Expression

In July 2012, Molon revealed three important changes he intended to include in substitutivo 2, issued on November 11, 2012. The first, article 9 on data traffic, was designed to further reduce possible loopholes for discriminatory network practices. This signaled that Molon and the CSOs that lobbied for it were not cowed by the obfuscatory and intimidatory tactics of the telecoms sector. The telcos, in turn, only intensified their efforts to thwart the bill's progress.

Those efforts would prove highly effective. Between August 2012 and June 2013, the Marco Civil was effectively frozen; as for any scheduled vote on the bill, the telecoms sector demanded the noncooperation of its congressional block. My web platform interviewee explained, "That was when people realized the force and the strength of the telecoms sector because they basically wanted to block network neutrality rules, they didn't really care about the rest" (2015).

Moreover, the Marco Civil no longer enjoyed the patronage of Lula da Silva, who was responsible for launching the project. Instead, the executive branch under Dilma Rousseff had effectively relegated the bill to a postscript on the governmental agenda. These obstacles were evidenced by two cancelled votes: one on August 8 due to lack of quorum (likely orchestrated through telecoms lobbying) and another on September 19 by order of the executive branch (Papp, 2014).

The inertia that had encompassed the bill must have been acutely evident to Molon, the man tasked with guiding its passage through the house. As such, the other two changes he included in this new version of the draft law were made with a view to breaking the deadlock. He intended to do so by driving a wedge into the sectorial interests of informational capitalism, which were interests that while not united, appeared in combination insurmountable.

One change was evidently a sop to the state security apparatus in Brazil. Article 12 on log storage for internet applications was completely rewritten in terms of the obligations of application providers (i.e., those companies providing online services, e.g., social networks). From being *prohibited from retaining* any connection logs, they were now *compelled to retain them* for one year.

The amendment antagonized privacy advocates who understood the implications of the security services gaining greater access to user data, implications learned painfully from twenty-one years of military dictatorship.

Those same advocates were also wary of the telecoms companies gaining access to users' navigation history, as they feared that data would be used to exploit them. By contrast, little to no attention seemed to be paid to the implications of the web platforms having access to the data. This blind spot can be attributed in part to the dominant paradigm of digital rights, which valorizes internet companies as guarantors of expression, innovation, and creativity but obscures the exploitative nature of their data-driven business models.

The third change in substitutivo 2 was the most radical. The addition of twenty short words signaled a major concession to some of the most powerful actors assailing the bill: the content production sector, including, most notably, Grupo Globo.

"Free" as in Beer: Expression and the Safe Harbor Paradox

Article 15 of section 3 on the "responsibilities arising from damages caused by content posted by third parties" now included a new subclause stating that "the stipulations of this article will not apply when it concerns the infraction of authorial or associated rights." This clause amounted to a radical alteration to safe harbors as a central principle of the Marco Civil, stipulating that online publishers would only be held liable for content if they had failed to comply with a court order for its removal. This change was the first attempt at what became solidified in the bill as a highly controversial IP carve-out, meaning that websites would be liable for copyright-infringing content. The inclusion of this new clause was significant because it signaled a tacit approval for the status quo: of notice and takedown, of backchannel agreements between platforms and copyright holders, and of the intimidation of small publishers to remove content deemed undesirable by economically or politically powerful actors in Brazil.

This amendment proved pivotal to the fate of the bill in terms of securing the support of powerful new allies and was predictably divisive. The nature of the contestation around safe harbors as free expression—a core digital right—is explored in the next subsection, although it suffices to state here that the battle lines divided two main groups. On one side were the IP-rights associations and content-production sector favored by the provision. They were, in turn, bolstered by pragmatists from within civil society who deemed it impossible to pass the Marco Civil unless they found a way to force Globo and the content-production sector away from the telcos.

On the other side were those idealists among the bill's civil society champions, who decried how this clause would provide the conditions for systematic censorship. Where both sides of the civil society divide did coalesce was in the notion that the limited liability of platforms served as a legitimate proxy for the expressive rights of its users; the only divergence was in the degree to which those rights were diminished by the IP carveout. The pragmatists considered it a sacrifice worth making for the greater good of the bill, while freedom-of-speech purists believed that the expressive rights of Brazilian internet users would be decisively undermined.

The debate around this point indicates once again the unchallenged assumptions about safe harbors: that the invulnerability of web platforms could represent a true substitute for the freedom of expression of Brazilian internet users. I reiterate now the essence of my critique: that safe harbors as a proxy for expressive rights privileges a mode of communication that is free only in terms of cost. Any advance of democratic or civic freedom generated by expression on those platforms is only ever a by-product of safe harbors, when the political economic underpinnings of the internet remain unquestioned. Such civic value is diluted by the reality that platforms commodify expression and use the ensuing power to algorithmically control the means of communication in a way that maximizes revenue at the expense of the public good. Ultimately, safe harbors represent the conflation of speech with profit, or as historian and political economist Dan Schiller described it, "a camouflaged preferment of electronic commerce" (2000, p. 72).

Defending the Commodity Form: The Case for IP

Molon's grand bargain was premised on securing support for the Marco Civil from the content-production sector, including its most powerful figurehead in Brazil, the Globo Group. The ability to effectively control the flow of its IP commodities was zealously guarded by the group. Across the breadth of its media empire in 2012, content and programming may have accounted for 25 percent of Globo's total revenues (compared to advertising at 71 percent), but it was the most rapidly growing segment of the group's enterprise (up 34 percent from 2011) (Folha de S. Paulo, 2013) and also the most vulnerable.

According to José Francisco de Araújo Lima, Globo's director of institutional relations, regulation, and new media, in 2012 the business issued 150 notifications per week for copyright-infringing content removal (Machado, 2012). As the executive explained in our interview, "It is necessary to maintain notice and takedown in the Marco [Civil] and to assign responsibility to the provider that does not comply with the request. Using a judicial order makes everything impractical with the ponderousness of the justice system and the cost of the process."

Lima's fellow Globo executive Camargo similarly bemoaned the content provisions in the Marco Civil. Clearly, Globo had a vested economic interest in ring-fencing the systemic logics of commodification and control that were integral to the profitability of the group. As Camargo explained, the prospect of a Marco Civil being legislated without the inclusion of IP protections was simply antithetical to the business goals of the group: "There has to be freedom on the web, but that doesn't mean that you relativize or end copyright. If you do, you end production. You end production" (interview, 2015).

Globo was obviously not alone in seeking to secure the continuation of notice and takedown. From the inception of the bill, the project had been assailed by the demands of international IP-rights associations, orchestrated primarily by the International Federation of the Phonographic Industry (IFPI), headquartered in Washington, DC. In a contribution submitted to the first round of public consultation, this organization—tasked with maintaining stringent IP protections worldwide to the advantage of the (predominately American) recording industry—wrote that "the approach of the Draft Proposal should therefore be rethought and amended substantially with the input of IP experts and the direct involvement of the copyright and cultural communities" (Ministério da Justiça, 2010, Contribuições recebidas).

The IFPI's Brazilian counterpart, the Association of Phonographic Producers (ABPD), also vigorously lobbied Molon and the PT government to secure an IP exception in the Marco Civil. The association's president, Paulo Rosa, cited data to justify its position, claiming that in 2011, eighty-thousand content-removal requests were issued, and "with a judicial order . . . the system will be overloaded." In a clear nod to the core of informational capitalism, Rosa also said, "It is not worth abandoning a practice that works in the United States and Europe" (Machado, 2012).

The largest internet companies also stood to gain from these proposed arrangements. An IP carve-out would simply replicate the familiar operating environment of the United States in Brazil, as well as maintain the practice of notice and takedown that had done nothing to inhibit the US platforms' dominance of the Brazilian internet. The web would never publicly declare their support for the IP exemption for fear of compromising their zealously guarded neutral status, although some press reports note Facebook's prominent role in the IP clause being introduced (Dias, 2012 July 10). Moreover, my web-platform interviewee related that in private the company urged the clause's detractors to be realistic:

The web companies said, "Listen, guys, let's be honest here. Even the Communication Decency Act in the US, which is the biggest safe harbor provision in the world, has a carve-out for copyright." . . . So, in a way our position ended up being a middle ground between these two extremes. . . . Web companies are happy with that. (interview, 2015)

The manner in which the carve-out was negotiated and included by Molon is the subject of conflicting accounts. What is indisputable is that the fact and manner of its insertion into the bill proved hugely controversial and consequential.

"Carve-Out," or Carve-Up? IP and Molon's Grand Bargain

The Ministry of Culture was one of the actors most often invoked in explaining the presence of the IP clause, and it did possess a strong vested interest in the issue. This is because in 2010 the Ministry of Culture had conducted its own public consultation to begin a proposed reform of intellectual property policy in Brazil. The existing copyright law (LDA) had been on the statute books since 1998, was considered highly restrictive, and had been badly dated by the mass adoption of the internet (Branco, 2016). Indeed, in 2012 an international consumer-rights association ranked Brazil as fifth worst in the world for access to information according to the strictures of its copyright law (Dias, 2012, August 14). A reform process had begun under Minister Gil, a fierce advocate for copyright reform, who sought to "establish a dialogue between the market and other dimensions of culture" (Silveira et al., 2013, p. 558). An online public consultation in 2010 under Minister Ferreira attracted eight thousand comments, but the draft law was quietly abandoned by Rousseff's appointee Ana de Hollanda, who increasingly pursued an approach to IP closely aligned with the goals of the content-production sector (Silveira et al., 2013; Branco, 2016).

In September 2012, a new minister of culture was appointed by President Rousseff: Marta Suplicy. Suplicy bucked the recent trend exhibited in the post by being more open to resuming the project of IP reform than her predecessor, de Hollanda (Abramovay, 2017, p. 132). For some observers, this offered a cogent explanation for what became the "official" version of events regarding the inclusion of the IP carve-out. According to this account, the new minister explicitly requested of Molon that the Marco Civil remain agnostic to the question of IP (or at least not impinge upon the status quo) so that she retained the policy space to reopen the IP-reform file.

This explanation was clearly a positive spin on the IP carve-out for supporters of the Marco Civil: the minister was simply paving the way for an eventual reform of IP law in Brazil. The reality, however, that Globo directly negotiated the carve-out with Molon presents a much-less palatable account for the bill's champions, one that does not gloss over how the foremost powerholder in informational capitalism in Brazil decisively shaped the bill according to its own interests and at the expense of Brazilian citizens.

It is undisputable that Suplicy was under acute pressure from Globo and its broadcaster coalition, ABERT, as well as the domestic- and international-rights lobbies, to leverage her influence to secure notice and takedown. Certainly, by November 2012 the pressure from these actors was intense. In what appeared to be a coordinated attempt to shape the bill according to its sectorial interests, the content-production sector led by the Brazilian Academy of Arts (ABL) and Grupo Globo made two high-profile interventions into the debate around IP and the Marco Civil.

The first such intervention was a November 5, 2012, public workshop ABL organized, translated as "Creators in Defense of Their Authorial Rights" (Academia Brasileira de Letras, 2012). The event was prominently reported by Globo in its newspaper (Machado, 2012) and was attended by heavyweights from the content-production sector, including Lima for the Globo Group; Rosa, director of ABL; and famed Brazilian author Ana Maria Machado.

Two days later, the Globo newspaper featured an impassioned tirade in an editorial headlined "Marco Civil da Internet Threatens Copyright." It criticized Molon's decision not to specifically make provisions for IP on limited third-party liability. The text argued that the burden of these arrangements would fall not on the "big editorial and media organizations that can mobilize battalions of lawyers to dispatch innumerable judicial notifications every day" but, instead, would be carried disproportionately by "the autonomous creators of content" (Marco da internet, 2012).

The notion that the Globo Group would concern themselves with the fate of "autonomous creators" would be laughable were their ambitions to mold the legislation around their own interests not about to be fulfilled so decisively. The hundreds of billable hours recorded by those "battalions of lawyers" was arguably the greater concern. Indeed, that a seismic shift in the Marco Civil occurred later the same day that this editorial was published should not be dismissed as happenstance.

Faustian Pacts and "An Industry of Private Censorship"

As mentioned above and according to multiple reports—in the press, social media, and subsequent academic accounts—the introduction of the

IP carve-out was less to do with any manipulation by the Globo Group but the result of a direct petition from Suplicy to Molon.

Molon himself tweeted the same day the clause was introduced that Suplicy had personally requested the amendment in order to facilitate reform of the copyright law (LDA) (Brito, 2015, p. 101). A year later Molon reiterated that claim in an op-ed, writing that the IP exemption was "not included . . . by business groups. The text was inserted in the bill in November last year at the request of the Minister of Culture" (Molon, 2013). The first press reports published after the amendment was made public also reference the Suplicy claim (Dias, 2012, July 10). Finally, academic texts examining the Marco Civil also contain numerous interviews from protagonists in the bill's development who reiterate this account (Abramovay, 2017, p. 132) or make obfuscatory claims regarding these events (Affonso Souza et al., 2017; Solagna, 2015, p. 90).

In my own interviews, for instance, Camargo from the Globo Group also stated that the IP carve-out was "an amendment proposed by the minister of culture." He went further by minimizing even Globo's role in pressuring Suplicy. He claimed that "who pushed this issue wasn't Globo. It was the association of broadcasters, that reunites three thousand broadcasters . . . so it was a sectorial position."

When I asked the Ministry of Justice's former chief of staff (and adviser to the ministry from 2011 to 2013) about how the introduction of the carve-out transpired, he was unclear:

> I'm not sure I recall well, and I may have left Brasília by that point. Because I went to the US in August 2013 [these events occurred in November 2012]. There was then pressure by IP owners, by Globo, different music-rights owners in the sense that they wanted to push a DMCA like provision. . . . Actually I think it was several things at the same time. By that time Marta at the Ministry of Culture was pressing because of some artists, I think Globo was pushing because of its content, and they were all trying to put their tentacles wherever they could to make things to one side or the other. (Almeida, interview, 2018)

My web-platform interviewee, for instance, concurred that there was a "huge pressure" from the media sector on Molon to accede to an IP carve-out. He went on to clarify, however, that "by the media sector, let's be honest here, it was the biggest Brazilian TV network, Globo, and of course copyright lawyers and copyright associations, the MPAA [Motion Picture Association of America], were really concerned *but the major player that made the changes was Globo*. Web companies are happy with that" (emphasis added). Although comfortable in revealing once again the web platforms' private satisfaction with the IP carve-out, he, too, was unable or unwilling to specify precisely how the amendment had come about.

One account published by the Electronic Frontier Foundation on November 9, 2012, and sourced from Guilherme Varella, an IDEC lawyer, tugged the veil of deception further away from the official version of events but still without identifying the central role of the Globo Group. According to the post, Varella recounted:

> This is the result of a clumsy intervention by the Ministry of Culture following constant pressure by the entertainment industry lobby, especially the Brazilian Association of Reprographic Rights [ABDR], the Brazilian Association of Phonographic Producers [ABPD], and the Motion Picture Association of America [MPAA]. Varella reports that the entertainment lobby has been camped outside the Ministry and the Congress for the past few weeks, pressuring the vote on the bill to be postponed until they get what they want. (Rossini, 2012)

In order to understand the circumstances in which many others believe this IP carve-out was indeed introduced, we must draw upon the account of one of my interviewees, one who observed the events in question and directly contradicts the "official" version of events. It is this account that implicates one of the progenitors of the Marco Civil as having brokered a deal with Grupo Globo that many civil society observers considered a near-mortal blow to the project's legitimacy as a framework of digital rights.

The individual in this case was a core member of the SAL team at the Ministry of Justice, and a technical adviser. He explained to me how the IP carve-out was inserted into the bill, revealing the central role played by Ronaldo Lemos, CTS director and author of the op-ed that laid the ideational foundation for the Marco Civil. He divulged the following:

> It ended up that Ronaldo Lemos took the lead and appeared at the Ministry of Justice with a representative of the Globo Group and offered this change as a way that Globo could help in getting the bill passed. . . . It was explicit, but it wasn't public. It was a meeting marked in the agenda and everything. But there was no press release about there being this amendment. It was a negotiation that wasn't arranged with the other civil society actors. Today there is a good part of those organizations that understands that it was a certain opportunism on Ronaldo's part that is reflected now in the fact that he has his own show on Globo News. At the time nobody understood, who wasn't there, they didn't understand why this happened and the doubt remained in the air. . . .

Some people found out what happened and the episode, let's say, got out. (interview, 2015)

His claim that this version of events was not widely known appears to be corroborated by my discussions with key figures around the Marco Civil, as well as a subsequent review of academic and media texts. This may have been the result of a genuine lack of insight into these events or because they were reticent about identifying Lemos on the record given his exalted profile within the conjoined fields of media, academia, technology, and civil society in Brazil.

One notable exception to this ignorance (willful or genuine) came from Amadeu, the free-software pioneer and professor who was nearly Lemos's equal in impelling the creation of the Marco Civil as a legislative project. In a later interview he stated, "Suplicy said that she didn't request the paragraph and that she wasn't interested in it," going on to add that the suggestion had come to her from representatives of Globo and the CTS team so that there was an agreement, and the project could go ahead (Papp, 2014, p. 80).

IPragmatism

Lemos himself has been repeatedly questioned about these events, but the responses he presents have always evaded the central nature of his role, as well as his possible motivations for doing so. For instance, his statement to Papp (2014) is well representative: "My vision is rational, I like to make things happen. What happened is that clearly the Marco Civil had died and didn't have the slightest chance of being voted. It had a lot of people against it. How do you pass a law like this? It's impossible! So we undertook a really good and difficult negotiation to align at least two of those interests" (p. 78, author translation). Or, in another exchange, "in that moment we realized that the people needed to create an alliance or the project was going to die" (Brito, 2015, p. 100). It is the nature of that alliance that requires critical analysis.

It is telling that Lemos describes the rationality of his vision. This description correlates closely with my earlier analysis of his op-ed, which I argue proved so formative for the Marco Civil as a framework of digital rights. This analysis flag how the technocratic tenor of Lemos's article effectively circumscribes the civic potential of the project. This rational vision was influential not only in discursively shaping the Marco Civil at its genesis but also appeared again now, guiding Lemos's decisive intervention in this midway point of the Marco Civil's legislative journey. By convincing himself that inserting an IP exception into the safe-harbor provision on behalf of the Globo Group was the only way to break the checkmate of rival powers that paralyzed the Marco Civil, Lemos also effectively negated any potential that the bill may have had in loosening the stranglehold of the content-production sector over the circulation of information online. This is because the inclusion of the IP carve-out in the Marco Civil would permit the continuation of the practice of notice and takedown for any *presumed* copyright violation. This is a process that has an enormous built-in power imbalance between individual users and/or posters on one side and platforms and/or rights holders on the other, that is highly opaque with little transparency or accountability on the part of the platform and/or rights holder regarding the grounds for content removal, and that can easily be abused—especially, when dealing with smaller websites and/or publishers—to remove material that is politically or socially objectionable.

Certainly, as per the assertion of my interviewee, the rational nature of Lemos's vision may also apply to the reward that accrued from his intervention. One can only speculate as to whether a *causal* relationship exists between the two events, but it is certainly plausible to link the fact that in 2013 Lemos was given his own TV show on the Globo News channel—*Navegador*, discussing salient technology issues (Castro, 2013)—with his acting as a go-between for Globo, the Ministry of Justice, and Molon. It is also entirely plausible that Lemos would have been selected to host this TV show based solely on his public profile and expertise. If nothing else, what this sequence of events does demonstrate is the closeness of the relationship between one of the most influential figures in the formation and development of the Marco Civil and the foremost powerholder in informational capitalism in Brazil. This fact provides another layer of reinforcement to the central argument of this thesis: that the Marco Civil as a framework of digital rights served to consolidate informational capitalism in Brazil rather than unsettle it.

Moreover, I believe that the other reason it is important to highlight these events is because they represent a powerful example of how discourses manifest reality and why therefore it is important to analyze them. In this case Lemos (2007) provided the ideational framework for the Marco Civil with his 2007 op-ed. Its focus on innovation and efficiency circumscribed the civic potential of the project, aligning it with the operational logics of certain sectors of informational capitalism, at the expense of establishing substantive communicative rights for Brazilian internet users qua citizens. It becomes clear in light of Lemos's later actions described here that the initial commonsense assumptions Lemos helped to establish around the Marco Civil would enable his actions to be viewed by many as a pragmatic and necessary course of action, rather than an act of betrayal. His expectations of this reaction surely emboldened him to pursue his action. Thus does discourse manifest reality.

Certainly, "pragmatism" was the watchword for many of the key figures working on the Marco Civil. As Molon explained to me, kicking the can of IP enforcement down the road would allow the government and civil society champions of the Marco Civil to isolate and possibly beat the telecommunications sector. Instead, "if we had confronted them all at the same time, maybe we wouldn't have done it. . . . The tendency is that people want everything resolved at the same time in a perfect fashion, but that's not always possible, right?" (interview, 2015).

In a different interview, Molon explained, "In Congress, it is very important not to increase your team of adversaries. . . . If we wanted everything, we were going to get nothing. What's the most important? The consensus was that it was net neutrality" (Papp, 2014, p. 76). And therein lies the essence of Molon's pragmatism: a politician's instinct as to the limits of the achievable and a belief that a grand bargain premised on securing net neutrality by isolating the telecoms sector and winning the support of Globo and the content-production sector, were justifiable. Almeida offered a similar justification as he revealed to me that by late 2012, "We were fighting so many battles at the same time that if we try to win them all, we might lose them all" (interview, 2018).

Pragmatism also abounded within civil society. Barbosa of Intervozes, for instance, directed me "to study the history of the Globo Group in Brazil, it succeeds in influencing political processes in a really strong way . . . so if it was against the text, openly against it, we certainly wouldn't have got the bill approved in Congress" (interview, 2015). The reaction to the insertion of the IP carve-out from within civil society was not uniformly sanguine. Groups such as the Electronic Frontier Foundation argued, "If the new language of Article 15 prevails, Marco Civil will fall short in regard to one of its main reasons for existence. From the perspective of Brazilian civil society, Article 15's second paragraph should be deleted from the Marco Civil" (Rossini, 2012). Meanwhile, Amadeu, academic and free-software champion, in a July 2013 editorial, said: "Globo wants to pervert the Marco Civil" (2013). In Amadeu's own words, the phrase that served as a lightning rod for criticism from civil society was "the magic word, that I knew would generate a problem, which is 'In the dead of the night, Globo inserts private *censorship* in the Marco Civil'" (Solagna, 2015, p. 91, emphasis added).

Following Barbosa's observation, it is indeed a stark reminder of Globo's sway over Brazilian politics to consider how two pieces that it published in November 2012 effectively bookended the controversial inclusion of the

IP exemption. On November 7, Globo published an editorial that sharply condemned the Marco Civil because of its failure to explicitly safeguard copyright among its provisions (Marco da internet, 2012). One week later, on November 14, Globo published a bland-description piece on the bill, describing how it compared with equivalent legislation in other countries (Jansen, 2012). Having secured one of its primary goals for the bill, Globo opted to break its news embargo on the Marco Civil with what amounted to a tacit validation of the project. This would set the tone for Globo's ongoing coverage of the Marco Civil. As my web-platform interviewee told me: "The moment they got the exception they wanted, they were suddenly heavy supporters of the bill. They came from radical opponents of the whole idea . . . to being very heavy supporters" (interview, 2015).

Just how heavy this support would get became acutely evident in April 2013, a period when the Marco Civil was still mired in a legislative morass. The signal that concerted support would now be the norm from the Globo Group came when the Brazilian broadcast association ABERT opted to cohost a seminar in Brasília with Lemos and his CTS team. It was at this event that the president of ABERT effectively bestowed his blessing on the bill by referring to it as "the Constitution of the Internet" (Papp, 2014, p. 79). One day later, Abranet followed suit with its own seminar that also publicly endorsed the bill (Abramovay, 2017, p. 134). Accordingly, two influential sectors within informational capitalism could now be counted among the supporters of the Marco Civil, with the isolation of the telecoms sectors as the official opposition, now even more pronounced.

It was not, however, until September 2013 that the question of copyright was resolved in the Marco Civil. This came as the result of a cataclysmic event in Brazil's international relations, the revelations made by Edward Snowden. The repercussions of this event for the Marco Civil and the curtailment of any of the bill's vestiges of civic potential are the focus of the ensuing chapter.

Conclusion

This chapter examines how the Marco Civil represented an object of dispute within the dynamics of informational capitalism once it reached the congressional stage of its development.

The chapter maps out the corporate and political maneuvers that prefigured the Marco Civil's entrance into Congress as a project of law. These machinations showed how powerful vested interests were positioning themselves to contest the Marco Civil and influence the digital rights according to their best advantage. The most notable of these groups was the telecoms sector, which brought its formidable arsenal of material and discursive power to bear in order to pursue its agenda for the Marco Civil.

Also analyzed is the digital right of network neutrality within the context of the operational goals of the telecoms, content-production, and web-platform sectors to demonstrate how this technolegal principle was decisively shaped by these divergent interests. The resistance of the telecoms sector to enacting substantive net neutrality protections was based in part on discursive strategies to exploit the low public profile of the issue and the limited technical understanding of Brazilian legislators. The concept was also systematically conflated with communism. I contend that these discursive strategies are particularities of the periphery, and further diminish any claims to the universality of digital rights.

This chapter proposes that the concerted resistance of the telecoms sector owed to their ambitions to pursue zero-rating as a business model, one that has become nearly ubiquitous as a mode of offering mobile internet access in the global south. However, given the value of juridical stability presented by the Marco Civil, as well as the sector's ambitions to extract greater value from user data, I contend that network neutrality may not have constituted the grave threat that the telecoms sector presented it as. I propose that the paradox of network neutrality in this case was that the greater the resistance exhibited by the sector, the more that civil society was convinced of its civic value and pursued it to the exclusion of any more substantive agenda.

Also demonstrated is how web platforms belied their public perception by offering a very limited defense of network neutrality. The global political economy of informational capitalism meant that the platforms were adverse to re-creating at the periphery confrontations between themselves and the telecoms sector from the system's core.

The final main insight provided here by the analysis of network neutrality is to highlight how the particular political economy of Brazil's media market created an intense rivalry between Globo and the telecoms sector that converted the media giant—otherwise a prominent antagonist on communication rights—into the foremost ally of civil society in its pursuit of network neutrality.

The chapter also analyzes the intense civil society advocacy around the Marco Civil, including most prominently the alliance of civil society with the state, the emphasis on securing civil rights, the acute vulnerability of communication rights, the significance of the internet as a tool for disintermediation, and the particular value of network neutrality in the context of an extreme level of media concentration. The discourse of social inequality proved to be a site of contention between the telecoms sector and civil society groups around network neutrality. Finally, the latter group, I argue, contributed to the hollowed civic value of the Marco Civil, the result of a paradoxical situation in which the politicization of consumption characteristic of the periphery drove the advocacy of consumer-rights groups for the Marco Civil, helping to produce a framework of civil rights that was built primarily upon the terrain of consumption. This analysis of civil society further demonstrates the contingency of digital rights upon local political economic and sociocultural factors.

Finally, the little-known circumstances that prompted the introduction of an IP exemption within the Marco Civil's safe-harbor provisions that threatened to neuter their already limited civic value are revealed. The importance of IP to Brazil's foremost media power, the Globo Group, is examined and showed that the Globo Group imposed the carve-out on the bill and negotiated it in secret via a go-between who was also the Marco Civil's most prominent advocate, bolstering my contention that the bill facilitated rather than challenged the logics of informational capitalism. What follows is an account of how the Snowden revelations became the catalyst for the Marco Civil's contested passage into law.

4

Cataclysm

Surveillance, Sovereignty, and Snowden at the Periphery

The cause of democratic media
reform . . . where the avoidance
of disaster passes for victory.
—John Nathan Anderson

The Marco Civil's rapporteur, Alessandro Molon, had sealed his Faustian pact with Globo and the content-production sector in November 2012, a bargain with Globo and brokered by one of the architects of the bill. The act of aligning the strategic goals of one of the most powerful sectors within informational capitalism even more tightly with the digital rights that comprise the Marco Civil was supposed to liberate the bill from its legislative morass. The beginning of 2013, however, was characterized by the same inertia that had defined the latter half of 2012; the draft bill was effectively deadlocked within the Brazilian Congress. Even with Globo's newfound support, the opposition of the telecoms sector was insurmountable.

The event that would prove pivotal in securing the passage of the Marco Civil was integral to the workings of informational capitalism. It centered on the sudden visibility of an otherwise-obscure component of the system. Specifically, the nexus of the security state and globally dominant web platforms exploiting their control over user data became suddenly apparent to the world.

The decision in June 2013 of a National Security Agency (NSA) defense contractor, Edward Snowden, to release a trove of highly classified NSA files into the public realm would have many repercussions. One of those was to create the necessary political conditions in Brazil for the Marco Civil to be voted into law. That fact was one of the few things on which nearly all of my interviewees concurred: without the Snowden files, the Marco Civil as a project of law would have likely languished indefinitely. It is the purpose of this chapter to explore precisely why the revelations of US state surveillance would weigh so heavily on the fate of a Brazilian bill of digital rights. The connections are not readily apparent, but Brazil's status at the periphery of informational capitalism, its claims to data sovereignty, and the country's history of perceived subordination to the United States would all play a key role in converting Snowden's revelations into the Marco Civil's most potent catalyst. The NSA files also had the effect of seeing digital rights thrust suddenly into the epicenter of geopolitics, while it both forced the Brazilian government to resolve the tension between digital rights and neodevelopmentalism and to cast the hypocrisy of forcing surveillance measures into the Marco Civil into even-sharper relief.

As well as surveying the influence of the Snowden revelations, this chapter examines how tensions within informational capitalism were eventually resolved vis-à-vis the digital rights contained in the Marco Civil. These include most notably the resolution of network neutrality in the bill despite the concerted opposition of the telecoms sector, the tug-of-war around data retention between civil society's privacy advocates and an alliance of the security state and the IP-rights lobby, and a fractious end to the détente between the Brazilian government and the major web platforms. After the early circumscription of what could constitute the Marco Civil's digital rights described in chapter 2 and the contestation of those rights by the principal sectors of informational capitalism analyzed in chapter 3, this chapter explores how those same actors acted to curtail any vestiges of the Marco Civil's potential to actually challenge the operational logics of informational capitalism.

Snowden's Shock Waves Reach the Periphery

Given the ramifications of the Snowden revelations within international relations, it might not be hyperbolic to compare them with a nuclear detonation. In this instance, the epicenter of the blast occurred in the United States (not coincidentally, the core of global informational capitalism), meaning that the ensuing shockwaves took longer to register beyond the blast center. In the case of Brazil, there was a lag of several weeks between Glenn Greenwald first breaking the story on June 6, 2013, and any direct connection with Brazilian national affairs.

The moment that the shock waves first reached Brazil can be identified quite precisely. Greenwald's coauthored article in the newspaper *O Globo* first alerted Brazilians to the fact that their calls and emails had been compromised by the NSA dragnet (Greenwald et al., 2013). That story, however, represents only the start of the fallout. A report on the September 1 edition of the weekly television news-magazine show *Fantástico*, broadcast on the main Globo channel, showed that President Dilma Rousseff had been the object of a targeted communications intercept operation by the NSA (Fantástico, 2013). This news heralded a massive intensification of the scandal.

The NSA program was revealed in a document titled "Intelligently Filtering Your Data: The Case Studies of Brazil and Mexico." It is dated June 2011 and appears to have been compiled to share best-practice techniques with other departments within the NSA, as well as the intelligence agencies of the so-called Five Eyes.[1]

One week later came the last and arguably most destabilizing shockwave from the Snowden detonation. On September 8, the same line of communication among Snowden, Greenwald, and the producers of *Fantástico* yielded revelations that the Brazilian state oil-company Petrobras had also been the target of US state surveillance (G1, 2013, September 8). Documents included in an internal NSA presentation showed how the agency was using new cryptographic techniques to monitor secure corporate networks, including those of Petrobras, provided by Google Brazil. This news contradicted statements by the NSA that it did not partake in industrial espionage.

As these shockwaves reached their destructive crescendo, between July 7 and September 8, the public reaction of the Brazilian government was initially limited to standard diplomatic maneuvers, such as summoning the US ambassador to the Ministry of Foreign Affairs (G1, 2013, September 1).

Beneath the surface of the Brazilian government's bland protestations, however, forces were shifting in a way that would have great consequences for the Marco Civil. It was clear to many of the actors and economic sectors with the greatest vested interests that the Snowden revelations opened a new window of opportunity to shape the bill according to their own agenda. Owing to the Marco Civil's status as a framework of digital rights, it was obvious that it could be presented by the Brazilian government as a riposte to the United States on the global stage. If the Snowden revelations could indeed compel the government to act decisively on the Marco Civil, to rouse the bill from its legislative coma, then those vested interests needed to act quickly to influence the form of the law before the "political opportunity structure" collapsed (Tarrow, 1996).

The next section examines some of the earliest moves to exploit that opportunity structure. These represented the initial skirmishes in what would become the final battle to shape the constitution of digital rights at the periphery of informational capitalism, with both the security state and the telecoms sector among those seizing the chance to realize its own interests.

Wounded Sovereignty and the "Craziness" of Data Localization

It took just twenty-four hours from the first Snowden revelations published by Globo on July 7 for the minister of institutional relations, Ideli Salvatti, to reveal that the government was studying proposals for a policy response to the NSA surveillance to be included in the Marco Civil (Mendes, 2013). Two days later, Molon announced a major amendment.

The measures constituted an extraordinary expansion in the scope of the bill: a new clause mandating the storage of Brazilian user data on Brazilian territory by any commercial-application provider. This clause included two further stipulations: that any communication occurring on these platforms in which even one participant was based in Brazil would also be stored locally and that Brazilian legislation would also apply in cases where Brazilian user data was stored outside of the country. These measures became known collectively as "data localization," and they proved to be one of the most contentious proposals to be added to the Marco Civil.

From the outset, Molon attempted to cast the amendment in the best possible light: "I consider this proposal . . . positive, it tries to reinforce the privacy protections for users" (Tozetto, 2013). In secret Molon must have known the amendment did no such thing, nor was it intended to do so. Indeed, he explained his private position in a later interview: "It was a political response from a president to an attack on our sovereignty. And it was important for a parliamentarian to support the head of state. But there (the Marco Civil) was not the proper place for it" (Abramovay, 2017, p. 141).

To understand why these data-localization measures did not, in fact, protect user privacy, one need only cursorily compare them against the NSA surveillance techniques. The incongruence between the two processes demonstrates clearly that protecting privacy was simply a façade.

The Privacy Fallacy

The data-localization proposal mandated that data about and by Brazilian users would need to be stored locally. Moreover, that data could not additionally be transferred to servers housed outside of the country (Ramos, 2013). However, the proposal did not specify what would occur in those instances when Brazilian users communicated with international users. The unspoken reality was that copies of those communications could and would be stored extraterritorially. Any notion of exclusivity would, after all, constitute a bounded Brazilian internet cut off from the outside world—an extraordinary proposition but one that would actually represent a meaningful block on NSA surveillance.

The practical reality of the almost inextricable nature of Brazilian and international user interactions across multiple global communication platforms—Gmail, Facebook, and so forth—meant that much of the Brazilian user data mandated to be stored locally would constitute simply a duplication. Thus, the NSA would continue to have ready access to the data stored on the servers of the US web platforms, which dominated internet use in Brazil, and exploiting its technical prowess could in any event likely access data stored on their Brazilian equivalents. As Christopher Soghoian, chief technology officer at the American Civil Liberties Union, opined at the time of the announcement: "It's not just about having servers in Brazil, it's about storing data on servers that are not run by US companies. Unless you're going to make it illegal to use Google, which would be a very high bar, you need to build domestic services that are equally compelling" (Toor, 2013).

Moreover, what was acutely evident to some was that not only were the data-localization amendments not going to provide a meaningful safeguard for privacy but also they would systematically undermine it. As Bia Barbosa of Intervozes, a communication-rights advocate, argued, "The more that you store data, even if it is here, the greater the risk of espionage." Moreover, the greater ease with which the Brazilian security state could access locally stored data and the power those forces held over every Brazilian user qua citizen meant that local storage constituted a much-graver threat to Brazilians' civil liberties than international espionage. As such, the data-localization amendment, rather than being an awkward appendage to the Marco Civil, should be considered a seamless addendum and as one more technolegal policy measure that would facilitate rather than challenge the systemic logics of informational capitalism.

The Periphery Strikes Back

What Minister of Justice Cardozo later described as "national data sovereignty" was not only embodied in the data-localization amendment, however (Azevedo, 2014). In September 2013, General Sinclair Mayer, head of the Brazilian Army's science and technology department, announced to lawmakers that Brazil would establish underwater internet cables linking Brazil to Europe and to Africa, in an effort to divert internet traffic passing through the United States (Romero & Archibold, 2013). Existing submarine infrastructure channeled around 90 percent of all outbound internet data from Central and South America through one data center in Miami named the Network Access Point of the Americas (Sparrow, 2013). Bypassing this surveillance choke point in the United States became an obvious policy target for Rousseff after the Snowden revelations. However, given the resources of the NSA—including the existence of a nuclear submarine dedicated to tapping transoceanic cables (Toor, 2013)—such measures would likely only make NSA surveillance costlier but not impossible. Moreover, it was only one year later that Google announced a new proprietary undersea cable connecting Brazil with Florida in the United States (Chant, 2014), exposing the futility of the Brazilian state efforts.

Finally, another related policy proposal that emerged in response to the Snowden revelations was a national email program. Conceived initially as a parallel measure to the Marco Civil, rather than an amendment to it, the service was named Digital Messenger (Época, 2013). Of significance, given the program's obvious benefits to the telecoms sector, was that the scheme was commissioned by the minister of communications—and staunch telecoms-sector ally—Paulo Bernardo. According to the minister, a national email service with local storage and cryptographic standards was essential in the wake of the revelations of NSA surveillance (Nery & Agostini, 2013). The service was slated for launch in early 2014, but with little support from other areas of government, the plan was quietly abandoned.

When assessing the plausibility of a national email service as a privacy safeguard, it is important to also note that in the initial development of the project, the designers were open to replicating Microsoft's or Google's advertising-based business model in order to cover the costs of the program (Época, 2013). With such a business model in place, it is certain that user communications would be under scrutiny from advertisers, thereby negating much of the defense of user privacy.

Given the profound deficiencies in these provisions as privacy safeguards, what was the real rationale for their development? To answer that question, consider two important dimensions of data localization in the Marco Civil: the discourse of sovereignty that accompanied the fallout from the Snowden revelations, and recognition of those sectors of informational capitalism with the most to gain and the most to lose from the territorialization of Brazilian data.

The Pretense (and the Reality) of Data Sovereignty

When Minister of Institutional Relations Salvatti first revealed the government's intentions to use the Marco Civil as a vehicle to respond to the

NSA surveillance, he also stated, "It is absolutely clear that the sovereignty of the country and the privacy of the Brazilian citizen is under threat" (Mendes, 2013). This claim of wounded sovereignty was later echoed by the other government figures, including Minister of Justice Cardozo.

Brazil was certainly not alone in articulating its outrage at the violation of sovereignty implied by the mass surveillance of the NSA and its partners. The government of Germany, as well as many others, issued similar laments (Bauman et al., 2014, p. 128). In the case of Brazil, however, the reference to sovereignty evoked a very particular set of connotations that pertain to Brazil's experience as a country at the margins of global capitalism.

As Brazil's first democratic president of the current republic, José Sarney declared in 1986 in justification of the country's informatics policy: "It is fundamental to our survival as a sovereign nation and for the welfare of our people that we exercise control over the scientific and technological instruments that will shape our future" (Crandall, 2011, p. 140). This policy was justified on nationalist principles and the idea that the country could only become Great Brazil by "the defense of national sovereignty through informatics" (Cukierman, 2013, p. 491). The contrast between Brazil's concerted efforts to assert technological autonomy from the United States in the late 1980s and the unfortunate consequences of what Edmund Amann calls "an erosion of technological sovereignty" evident by the 2000s was stark and clear (2002, p. 886).

The Workers' Party (PT) government of Lula da Silva, first elected in 2002, had taken stock of the parlous state of Brazilian technological development and devised several policies to address it. In keeping with the neodevelopmentalist model of government adopted by this PT administration, it promoted industrial policy for economic sectors that it deemed a national priority, such as the IT sector. The most notable of these was the Strategic Program for Software and IT Services launched in 2012. This included tax incentives, state subsidies, and assistance for new business through an accelerator fund called Start-Up Brasil (Ramos, 2013). Furthermore, the development of internet exchange points (IXPs) within Brazil, and the build-out of undersea internet cables was a core part of this initiative (Woodcock, 2013).

The affront of violated sovereignty could also be connected to the PT's hallmark foreign policy. Certainly, in opposition, PT had developed a foreign policy in which the assertion of national sovereignty was one of its main planks (Bourne, 2008, p. 153). In government, moreover, a policy of assertive diplomacy designed to boost Brazil's global profile was a defining characteristic of the Lula administration (Saad-Filho & Morais, 2017, p. 97).

Finally, as mentioned before, the fear of the United States thwarting Brazil's global geopolitical ambitions was a recurring theme in popular and media discourses in Brazil. For instance, a trope emerged in the early 2000s that was popularized in Brazil, that Brazil's sovereignty over the Amazon region was threatened by US "forces" who coveted the resource-rich region (Rohter, 2002) that was dubbed "Amazon Paranoia" (Viola & Franchini, 2018).

The scenario, therefore, in which Brazil found itself in 2013 evoked numerous associations that were characteristic of Brazil's peripheral status, current and past. Moreover, the discursive articulations between the violation of sovereignty implied by the NSA state surveillance and these particularly Brazilian discourses of sovereignty provided both rhetorical cover for possible government policy responses (that might advance another more obscure agenda), as well as exerting additional pressure to react decisively. I believe this dual function of the discourse of data sovereignty is essential to understand the inclusion of data localization in the Marco Civil: it offered a plausible justification for a measure designed to further other less palatable goals (discussed shortly) and helps to explain the pressure on the Brazilian government to be seen to offer a strong policy response.

The twin defenses of privacy and sovereignty were not sufficient, however, to avoid a barrage of criticism for the data-localization provision. Civil society supporters of the Marco Civil, particularly, those aligned with the technical community, such as the Brazilian Internet Steering Committee (CGI.br), were amongst the most vocal. CGI.br cofounder and Brazilian internet pioneer Carlos Afonso (Caf) explained to me in interview: "We had a problem with this idea of sovereignty which I already told you, the government started to make proposals, absurd proposals that all data centers should be located in Brazil," describing them also as "completely impossible . . . so silly" (2015). Another pioneer of the Brazilian internet, Demi Getschko, described the measures as "imprecise . . . and incoherent" (Romer, 2013). Ronaldo Lemos also spoke out against the proposal, highlighting how it would make Brazilian internet users "clandestine, second class citizens" as global platforms would bar them in order to evade these obligations (Honorato, 2013).

A coalition of civil society groups published an open letter to Brazil's Congress in August 2013 in which, among several demands, they decried the fact that "data would continue to be sent to the country of origin of the web company, and therefore subject to their inspection" (Altercom et al., personal communication, August 7, 2013).

Overall, the suite of measures advanced by the PT government under the banner of data sovereignty was not intended to usurp or replace informational capitalism. It was intended to realign power relations within the system and to wrest some control over the flow and commodification of data away from the epicenter and toward the periphery. In that respect, the parallels with Brazil's earlier efforts to induce technological sovereignty are clear. As Yuri Takhteyev (2012) notes, the key actors responsible for Brazil's sovereigntist efforts in the 1970s did so not "seeking to isolate Brazil from foreign influences. Rather, each group *was looking for a way to participate to the fullest extent possible in global practices* . . . and, more generally, to promote the modernization of the country" (p. 109, emphasis added). In the present case, if enacted, these measures would represent a significant riposte to the nexus of the US security state and the globally dominant web platforms. The logics of informational capitalism would not be challenged, however, as actors within Brazil—notably, the telecoms sector and the Brazilian security state—would simply gain greater advantage from the commodification and control of Brazilian user data.

In terms of data localization specifically, the most vocal and concerted opposition came from the sector with the most to lose from the proposal: the web platforms. Indeed, it is by analyzing this opposition that we can identify the agenda that drove the government to shoehorn data localization into the Marco Civil under the pretense of securing user privacy. Moreover, we will see that the dispute around data localization exposed a core tension within informational capitalism, one that exists between the security state and the web platforms over which sector directs the mechanic of enclosure to its best advantage.

The "Google Amendment"

As detailed in chapter 1, one of the defining characteristics of informational capitalism is the tension between data flow and data enclosure and the ways different sectors compete to employ those mechanics in order to channel the systemic logic of control. This antagonism is most clearly embodied in the ongoing disputes between states that seek to impose data enclosure for the purposes of securitization and the web companies' operational need for data flow. Tim Jordan (2015) argues that such state attempts at data enclosure go "against the flow" of information power, while Blayne Haggart and Michael Jablonski describe this as the "protection-dissemination tension" inherent to American information policy (2017, p. 104).

This is the systemic tension within informational capitalism that explains the real rationale for the government proposal of data localization and why it was so fiercely resisted by the web platforms.

The most significant consideration for the web platforms was the cost implications of being forced to construct a parallel set of data infrastructure in Brazil. In the case of Google Inc. (now Alphabet Inc.), for instance, in the last quarter of 2013, the company had already invested US$7.3 billion in data infrastructure, from earnings of $59.7 billion, or 12 percent of total revenue (Miller, 2014). Each of its data center projects in the United States in 2013 constituted a cost of $200 million to $600 million (Miller, 2014). The cost, however, of creating standalone *national* data infrastructure sufficient for Google's approximately forty million Brazilian users would likely be much higher. This cost would, moreover, be exacerbated by the higher cost overall of building data centers in Brazil (Ramos, 2013).

Of course, given the enormous cash reserves of the likes of Microsoft, Facebook, and Google, the one-time capital expenditure for complying with data-localization provisions in Brazil could ultimately be easily absorbed. The real fear, though, was that other governments would see the opportunity in the wake of the Snowden revelations to roll out their own data localization measures, and in this case, Brazil would be the first domino to fall.

Google CEO Eric Schmidt articulated this fear at an event in New York in September 2013: "The real danger . . . is that other countries will begin . . . to essentially split the internet and that the internet's going to be much more country specific. That would be a very bad thing, it would really break the way the internet works, and I think that's what I worry about" (Holpuch, 2013). And as my web-company interviewee similarly advised me, "You can imagine the cost and you can imagine the domino effect if Brazil wants that. Then Turkey, China, Russia" (2015). In effect, data localization writ large could amount to a coup attempt by the periphery, to realign power within informational capitalism away from the epicenter.

Accordingly, the web platforms embarked on a campaign of lobbying to try and persuade the Brazilian government to withdraw the data localization amendment. Representatives of the major US platforms increased their presence in Brasília, conducting meetings with legislators, presenting at senate and house committees, and giving interviews to the mainstream press. Hostility to the sector was, however, evident from some of the coverage in the popular press. The fact that article 12 was known colloquially as "the Google amendment" made that clear (web platform executive, interview, 2015).

The "June Journeys" and the Need for Data

In public the web platforms developed an obfuscatory narrative, one that would not further antagonize the Brazilian government or their Brazilian user base. On one hand, they were at pains never to reveal their primary concern that Brazil could trigger a cascade of data localization proposals around the world. On the other, the web companies also opted to play along with the Brazilian government's narrative of sovereignty and privacy, even though in private they were clear that this was only a façade. My web-platform interviewee explained:

> Snowden happened and the Brazilian government played the card that the Marco Civil was going to be the solution for Brazilian sovereignty, to safeguard Brazilian rights . . . but if you take a look at it with less anger in your eyes, you realize that what they were trying to do is to make sure that local authorities had that level of access that they were perceiving the US government to have in the first place. (2015)

By applying this rationale, the conundrum of why the government would promote data localization as a safeguard for user privacy when its deficiencies were so glaring is quickly resolved. Data localization would permit the Brazilian security state untrammeled access to data about Brazilian citizens that had for years been denied to them by American internet companies. One only need to review the data from Google's biannual transparency reports to understand why a sense of frustration and urgency would have been building within the Brazilian government. The data in table 4 shows how more requests for user data from the Brazilian government were being denied by Google Inc. each year from 2011 to 2013.

Mutual legal assistance treaties (MLATs) are the principal means to request information from a foreign government to aid in a criminal

TABLE 4. Brazilian government requests for user data from Google Inc., 2011–13

Reporting Period	Data Requests	Requests Where Data Disclosed (%)
January–June 2011	703	87
July–December 2011	1,615	90
January–June 2012	1,566	76
July–December 2012	1,211	66
January–June 2013	1,239	65
July–December 2013	1,085	49

investigation. The process may not, however, be especially efficient, nor would it guarantee success. Certainly, my web-platform interviewee was clear that the Brazilian authorities resented having to resort to an MLAT:

> Web platforms . . . kind of shot themselves in the foot. . . . [If there was a request for user data,] what we would say as web platforms is basically that this is actually in conflict with US law, and because the services are controlled by the US parent company, you actually need to go through the MLAT process . . . and that was a thesis that has always held a lot of water anywhere else in the world but *the Brazilian authorities . . . even said that it was humiliating to go through the MLAT process.* (2015, emphasis added)

The frustration of the Brazilian state security apparatus regarding the MLAT requirement was not the only driver of the data localization provisions, however. In June 2013 a loose collation of protest groups took to the streets in mass rallies across Brazilian urban centers. The massive and rapid scaling of the so-called Jornadas de Junho (June Days) took the Brazilian authorities by surprise. As such, it was a logical development that during the protests, the Brazilian Intelligence Agency (ABIN) announced that they had launched a surveillance program to monitor social networks to preempt future unrest (Rizzo & Monteiro, 2013).

This move by the Brazilian state toward securitization had two important effects with regard to the data localization measures. On one hand, the June protests would have made much more urgent the Brazilian authorities' desire to access user data held by US web platforms. The other is that a discourse of securitization already in effect in the wake of the street protests would have emboldened the Brazilian state to authorize such an extraordinary proposal as data localization.

According to many civil society actors, as well as academic observers, such as Pedro Abramovay (2017), the inclusion of the data centers constituted a "clear rupture" with the early promise of the bill as a framework of digital rights (p. 143). I argue, however, that the evidence pointing to the real rationale for the inclusion of data localization in the Marco Civil demonstrates that it was entirely coherent with the overall tenor of the bill. Indeed, the dispute over data localization was really a struggle as to which sector of informational capitalism stood to gain the most: the security state or web platforms. This corroborates the thesis that as a bill of digital rights, the measures would consolidate rather than challenge the systemic logics of informational capitalism.

Nuclear Options

Given the potential ramifications of the Brazilian data center proposals for the web platforms, it should not be surprising that given their abundant resources, they would consider using their power to influence a political outcome at the periphery. To what lengths, though, would the web platforms be willing to go to have data localization effectively disappear as a problem? According to my interviewee, they were prepared to try and eliminate the Marco Civil entirely. The comments here merit reproduction in full:

> It would be a very schizophrenic scenario in which we had been some of the major supporters of the bill moving forward and suddenly we would have to actually try and halt it, try to change parts of it . . . and data localization provisions which was basically such a huge problem inside of the company. . . . Every US company actually gave the order from HQ to all of the policy folks on the ground here . . . everybody that you can think of. *If it comes to that we prefer you to nuke the entire bill,* we prefer to lose the safe harbors that we are going to get than have to comply with this craziness of data localization. (2015, emphasis added)

Beyond simply trying to prevent the inclusion of data localization measures in the bill through standard lobbying practices, the web platforms were apparently prepared to try and impel the complete abandonment of the Marco Civil as a legislative project. My interviewee did not elaborate on how they might make that happen, but one can draw three likely conclusions from this revelation.

The first is that in terms of how the provisions of the Marco Civil corresponded to the sectorial needs of the web platforms, the negative implications of data localization outweighed the positives of safe harbors. Although categorized as "really the thing to get," the web platforms were willing to forego the benefits of limited liability and the unimpeded data flow represented by safe harbors to avoid the prospect of Brazilian data localization catalyzing a balkanized global internet.

The second is that any notion that the web platforms constituted a steadfast ally of civil society on the topic of digital rights should be abandoned. Although both sectors based their defense of the Marco Civil on the tenets of the digital discourse, any alignment between civil society supporters of the bill and the web platforms was based purely on the pragmatic pursuit of their sectorial needs.

Thirdly, and of most significance for this study as an analysis of how digital rights are constituted and contested at the periphery of informational capitalism, the web platforms possessed the will and also likely the means to sabotage a bill of law supported by multiple civil society groups and a democratically elected government. This vividly illustrates not only the power differential between center and periphery within the global system of informational capitalism but also justifies in the first instance why the analytical perspective offered by informational capitalism is so important: it foregrounds information as both the goal and means of power.

By Hook or by Crook: Jurisdictional Battles

In the closing months of 2013, the repercussions from the Snowden revelations continued to play out in Brazilian politics, and in November 2013, Molon issued version 3 of the Marco Civil, formally including not only the data localization amendment but also a new provision that amplified the pressure on the web platforms.

A new article, article 11, was included in this version of the bill, stipulating that in any instance of the "collection, storage or treatment of personal data, registration data, or communications by connection providers or internet applications in which at least one of these acts occurs on national territory, Brazilian law should be respected" (Brito, 2015). This jurisdictional provision was designed to further consolidate the reach of Brazilian security services into data about Brazilian users collected by US web platforms. It signaled perhaps an awareness from within government that the data localization provisions might not survive the lobbying efforts of the US web platforms or the resistance of the Brazilian technical community. Another significant reason for the addition of this jurisdictional provision was the influence of the telecoms sector.

The director of the Brazilian Telecoms Association revealed to me in an interview that they had compelled Molon to add the provision: "He didn't want to put it in. . . . It was us that forced it. If it's awful for us, it should be awful for others, too" (2015). Beyond a simple expression of spite, however, the telecoms sector would have been aware that imposing jurisdictional provisions on the web platforms would help to level the playing field in terms of limiting their capacity to commodify user data: a revenue source that the telcos dearly coveted. Accordingly, lobbying for this amendment was simply another skirmish in the battle for primacy within informational capitalism.

My web platform interviewee asserted that for the Brazilian government, data localization had only ever been a means to secure the jurisdictional provision, in effect, the invocation of an apocalypse, to make a disaster seem palatable: "Brazil never actually wanted data localization in the first place. The real issue on data localization was jurisdiction. . . . It was basically as if they had written, 'If your company is called Google or Facebook or Microsoft, you have to comply with this, or else not a problem'" (2015).

It is impossible to determine if data localization represented little more than a bargaining tool on the part of the Brazilian government to ease the passage of the jurisdictional provision. What we can infer with confidence from the various machinations surrounding the insertion of articles 11 and 12 in the Marco Civil is that they represented one more instance of digital rights serving as the terrain for the powerholders of informational capitalism to vie for systemic advantage.

The Triumph of Digital Rights over Data Sovereignty

In the wake of the initial revelations, Rousseff explained to the press, "I want to know everything there is . . . beyond what was published in the press, I want to know everything there is related to Brazil. Everything" (G1, 2013, September 8). Within days Rousseff would discover more about the scope of the NSA surveillance program targeting Brazil.

On September 8, news broke that Petrobras had also been the object of US surveillance. This revealed that the US security state was pursuing not only an agenda of securitization but also seizing access to commercial data that could provide American energy companies with a competitive advantage. Petrobras was the worldwide leader in offshore oil exploration making it not only the crown jewel of the Brazilian state in terms of revenue generation but also an emblem of its sovereignty. As such the Brazilian government needed to amplify its reaction.

The data localization amendment had already been added by this point but given the critical reaction it had received from civil society, the Brazilian government required a more categorical response that would signal to the public its resolve to stand up to the Americans. This was particularly important because, according to Robert Muggah, the research director of Brazilian security think tank Igarapé Institute, "for many on the Brazilian left, the NSA program harkens back to the military dictatorship and the US support that brought the military to power" (Toor, 2013).

Righting the Ship: Dilma Leverages the Marco Civil

According to multiple accounts (Abramovay, 2017; O'Maley, 2015; Papp, 2014), Rousseff felt under acute pressure to deliver a fitting riposte to US surveillance on the international stage. Partly this was due to electoral calculations. Rousseff's approval ratings had plummeted in the wake of the June protests—from 60 percent to 27 percent in the space of one month (Santos & Guarnieri, 2016, p. 485)—and the elections were less than twelve months away. This meant that the Snowden revelations represented an opportune distraction, from which Rousseff needed to extract maximum political value. It was at this juncture that she started to take personal interest in the Marco Civil as a tool with which to confront the United States and to improve her public image. This represented a major pivot because after the transition of power from Lula to Rousseff, the Marco Civil clearly constituted a low-priority issue for the latter administration. Guilherme Almeida characterized the difference to me: "With Lula it was more a political support, but with Dilma it was more of a technical perspective until Snowden arrived, and then the energy raised" (2018). Given the obstacles within Parliament erected by the telecoms sector, the passage of the Marco Civil could not be impelled by force of political will alone. Indeed, by late 2013 Rousseff's political capital was much diminished. In the last year of her first term, Rousseff only managed to secure the passage of 16 percent of her proposed bills (compared to an average of previous Brazilian presidents of 60 percent in their final year) (Santos & Guarnieri, 2016, p. 490). A sleight of hand was needed.

As such, the Brazilian government announced that it was applying the status of constitutional urgency to the bill. According to the federal Constitution, the president has the prerogative to apply this to any bill of law meaning that Congress has forty-five days to pass it, and if it fails to do so, no other bill can be voted upon. This effectively shutters the legislature. Accordingly, this provided a clear signal to both the opponents and defenders of the bill that passage of the Marco Civil had become the priority policy item for Rousseff's government. As such, the assignment of constitutional urgency marked the beginning of the end game for the Marco Civil, a period defined by the curtailment of any residual potential for the Marco Civil to establish a substantive set of civil digital rights.

A "Steering" Committee, Indeed

Another pivotal moment for the fate of the Marco Civil was the decision by Rousseff to convene a meeting with the Brazilian Internet Steering Committee (CGI.br) in order that its members might guide her in planning the government's next steps. This was a pressing consideration as Brazil was due to give the opening address at the General Assembly of the United Nations on September 24, an obvious opportunity for Rousseff to deliver her response to the United States.

The meeting with CGI.br and the president was arranged for September 16, and according to five of my interviewees who were present, as well as the statements of other participants published elsewhere, the discussions therein were a determining factor in impelling the Marco Civil toward its passage into law six months later. In essence the advice offered by the members of the steering committee to the president consolidated her belief that the Marco Civil should form a core plank of her response to the NSA surveillance programs. As evident in her UN address, the Marco Civil was not intended to be the only weapon in her armory, and Rousseff played a careful double game intended to reconcile Brazil's status both as defender of digital rights and as a peripheral country advancing its technological sovereignty through infrastructural development.

This double game was principally rhetorical, however, and in terms of impelling actual policy, there was a clear emphasis on the side of digital rights. Indeed, the testimony of the CGI members appeared to guide the president toward that direction. As argued earlier, the pursuit of data sovereignty constituted a means to partially redress the power imbalance within informational capitalism from the epicenter to the periphery. Rousseff's eventual focus on digital rights and the gradual erosion of government support for data sovereignty constituted another important instance of the Marco Civil maintaining the status quo of informational capitalism, rather than disrupting it.

Securing Rousseff's support for digital rights over data sovereignty would also play a large role in determining how sectorial tensions within informational capitalism were eventually resolved in terms of the digital rights contained in the Marco Civil. Accordingly, this meeting on September 16 played a decisive role in the resolution of some of the most contentious elements of the bill: network neutrality, the IP carve-out, and the role for multistakeholderism.

Before analyzing the details of the meeting and its implications, we must account for the nature of Rousseff's interlocutors in this meeting. The fact that it was the Brazilian Steering Committee (CGI.br) was, I argue, highly significant in continuing to circumscribe the scope of digital rights within the bill. As chapter 2 shows, the CGI.br espoused a vision of digital rights squarely aligned with the dominant paradigm. Accordingly, the tremendous opportunity to advance a more substantive vision of digital rights implied by Rousseff's newfound interest in the Marco Civil was effectively nullified by the fact that she sought out the guidance of the CGI. As we will see, the demands they articulated at this encounter amounted to little more than damage control to preserve an already deeply compromised vision of digital rights.

Discrediting the Telcos

The first outcome from this meeting worth noting was how CGI's efforts to sideline the telecoms sector resulted in the marginalization of then minister of communications, Bernardo, a man who, according to the judgment of CGI cofounder Carlos Afonso (Caf), was "completely in the hands of the telcos" (Afonso, interview, 2015). He went on to highlight the importance of the fact that Bernardo was present at the meeting and was compelled to listen as the CGI board members denounced the telecoms sector's position on the Marco Civil.

The discrediting of Bernardo as a credible adviser to the president was significant because proposals backed by Bernardo, such as the national email program and national data centers, lost legitimacy. This suggested that although further governmental responses would continue to assert data sovereignty, the principal focus would be on digital rights. Also, given that Bernardo served effectively as a proxy for the telecoms sector within government, that lead to a commensurate rise in profile of the "telco Rasputin," Eduardo Cunha, as the telecoms sector began to advance its agenda through him.

Another significant concern for the CGI members present at the meeting was the IP carve-out that had been introduced amid such controversy and subterfuge nearly one year prior. The end result of the meeting was a later (and final) amendment added by Molon, article 20, stating that the application of limited third-party liability in any cases of copyright infringement would depend on future "specific legal provisions." In effect, the entire issue of intellectual property would be deferred until copyright reform was revisited. In the continued absence of this reform, however, this amendment did little other than to consolidate the status quo practice of notice and takedown for copyright violations, to the benefit of the content-production and web platform sectors.

For the most part, civil society groups accepted that the amendment was as great an improvement as they could expect given the power of the organizations that backed an IP carve-out. As such, they swallowed their medicine. This tone of resignation regarding the permanency of the IP carve-out was expressed to me by the manager of the public consultation, Paulo Santarém: "What is undeniable is that it facilitated the approval of the Marco Civil. By the same token, it is also undeniable that it weakened the project. It would have been stronger if it had been approved without that point" (interview, 2015). In such a way, the flawed equivalence of freedom of expression with safe harbors saw its civic value further diminished.

Sovereigns and Stakeholders

Brazil's support of multistakeholderism as the preferred model of internet governance, both globally and domestically, was the final agenda item that the CGI members sought the opportunity to advance at the September meeting. Brazil's approach to the governance of the internet does require some contextualization, as it suffered from a lack of coherence between its domestic and foreign policies; a disjuncture that once again signals the tension between pursuing data sovereignty and digital rights, as well as highlighting the stratified global political economy of informational capitalism.

From 1995 Brazil established a model of governance for its national internet based on multistakeholder principles through the foundation of the CGI.br. By contrast, at more-recent International Telecommunication Union (ITU) summits, Brazil had sided with voting blocks of mostly developing nations—prominently led by Russia and China—that sought greater government control of the internet. Indeed, at the 2012 World Conference on International Telecommunications (WCIT) in Dubai, Brazil voted for the ITU to wrest control of internet governance away from the Internet Corporation of Assigned Names and Numbers (ICANN). The fact that the other voting block was populated most notably by the United States and European Union states led *The Economist* magazine to dub this "a digital cold war" (L. S., 2012). What then accounts for Brazil's seemingly schizophrenic approach to internet governance?

It is important to note that those nations voting for greater government control of global internet governance corresponded largely with the Group of 77 (G77) that in turn could trace its roots to the Cold War–era nonaligned movement. These countries were opposed to US geopolitical hegemony, generally, and sought to assert their sovereignty in international forums whenever possible. More specifically, these nations were antagonistic to and skeptical of US control over ICANN and the influence this control afforded the United States over global telecoms infrastructure (Mueller & Wagner, 2014, p. 2). As noted earlier in this chapter, the PT government pursued a neodevelopmentalist agenda that sought to assert national sovereignty in various policy arenas, including foreign policy and national technology development. Accordingly, Brazil's position at the WCIT was coherent with these goals. Additionally, other factors more specific to the operation of telecoms at the periphery help to explain Brazil's earlier position on internet governance.

As per the analysis of global communication scholars Milton Mueller and Ben Wagner (2014), countries in the pro-sovereignty block pursued international communications policies that "tend to be driven by government ministries that have close and sometimes incestuous ties to incumbent telecommunications operators" (p. 3). As frequently noted by Brazilian academics, civil society, and political figures, the Ministry of Communications, as well as the state telecoms regulator, Anatel, were heavily influenced by Brazil's telecoms corporations. As such, Brazil's international position on internet governance was likely driven in part by the calculations of Brazil's telecoms sector that greater government influence in internet governance arrangements would benefit them more than a multistakeholder model that permitted its principal antagonists—web platforms and civil society—a voice at the table.

My discussions with a senior executive at Anatel on this topic presented a slightly different perspective. He claimed that the ITU conference in Dubai was unfortunately politicized and miscast as a polarization between those seeking to control the internet and those seeking to leave it "free." In fact, Brazil's more nuanced position was based on economic and developmental considerations (interview, 2015). What he was alluding to was the other major reason why Brazil might have backed the pro-sovereignty block at the WCIT.

The incisive analysis of Mueller again points the way: "The most important battleground in the WCIT is not censorship or security but interconnection and the flows of funds among carriers attendant upon interconnection agreements" (2012). Indeed, while it might have suited the American delegation to claim that the dispute at WCIT was an attempt to censor the internet, really it centered upon the desire of nations at the periphery of informational capitalism for their "national regulatory authorities to have more collective control over ISPs generally, and American ISPs and Internet services specifically" (Mueller, 2012). Canadian political economist Dwayne Winseck (2017) also observes, "Some telecoms operators in the Global South, with backing from their respective governments" consider "traffic from internet giants such as Google, Facebook, Amazon, Apple, Baidu, Netflix, and so on as bypassing the traditional international revenue settlement agreements they have relied on in the past for profits and to finance their network investments" (p. 246).

Essentially, the international telecommunications regulations (ITRs) that were being renegotiated offered telecoms companies in peripheral nations the opportunity to reset the economics of interconnection that favored content providers in informational capitalism's core. The proposal was to secure revenue by enshrining "the principle of sending party network pays." By contrast, the status quo of multistakeholder governance of the internet through US-led bodies like ICANN upholds a market-led, distance-agnostic model favoring US-based web platforms and internet services. In sum, the dispute over ITRs at the WCIT in 2012 represented a zonal conflict between center and periphery within the global system of informational capitalism, a battle over who controls and profits from information flows.

Six months on from these events and the Snowden revelations presented Brazil's government with a dilemma in how to orient its approach to internet governance. The government could ride the wave of criticism directed at the US surveillance programs and continue to pursue greater sovereignty within international internet governance arrangements. Or it could align its direction with the dominant digital rights paradigm and advocate for multistakeholderism and internet freedom, leaving the power structure of informational capitalism untouched. Ultimately, as will be seen, Rousseff opted for a variant of the latter, a "third way" as Lemos describes it (2014, p. 8).

The CGI members were given a tremendous opportunity to validate Rousseff's instincts as they proceeded to help her draft her UN address in a way that incorporated nearly all of the decálogo principles, including an affirmation of multistakeholder governance.

UN versus NSA, and Rousseff's Double Game

The day after the pivotal meeting between President Rousseff and the CGI board members, on September 17, the Brazilian government announced that it was canceling Rousseff's scheduled state visit to the United States in October 2013, a visit that was to include the rare honor of a full state dinner at the White House (Balza, 2013). As a statement of the Brazilian government's displeasure, the cancelation was a clear one. Rousseff, however, would still soon be traveling to the United States to deliver a more categorical rebuke. This because on September 24, Brazil was due to make the inaugural statement at the opening of the sixty-eighth session of the UN General Assembly.

The meeting with CGI.br eight days prior had served to prepare the president for this engagement, and she duly presented a speech in New York on September 24 that was in large part premised upon the principles of the Marco Civil, derived in turn from the CGI's decálogo. Rousseff claimed, "Brazil will present proposals for the establishment of a civilian multilateral framework for the governance and use of the Internet" (United Nations, 2013), a framework that would contain five of the first six "Ten Commandments": freedom of expression, individual privacy, and respect for human rights; open, multilateral, and democratic governance; universality that ensures social and human development; cultural diversity; and network neutrality (United Nations, 2013).

Rousseff found in both the decálogo and the Marco Civil a framework of digital rights that translated readily into the language of universal human rights that was the lingua franca of the United Nations. Hers was a discursive strategy that obfuscated the central tension implied by the role of the state in both the UN discourse of human rights and the digital discourse that was formative for the Marco Civil. In effect, she employed an articulation between the digital rights informed by the digital discourse in which the state is a threat to be contained and the UN discourse of human rights in which the state constitutes a guarantor of rights.

In her speech, Rousseff made reference to the NSA "violating fundamental human rights" and claimed that "harnessing the full potential of the Internet requires . . . respect for human rights" (United Nations, 2013). Her address was not limited to this vocabulary of human rights, however. Rousseff also sought the opportunity to assert Brazil's sovereignty, as well as to underscore the particular implications of the NSA surveillance for a society at the periphery. As per the analysis of several prominent sociologists, "the game that Brazilian authorities are playing is actually an attempt to reconcile individual autonomy, state sovereignty, and universal rights" (Bauman et al., 2014, p. 129).

In the following statement, Rousseff made clear that there was an economic dimension to the NSA's digital surveillance and that her government was prepared to defend its informational resources and data sovereignty from the forces at informational capitalism's core:

> Brazil, Mr. President, will redouble its efforts to adopt legislation, technologies and mechanisms to protect us from the illegal interception of communications and data. My government will do everything within its reach to defend the human rights of all Brazilians and to protect the fruits borne from the ingenuity of our workers and our companies. (United Nations, 2013)

The technologies and mechanisms here refer to the bundle of policy measures conceived to assert Brazil's data sovereignty: the undersea cable to Europe, the national email program, and data localization. Finally, Rousseff invoked Brazil's peripheral history of military dictatorship to proclaim, "As many other Latin Americans, I fought against authoritarianism and censorship, and I cannot but defend, in an uncompromising fashion, the right to privacy of individuals and the sovereignty of my country" (United Nations, 2013).

In sum, Rousseff used her UN pulpit to play a careful double game. On one hand, she presented Brazil as the champion of digital rights and carefully articulated the individual rights of the Marco Civil with the vocabulary of universal human rights expected at the United Nations. This gambit was designed to stake the moral high ground in contrast to the "skullduggery" of the United States and as such to appeal to voters in Brazil. In juxtaposition to the Marco Civil's digital discourse of individual rights grounded in expression and creativity, Rousseff also drew upon the discourses of sovereignty and neodevelopmentalism as another means to rhetorically confront the United States. These references were intended to reconcile the core PT policy commitment to technological sovereignty with an appeal to those voters whose desire for economic nationalism was offended by the Snowden revelations.

Ultimately, Rousseff's post-Snowden balancing act between sovereignty and multistakeholderism, the digital and neodevelopmental discourses, and accommodation or confrontation with the core of informational capitalism would soon reach its resolution.

Echoes of Media Tyranny

Despite President Rousseff championing the Marco Civil, the bill was still effectively frozen in Brazil's Congress. This occurred because of the continued obstructionist tactics of a block of parties within Congress, orchestrated in support of the telecoms sector but also by an ad-hoc alliance of six parties acting on behalf of the federal police. In order to overcome these obstacles, Molon opted to introduce four last-ditch amendments to the fourth—and penultimate—draft of the bill (substitutivo 4) issued on December 11, 2013. One of these changes was intended to placate the telecoms sector and its allies and is analyzed in the next subsection.

Another of the four amendments was widely seen as a concession to representatives and senators anxious to retain control over politically damaging material published about them online. Clauses 3 and 4 stated that online content deemed damaging to "reputation, honor, and personal rights" could be attended to by specialist courts. This amendment also drew the ire of CSOs that recognized the naked self-interest of politicians in Brazil.

The fourth and final amendment was a significant change to the provisions on data retention. This was widely perceived to serve the interests of the Brazilian state security and law-enforcement authorities. What was less visible to outside observers was the vested interests of other sectors of informational capitalism, namely, the web platforms and the copyright lobby.

Those two sectors, examined next, possessed strong commercial interests in further diminishing the Marco Civil's limited privacy safeguards.

What's the Matter with Metadata?

In a new article, 16, in a newly added subsection, "Storage of Access Registries for Internet Applications," the draft stated that commercial application providers need to retain data for six months and that any application service provider—even if noncommercial—could be mandated by judicial order to retain data pertaining to specific events over a longer time frame. These transformed the initial article 13 on the matter, which had remained unchanged from the first iteration of the bill and had specified *no* data retention obligations for application service providers.

The main implication of this modification stemmed from the newly enabled capacity of security services to combine connection and access records. ISP connection logs were mandated for retention from the inception of the Marco Civil. Connection logs meant data pertaining to time, frequency, duration, and IP addresses of internet connections. These metadata constitute technical information that might aid with a criminal investigation but in isolation yield a limited understanding of an individual's behavior. Access logs, however, mean metadata pertaining to sites visited, software used, files downloaded, and the like. These evidently constitute a detailed portrait of user behavior. By combining them with connection logs and with communication content, security analysts would gain access to a trove of personal information.

The amendments on data access need to be considered in conjunction with changes made to the previous substitutivo (3) issued the month prior: specifically, two new clauses added to article 10 in the "Section on the Protection of Registries, Personal Data, and Private Communications."

The first clause, included within an article otherwise oriented toward user privacy, stated that "the content of personal communication can only be made available through a court order." This was the first time that any reference to communication content had been included in the bill. The second relevant clause stipulated that access to user data held by connection or application providers and related to "personal identity, affiliation, and address" could be sought by "administrative authorities that possess the legal competency for its requisition." This meant that connection and access data could be integrated with detailed offline-identifying metadata, as well as communication content, creating an integrated whole. Moreover, the vague wording of this second clause would enable access to this information for a huge swathe of state actors without necessarily having to seek a judicial order.

Cumulatively, the provisions concerning the retention of user metadata, access to personal information and communication content, and establishing lenient conditions under which that information could be divulged to state authorities, constituted a tremendous expansion of the Brazilian surveillance state.

Communication content, after all, can reveal only so much. It is metadata pertaining to cookie identifiers and global positioning system (GPS) coordinates that provide the means for security services to connect persons with other surveillance targets and to cast a dragnet. And if access to metadata provides the means to extend surveillance, then it contributes significantly to the chilling effects that are so corrosive to democracy. As Parsons (2015) explains, "as a result of being always in a potentially-targeted category, individuals may alter their behaviours to try to secure their telecommunications from third-party monitoring" (p. 4). Surveillance practices do not only impede the development of *individual* autonomy, however, but also alter "the environment of social relationships and thereby undermines *collective* self-determination" (Stahl, 2016, emphasis added). Ultimately, increasing the surveillance capacities of the state security apparatus increases the dominion of state over citizen and amplifies the coercive power of the former over the latter. For these reasons, the surveillance practices of the security state constitute one of the many ways that the logics of informational capitalism are inimical to democracy.

Accordingly, the changes enacted in this fourth iteration of the bill need to be understood as one of the central contradictions of the Marco Civil as a framework of digital rights: at the same time as some provisions in the bill purported to safeguarding individual privacy, others were explicitly conceived to enable the surveillance state.

A "Big Defeat"? Civil Society Finally Reacts

The fact of this contradiction did not go unnoticed by Brazilian civil society organizations and explains some of the most concerted resistance displayed by CSOs during the Marco Civil process. Moreover, the timing of these amendments contributed to the jarring sense of incoherence. Within six months of the Snowden revelations generating such outrage in Brazil and of Dilma Rousseff taking the role of global spokesperson against the practices of state electronic surveillance, it was shocking to see surveillance measures added to the country's landmark digital rights law.

Of course, the Snowden revelations were not the only political event to agitate Brazilian politics in the middle of 2013. The Jornadas de Junho served to sharpen the ambitions of the surveillance state. Intelligence and security services in Brazil were emboldened to demand tools, such as mandatory data-retention provisions in the Marco Civil, however incongruous they may have appeared in a bill of digital rights.

Flávia Lefevre of the CSO Proteste was forthright in her condemnation of the bill's incoherence: "Here in article 10, this third paragraph I think is terrible, a loss. Here you have a great protection. But then . . . you have . . . the process of metadata, this is a big thing. . . . In my opinion it's a big defeat: either you have data protection, or you don't" (interview, 2015).

Communication-rights activists were justified in their concerns, as Brazil's state security apparatus was already a prolific user of surveillance technologies. As Freedom House's 2012 press-freedom report for Brazil recounts, "in August 2011 alone, the judiciary granted over 17,000 wiretaps, many of them to Voice over IP (VoIP) lines" (2012). Moreover, Luiz Moncau, senior researcher at the Getulio Vargas Foundation (FGV), recounted to me how the security services would employ extralegal measures to intimidate smaller web companies and ISPs into divulging user data: "We hear about the use of different kinds of pressures such as . . . bringing the police to the door of the house of the director of the company and there is this concern among the neighbors, 'Oh, was this guy corrupt?' There is this kind of pressure to get at the data" (2015).

Concerns about judicial overreach and the abuse of state power were also echoed in a statement published by the Partido Pirata on December 13, 2013, one day after the contested provisions were announced by Molon in Congress. The Pirates decried what article 16 could mean for the "monitoring and intimidation of social movements that organize on the internet in order to demand change in Brazil" (Partido Pirata, 2013). A tract from the Pirates' statement deserves particular attention as it signals how those few CSOs that rejected the tenets of the digital discourse appeared more attentive to the corporate capture of the Marco Civil: "Political games ensured that economic interests and the maintenance of current power structures were privileged. These above all were the business models of the telephone operators and the other holders of communication infrastructure, as well as the big media conglomerates, copyright holders and political parties" (2013). Indeed, the Party considered the amendments on data retention so egregious and antithetical to their values that they announced their intention to withdraw support from the project until article 16 was reformed.

Such a move was resisted by Barbosa, one of the highest-profile coordinators within the Marco Civil coalition. Her position was that it was essential to retain a united front in order to effectively pressure members of Congress to pass the bill: "If we started to divide, it was going to be very easy for them to not approve the text" (interview, 2015). Walking united required hewing to a centrist line and arguably led to civil society groups other than the Pirate Party capitulating to the systemic needs of informational capitalism.

The Economic Imperative for Data Access

The fact that the furor around article 16 did not include the US web platforms was perhaps simply a tacit recognition that the data-retention provisions did not imply an obligation for them; their business models were already premised on complete data capture and its long-term retention. The principal novelty for the likes of Google, Facebook, and Microsoft lay in the means by which user information could be requested by actors within the Brazilian state. As such, this sector of informational capitalism was a strong advocate of article 16, again pitting its interests against the Marco Civil's civil society backers.

In 2012, Brazil was ranked the third-highest country worldwide for state-initiated user-data requests (following the United States and Japan). This was according to data divulged by Google (2,777 requests) and Twitter (34) (Freedom House, 2013). In the first half of 2013, for Google that number had dropped to 1,239 requests for data regarding 1,515 Brazilian user accounts (Google, n.d.). Facebook at this time did not systematically report such requests.

Complying with this volume of user-data requests might not imply more than a nuisance for companies with the operational scale of the US platforms. However, the concerns arose from the lack of legal clarity in how these requests should be addressed and the consequences of noncompliance. According to my web platform interviewee, clarity on data-retention provisions was near the top of their agenda for the Marco Civil: "Of secondary importance . . . but not nearly as important as the safe harbors were the regulations on what kind of data to retain, for how long, to which authorities they should disclose . . . because that has always been a mess" (2015). He went on to add that in Brazil there is no subpoena or middle ground like in the United States, but there is either a court order or an unofficial request. Some judges, apparently, would accept a letter from the police as legal authority, but his company would always demand a court order.

The result of this opacity was that the web platforms would often confront the dilemma of divulging user data without due process or antagonizing the Brazilian security state. The implications of the latter were vividly illustrated when in September 2012 a Brazilian court issued arrest warrants for two senior Google Brazil executives "for failure to remove content prohibited under electoral law" (Freedom House, 2013). Given this scenario, it is perhaps unsurprising to learn that "of course we tried to influence the system so it would be in compliance with our own practices, which is basically that you always needed a court order" (web platform executive, interview, 2015). What this statement does not address is that the changes made to article 10 in the Marco Civil would permit web platforms and ISPs to divulge personal user information to a broad array of state actors *without* a court order. This change would certainly establish legal certainty for the web platforms in terms of user-data requests but would also massively facilitate the sharing of that user data with the Brazilian state and without the oversight implied by judicial intervention. In this respect, once again, the operational needs of the web platforms ran counter to the demands of civil society.

The web platforms were not the only sector of informational capitalism with a commercial interest in securing the new data-retention provisions. IP-rights holders also benefit significantly from access to user data in order to combat online piracy; the longer that web platforms and ISPs are compelled to retain access and connection data, the stronger the basis for identifying and processing copyright violations. It was well established that the concerns of the international IP-rights holders were one of the main drivers of the ill-fated cybercrime bill, the Lei Azeredo. And outside of Brazil, it is a routine feature of copyright legislation that IP-rights associations pressure governments to implement data-retention provisions.

In the case of the Marco Civil, Carlos Afonso (Caf) indicated to me that the data-retention provisions would remain in the bill because "the IP community are very strongly interested in keeping that." Moreover, as well as global IP-rights associations, such as the Motion Picture Association (MPA) and International Federation of the Phonographic Industry (IFPI), Brazil's media sector (i.e., Globo) "were desperate on the articles on metadata because they are the prime representatives of the IPR [intellectual property rights] community, so the process took over and it was really, really difficult" (2015). According to this well-positioned observer then, the amendments to article 16, as well as a boon to the Brazilian surveillance state, represented another instance—to be added to the IP carve-out—of the content-production sector safeguarding the logic of control within informational capitalism.

The outrage of many civil society organizations generated by the revision of article 16 was vividly manifested in the #16igualNSA protests (i.e., article 16 equals the NSA, explored in the next subsection). International condemnation, by the likes of the Electronic Frontier Foundation, also followed (Rodriguez & Pinho, 2015). Such consternation was not, however, necessarily reflective of the wider Brazilian population. In one of the main contradictions around the concept of privacy in the Marco Civil, at the same time as the data-retention provisions evoked Brazil's recent history of military dictatorship and state control, for many others another concern ensured a more sanguine reaction to the amendments. This was the fear of crime that is pervasive in Brazil.

Running parallel with and no doubt connected to its status as one of the most unequal societies in the world, Brazil also heads global data tables in terms of crime. Between 1980 and 2010 there were one million violent deaths in Brazil, providing it with the unwelcome distinction of having one of the highest homicide rates in the world (Murray et al., 2013). From 2008 to 2013, Brazil's incarceration rate increased by 40 percent (Human Rights Watch, 2013) and resulted in the country having the fourth-largest prison population in the world (Murray et al., 2013). Vigilante actions perpetrated by urban militias, as well as high rates of extrajudicial killings by law-enforcement authorities (Human Rights Watch, 2013), contribute to the cycle of violence and the perception of insecurity. Such chilling statistics can, in turn, be connected to the policy failures of a weak peripheral state.

Moreover, the result of such high societal sensitivity to crime is that moves toward securitization can find favor in the general public. The consequences of this were disheartening for Bia Barbosa in terms of repealing the article 16 amendments: "It is a difficult debate to make in Brazilian society because you have this whole discussion on pedophilia, of financial crime. There is this logic that people have, that if they're not doing anything wrong, they don't have any problem with having their data retained. . . . If privacy was a stronger value in Brazilian society, perhaps we would have one on this issue" (interview, 2015). Indeed, in the absence of any significant public reaction, article 16 reached the final version of the bill.

In Sum

In sum, the addition of these data-retention clauses in the Marco Civil was significant for three reasons. The first is that they constituted one more instance, perhaps, more explicit than most, of the predominant powers of informational capitalism securing protections for their systemic logics within the Marco Civil. Primarily, these protections favored the security state but also IP-rights holders. For both sectors, mandatory data retention allowed them to more effectively surveil and discipline citizen-users.

The second reason relates to the failure of the digital rights contained in the Marco Civil to address the practices of commercial surveillance. The mass collection and commodification of behavioral data by web platforms, legitimated through the provisions of article 16, were never substantively addressed in the Marco Civil. The nature of civil society reaction to the data-retention clauses, particularly, the tunnel-vision focus on the implications of increased state surveillance, without considering the oppressive potential of commercial data collection for Brazilian citizens, was indicative of this enduring lacuna. I argue that the fact of this blind spot demonstrates not only the influence of the digital discourse in delineating which actors needed to be conceptualized as threats through digital rights but ultimately made the Marco Civil an expedient for, rather than a check upon, the logics of informational capitalism.

Finally, the third reason why these data-retention provisions are significant is because they cast into relief one more dimension of the way that digital rights were contested at the periphery. In this case, privacy was contested fiercely by some activists and CSOs because increasing the powers of the surveillance state evoked memories of Brazil's history of military dictatorship and the manner in which citizens were systematically monitored, classified, and oppressed. For many other Brazilian citizens, however, privacy was a social good of limited value when compared with the fear of criminal victimization. This fear stemmed from the perilous levels of insecurity born of life in a "disjunctive democracy" (Rodrigues, 2006).

The next and final section of this chapter focuses on the resolution of network neutrality in the Marco Civil. This represents the last major instance of curtailment for the digital rights contained in the bill. This is because the laser focus on net neutrality by the CSOs that advocated so tirelessly for it meant that not only did they fail to consider policy alternatives that would more fully address the inequities of informational capitalism but they also ended up with a version of net neutrality that was compromised in some key respects.

That Most Corporate of Digital Rights

Alongside the data-retention provisions introduced in the fourth and penultimate version of the Marco Civil, the other major novelty was an amendment that had long been coveted by the telecoms sector in Brazil and was intended to win their support for the bill. This was a grim necessity for Molon, as the telecoms sector, represented with brutal efficacy in Congress by Eduardo Cunha, continued to block its passage.

Although no observer of the Marco Civil was in any doubt that this amendment pertained to the legislation of network neutrality, the change did not appear in article 9, which was dedicated exclusively to the topic. Instead, the divisive amendment was added to article 3, which outlined the fundamental principles of internet usage in Brazil. Alongside such civic ideals as "protection of privacy" and "guarantee of freedom of expression," a new principle baldly protected "the freedom of business models developed on the Internet, so long as they do not conflict with the other principles established in this law."

It was clear that the clause was intended to address the long-standing concern of the telecoms sector that network neutrality in Brazil would prevent them from offering potentially lucrative new services. These plans were never explicitly articulated but likely referred to zero-rating for mobile internet users and high-speed prioritization for content providers and corporate services. The ambiguous nature of this clause would provide the telecoms sector a secure foothold from which to contest the most inconvenient aspects of network neutrality in the regulatory phase of the Marco Civil. According to aggrieved civil society observers, the clause would create a "war of interpretations around the concept of neutrality" (Observatório da Sociedade Civil, 2014).

Backed by President Rousseff's newfound commitment to net neutrality, as well as the indefatigable support of the bill's core of civil society advocates, over the course of the two versions of the bill issued in 2013, Molon had added new clauses to strengthen net neutrality, such as the obligation for network operators to "act with proportionality, transparency, and isonomy" as well as to "offer commercial services that were nondiscriminatory and to abstain from anticompetitive practices" (Solagna, 2015).

In addition to these amendments, the telcos frequently claimed to be indignant about the prospect that the Marco Civil would prevent the marketing of internet subscriptions based on connection speeds. As Molon repeatedly insisted this was not the case (Estadão, 2013), this was likely a negotiating tactic for the telecoms sector to secure the capacity to offer mobile and fixed internet plans based on data packets, as this had been in genuine doubt. Establishing clarity on this matter would put the sector a step closer to the desired goal of legally enacting positive discrimination. As Sinditelebrasil executive Alex Castro explained, "the concern was that the activists did not want mobile plans based on [data] capacity. They said that it violated the concept of neutrality network." But as he also added, "we won on this" (interview, 2015).

The "win" for the sector came about as the result of a meeting on December 6 between Molon and Eduardo Levy, the executive director of Sinditelebrasil. According to Levy, "now the telecoms sector is favourable to its passage" (Papp, 2014, p. 107). Tellingly, the fourth version of the bill was issued a week later, one including the clause on "freedom of business models."

The tactics of the sector, acting hand in glove with Cunha's opposition coalition, *o blocão* (the big block), had forced Molon into granting this concession, even as it represented a time bomb for the bill's subsequent regulation. The president's declaration of constitutional urgency had done little to counter the obstructionist maneuvers that had stymied the bill's progress until then. According to Proteste executive lawyer Flávia Lefevre, after "urgency" had been declared, the telecoms sector "turned their attention to removing the article on network neutrality and Molon was so assailed by their demands that the only way to achieve consensus was to include the [clause in] article 3" (interview, 2015).

The sector advanced these demands by blocking the bill every time it appeared on the voting agenda for Congress. At the end of 2013, the bill was deferred on ten occasions, with a further fourteen occurring in the first months of 2014 (Solagna, 2015, p. 104). Congresspeople allied with the telcos exploited the opportunity to bombard the bill with amendments that would undermine protections for net neutrality (web platform executive, interview, 2015). These amounted to more than thirty such changes, leading Molon to declare indignantly that "amendments that distort or disfigure neutrality . . . will be rejected" (Papp, 2014, p. 97).

Realpolitik Meets Digital Rights

During the Brazilian Congress's lengthy Christmas recess, many actors were actively developing strategies for the Marco Civil's resolution, to shape the bill according to their own agendas. Fears of the implications of an expanded surveillance state in Brazil prompted new measures by the recently established civil society coalition MarcoCivilJá (Marco Civil Now). One was to launch a social media campaign. Developed around the hashtag #16igualNSA, the campaign was designed to flag the hypocrisy of the PT government in concurrently spearheading outrage to US surveillance abroad while adopting new surveillance tools at home. Another measure by the coalition was to threaten to withdraw its support from the bill if the provisions on data localization, data retention, and content removal were not substantively reformed (Observatório da Sociedade Civil, 2014). In an open letter published on February 10, cosigned by sixteen CSOs,[2] the authors were explicit in denouncing the repressive history of state power in Brazil and the increased risk for political dissidents:

> Even if the data is only released following judicial deliberation, they will be collected in an open-ended way, turning everyone into a suspect. Given how the judiciary functions in Brazil, it is not hard to imagine that a

climate of vigilantism will be created, particularly against the "undesirables," *those that contest established powers*. (Observatório da Sociedade Civil, 2014, emphasis added)

On the same day as Molon issued the latest substitutivo for the Marco Civil, it became clear that civil society groups had not been alone in developing new strategies for the Marco Civil during the congressional recess. Cunha, leader of the conservative PMDB, the main coalition partner for the governing PT and the conduit through which the demands of the telecoms sector were conveyed into Congress, announced to the media that his party would no longer be supporting the government agenda. Moreover, their "political position was to defeat any project that has been granted urgency." That meant the Marco Civil (Passarinho, 2014, Aliados).

The pivot from reluctant ally to outright opposition by the PMDB was consolidated days later with the announcement of a significant arrival in Brazilian politics: the blocão. A group of right-leaning political parties had forged a formidable new alliance. Formally unveiled to the media on February 25, 2014, the group consisted of seven parties previously allied with the PT-led government, including Cunha's PMDB, and one opposition party. The group would go on to play a pivotal role, not only in the conclusion of the Marco Civil but in Brazilian politics writ large. The group was formed to a large degree born of the frustration of seeing its legislative proposals frozen within the regime of urgency invoked for the Marco Civil. However, the group had another goal that would contribute to what became a cataclysm in the Brazilian polity (Passarinho, 2014, PMDB).

The blocão announced its intention to establish an investigative committee to probe claims that a Dutch oil company had paid millions in bribes to executives of the state oil company Petrobras (Passarinho, 2014, PMDB). The intention was to put pressure on the PT government, and these allegations would later form part of the sweeping corruption investigation, Operation Lava Jato (Car Wash), that would contribute to President Rousseff's impeachment in 2016 and the imprisonment of her predecessor, Lula da Silva, in 2018.

In terms of the Marco Civil, the implications for the bill were significant. Given that the new group was led by Cunha, the priorities of the telecoms companies would be made paramount. Indeed, at the media announcement, the group demanded that Molon include a provision in the bill to permit internet plans based on different speeds (Passarinho, 2014, PMDB).

The new political alliance continued to obstruct the bill's passage through the early months of 2014, and in keeping with the strategy of explicit opposition, on March 13 Cunha was emboldened to attempt a radical transformation of the bill that would have aligned the provisions of the bill tightly with the goals of the telecoms sector. The principal changes included explicit allowances for the sale of differentiated services, such as social media packages, and exempted internet services, in general, from net neutrality obligations.

The attempt to put this transformed version of the bill to a vote was ultimately defeated due to a lack of consensus. However, it demonstrated the degree of political capital the conservative alliance within Congress was willing to expend to shape the legislation of network neutrality in the interests of its corporate backers. An event in the Brazilian media sphere, however, proved pivotal in dampening the oppositional resolve of the blocão. On March 15 the current-affairs magazine *IstoÉ* published a feature article analyzing the power wielded by Cunha within Congress, influence that had been hitherto unknown outside the political bubble of Brasília (Dantas & Torres, 2014). The front page features a Photoshopped image of Cunha's head atop the iconic throne image of Kevin Spacey from Netflix's political thriller *House of Cards* and a headline reading "Saboteur of the Republic." The publication sent shockwaves through the Brazilian polity.

As a PT policy adviser explained to me, the consequence of the *IstoÉ* article was that "for the first time he [Cunha] became a relatively public figure. . . . This generated a tremendous anger on his part, and a major public pressure finally turned against him. For the first time, the telcos became more withdrawn, and this was a major victory" (interview, 2015). This was clearly a highly significant development: Cunha and the telecoms sector were accustomed to operating in the shadows, and given the low esteem in which Brazil's major telecoms companies were held by the public, it became prudent for them to refrain from further attempts to derail the Marco Civil.

Resolving Neutrality

Indeed, by the end of March 2014, a combination of elements was in place that finally enabled a successful vote on the Marco Civil. The *IstoÉ* exposé limited the room for maneuver for Cunha's blocão and the telecoms sector. It appeared that a decision was made by the telecoms sector at this stage to move ahead with the Marco Civil with the concessions that had already been won. As Guilherme Almeida explained to me, "part of the compromises they tried to force could be seen as part of their legal strategy to minimize the effects of network neutrality. It seemed to me like one of those chess games where they had less pieces but they could lead to a tie" (interview, 2018).

The most significant compromise "forced" by the sector that was retained in the final version of the bill was the principle of freedom of business models. This coupled with the general tendency in the Marco Civil to keep "limitations to network neutrality that were generic and open" made the "legislation a bit less self-enforceable." This was, in Almeida's estimation "a victory" for the sector. Moreover, the final provision that any future regulation of network neutrality would be based on presidential decree was based on the sector "counting on having more influence at the regulatory agency and more influence with future governments to revise any potential defeats" (G. Almeida, interview, 2018).

The head of the telecoms industry association, Alex Castro, buttressed Almeida's assertion that at some point the sector realized that it had wrung every concession it could from the Marco Civil at the legislative stage and had to refocus on shaping network neutrality at the regulatory level:

> So, we're only going to work on the exception, not on the concept any more. Reinventing network neutrality? That passed, that phase has gone. Network neutrality is done. *Now it's about seeing where I can, in what situations I can, break network neutrality.* (interview, 2015, emphasis added)

Finally, as was repeatedly emphasized to me by figures within the major economic groups contesting the Marco Civil, almost irrespective of its particular provisions, the juridical assurance implied by the bill would prove a boon for investment. The prevailing opinion was that establishing legal clarity would assuage the fears of prospective investors in Brazil's digital economy that rogue judges could implement ad hoc rulings that jeopardize investments. This was encapsulated most neatly by Tonet Camargo from the Globo Group: "Juridical certainty leads to what? Investment, in very clear reasoning. The less juridical certainty you have, the greater the difficulty you will have for investment" (interview, 2015). This was likely more true of the telecoms sector than any other because of the huge capital costs required for physical infrastructure. Accordingly, despite its overt hostility to the legislation and despite the prevailing opinion by civil society observers, I contend that the passage of the Marco Civil was ultimately a positive development for the telecoms sector.

As well as the strategic shift by the telecoms companies, other sectors of informational capitalism combined to finally impel the passage of the bill. In the case of those other sectors, they continued to exert pressure so that the key provisions that benefited them would finally be written into law. According to Pedro Abramovay's later appraisal (2017) of the Marco Civil's "home straight," the pressure of the web platforms, the Globo Group, and the security state were all decisive in dampening the obstructionist ardor of the blocão (p. 145).

The Seductive Vision of Innovation

The last remaining concern of the web platforms was the clause on data localization. The principal US platforms—Facebook, Google, Microsoft, and Twitter (now X)—had lobbied the government relentlessly to strip this last vestige of data sovereignty from the Marco Civil. The web platforms wanted the government to do away with an obligation that could be ruinously expensive if it was replicated on a global scale. As my web company interviewee explained, "we did a major campaign explaining the problems with data localization. We were successful in convincing pretty much everyone in Congress of the problems that it would cause" (2015).

This executive went on to ascribe the reason for this success, and it was an important factor not only in the debate over data localization but in explaining how the final version of the bill aligned with nearly every point on the web platforms' agenda. This factor was the seductive vision of innovation that the web platforms sold as part of their lobbying:

> I guess part of the reason we were so successful compared to the telcos was *we wanted to tell the good stories.* Basically, we were saying . . . Brazil really wants to attract more digital entrepreneurs, Brazil really has all this creativity. Look at the local start-up ecosystem. Look at all of these things. So, data localization is a bad idea for these reasons. . . . Web platforms don't do any support of Congress . . . so, *essentially it was the power of the arguments.* (interview, 2015, emphasis added)

The power of this argument can, I argue, be explained in large part by Brazil's place at the periphery of informational capitalism. The policy direction of the PT government under Lula da Silva was explicitly oriented toward technological sovereignty. The web platforms were, therefore, very astute in making the connections between establishing the policies that would benefit them and creating the conditions for a viable, local high-technology sector.

One of the few public statements issued by the web platforms on the Marco Civil, two years earlier, offers insight into the kind of argument that they would likely have been making privately in the corridors of the national Congress. In an open letter published in 2012, Google, Facebook, and Microsoft argued strongly in favor of limited third-party liability:

> Protection of content providers boosts national innovation. The next online revolution is just an idea at this time. Innovation on the internet

requires a balanced judicial system that protects providers from responsibility for the acts of their users. The absence of such safeguards tremen-
dously increases costs for entrepreneurs, small businesses, and Brazilian
start-ups, creating disparities that undermine national innovation and
scare away foreign investments. (Facebook, Google, and Mercado Livre,
September 18, 2012, PDF in author's possession)

The other main factor that explains the power of these arguments is the
extent to which they cohere with the tenets of the digital discourse. Entrepreneurialism, creativity, and innovation are all metasignifiers within the
discourse that are established common sense in matters of technology and
associated policy. It is also, of course, the discourse that legitimated the
logics of informational capitalism and facilitated the economic might of
the web platforms. Finally, as demonstrated in chapter 3, innovation was
the orienting framework for the Marco Civil from the outset owing to the
discursive intervention of Ronaldo Lemos. By invoking that founding value
in their arguments, the web platforms were staying true to the origins of
the bill as a framework of digital rights and were ultimately successful in
removing the maligned data-localization clause.

The Unbearable Lightness of Data Finality

The resolution of the Marco Civil did not entirely favor the interests
of the web platforms, of course. Article 7 of the approved bill, establishing "the rights and guarantees of users," contained several limitations on
commercial data storage for web-application providers. These approved
provisions stipulated notably that user data could only be shared with third
parties with explicit user consent and that users could request the permanent
deletion of their data upon terminating subscription or membership of a
particular application. These moves toward data finality were welcomed by
communication-rights activists (Barbosa, interview, 2015), even though it
was clear that the business model of the web platforms premised on commodifying user data would be unaltered.

It is worth noting legal scholar Julie Cohen's (2019) critique of such
measures here, as she argues that it is "unclear what, if anything, individual data subjects might gain from the opportunity to navigate an additional layer of complexity in aid of making wide-ranging and imperfectly
informed decisions about an uncertain future" (p. 262). Indeed, following
Jonathan Obar's argument of the "fallacy of information self-management"
(2015), the notion that reams of dense legalese might constitute the free
and informed consent of the average user represents another instance in

the Marco Civil where digital rights were hollowed out and incapable of addressing the exploitation inherent to informational capitalism.

Another reason that even those CSOs with the greatest expertise in matters of communication and consumer rights were willing to accept the weak provisions of data finality was because of the asymmetry, oft-noted in these pages, between the acute concern of many Brazilian citizens about state surveillance and their relative ambivalence on issues of corporate "dataveillance." Partly this can be interpreted within a peripheral frame, as the result of Brazil's history of military dictatorship, but also with a discursive interpretation, as a product of the web platforms' status within the digital discourse as champions of free expression and creativity.

The web platforms, too, were sanguine about the user-rights provisions contained in article 7. Although these represented some of the most onerous obligations heaped them, the companies were conspicuously silent on the matter. Their reticence to obstruct the data-finality provisions can be ascribed in part to the civic tenor of the bill and how incongruous it would be for the web platforms—the perceived allies of civil society—to be seen to resist particular digital rights.

One should recall that as a matter of private strategy, the web platforms contemplated doing whatever they could to "nuke" the bill if it proceeded with data localization measures. They were clearly therefore willing to resist, just not to do so publicly. Although the web platforms also opted against lobbying publicly for network neutrality for fear of catalyzing a major conflict with the telecoms sector, it would have been abundantly clear to those within government that the decision to implement the policy meant favoring either the web or the telecoms companies. As Brazilian telecoms law scholar Pedro Ramos opined, "It seems clear that network neutrality is a question of choice: it is, at its base, a trade-off between incentivizing the software and IT sector, reducing the economic potential of the telecoms sector; or promoting the telecoms sector, and reducing incentives for Internet applications" (2014, p. 6).

Given the economic power and political influence of the telecoms lobby, it would have been understandable if the PT government had decided to side with it in the conflict over network neutrality to diminish or even eliminate the most contentious provisions. The fact that the government was resolute in including network neutrality in the final version of the Marco Civil requires some explanation.

One important factor was the web platforms promoting the potential for domestic technology innovation in Brazil, a seductive vision for the PT government, as explained above. Moreover, CSOs that championed the bill were indefatigable in their defense of net neutrality. In what I describe as the "paradox of network neutrality," the greater the opposition of the telecoms sector, the more entrenched the belief became among activists and CSOs that it was an essential part of securing digital rights in Brazil. This precluded consideration of structural reforms that might have challenged the logics of informational capitalism.

The support of the CSOs, in turn, buttressed the resolve of Molon. He described neutrality as "the heart of the bill," and in interview with me he dismissed the benefit of the measure to the web platforms as incidental: "The guarantee of neutrality, for me, it is principally of interest to the user. And it's good for Google as well. That doesn't interest me. My focus is not on Google, my focus is on the user." I argue that this view neatly encapsulates the blind spot that dominated the defense of the Marco Civil by its civil society and state champions: it was a failure to anticipate that favoring the operational needs of the web platforms was not merely a secondary effect of securing digital rights *but in fact would actively undermine them.*

There were also important electoral considerations for the PT government in early 2014 in continuing to defend network neutrality. A federal election was only six months away, and the popularity of Dilma Rousseff had been badly eroded by the massive street protests of 2013. The government could ill afford to be perceived to be acting in favor of entrenched economic interests and against the will of the people by capitulating on net neutrality. The advocacy work of CSOs and activists, such as MarcoCivilJá, was very effective at establishing this as the stark choice implied by net neutrality. The popular slogan used by defenders of the bill, "Democracy yes; corporations no," made this quite explicit.

Finally, the media power of the Globo Group, for which network neutrality was of fundamental concern, would have been influential in the government's decision. As discussed in the previous chapter, several of my interviewees reported that positive coverage of the bill increased markedly on Globo's various television holdings after the group secured its coveted IP carve-out. Although references to the Marco Civil in the *O Globo* newspaper in 2013 and 2014 were still relatively modest, given that Globo's free-to-air TV stations boasted a daily average audience of ninety-one million people in 2014 (Globo domination, 2014), it is likely that any coverage of the bill would have substantially increased public support. Luiz Moncau explained to me how Globo advanced that agenda by using its strategic assets: "Broadcasters were really smart, and they didn't come up to the front. They won on network neutrality. They used media right, so this is a lot." And as the communication rights advocate Bia Barbosa explained to me in stark terms: "If you want to study the history of the Globo Group in Brazil, it has managed to influence political processes in a really profound way . . .

so if it was against the bill, openly against it, then we would certainly not have secured its approval in Congress" (interview, 2015).

Moreover, data regarding the levels of state expenditure by all of the PT administrations on advertising in the various Globo holdings (6.24 billion reals or US$1.7 billion from 2003 to 2014) (Marinoni, 2015, p. 12) demonstrates the reciprocal levels of influence that existed between Grupo Globo and the government. Indeed, just in 2013, state funding on advertising was equivalent to 25 percent of all Globo's revenues (Marinoni, 2015, p. 12). These facts corroborate the cynical thesis that the Brazilian government's support for network neutrality was driven as much by the influence of Brazil's preeminent media power as by dedication to the rights of its citizenry.

By late March it appeared that most of the conditions were in place for the Marco Civil to be finally viable as a bill of law: the government was motivated by the looming deadline of the global net-governance forum, the NetMundial summit to be hosted in Brasília in April, which was to be the showpiece of their global leadership on resisting US surveillance (and with a newly passed Marco Civil its crown jewel); civil society organizations had ratcheted up pressure on congresspeople to finally pass the bill, which was doubly significant in an election year; Cunha and the blocão were temporarily cowed by the *IstoÉ* exposé; the telecoms sector finally resigned itself to fight for net neutrality loopholes at the regulatory phase of the Marco Civil; the security state and IP-rights holder were keen to lock down valuable surveillance provisions in the bill; Globo used its power to pressure congresspeople to secure network neutrality and limited third-party liability, including the IP carve-out; and web platforms pushed for resolution of the bill once the government finally abandoned data localization on March 19, 2013 (Abramovay, 2017, p. 145). Cumulatively, the stage was finally set for a successful vote on the Marco Civil.

Passage

On March 25, 2014, I arrived at the national Congress late into the night and with the security clearance of a parliamentary aid, was permitted to view proceedings on the floor of the Congress as the vote concluded. Five months after the bill was subject to constitutional urgency, it was finally passed with near unanimity. Even Cunha voted in favor of the bill, although in a telling declaration as he submitted his vote, he confessed: "I do this with the residual fear that the Internet only got where it is due to the absence of regulation" (Nascimento, 2014).

In one abstention worthy of note, Jair Bolsonaro, virulent congressman and future president, declared, "I prefer Obama to be reading my emails than a gang set-up by the PT." When he was rebutted by a PT congressperson, Bolsonaro's response evoked the telecoms-sector strategy of connecting the Marco Civil with communism: "You are Cuban! Get to Cuba! Get to Cuba, Cubano! They've got Internet there!" (Papp, 2014, p. 122).

These bombastic statements, however, were the exceptions to the rule. The vast majority of the speeches made as votes were cast, irrespective of party affiliation and ideological hue, praised the significance of the bill and recognized its civic legitimacy. Barbosa of Intervozes interpreted this as the fruit of all of the civil society coalition's tireless advocacy work: "I think it was all well done in the end because . . . all the parties voted in favor of the bill with speeches saying, 'This is an important project for the country,' or 'This is important for society.' It stopped being the speech, 'This is a government project so it should be defeated'" (interview, 2015).

Another observer of the vote took a more cynical position: "It was almost like we were watching a science-fiction movie, because these guys who were fighting each other like a week before, and suddenly everyone was like, 'Yeah, this is for the benefit of Brazil and the internet ecosystem!' 'Yeah, let's approve the Marco Civil!' It was kind of hilarious to see that. But that's politics, right?" (web platform executive, interview, 2015).

Less than one month later and the result of concerted government pressure, on April 22 the bill was unanimously approved by the Brazilian Senate. President Rousseff secured her coveted goal of being able to sign the bill into law, before a global audience, on the opening day of the NetMundial summit.

Thus, after five years of internecine conflict between competing sectors of informational capitalism, bitter political factionalism, the relentless campaigning of a small band of technology activists and communication and consumer-rights advocates, and a singular act of courage by a US government contractor, Brazil had its bill of digital rights. Still structured around the three pillars of network neutrality, data privacy, and freedom of expression first proposed at the public consultation, the final Marco Civil da Internet had been decisively shaped by the discursive and material power of informational capitalism, as well as by Brazil's present and historical status at the periphery of the global capitalist economy.

Many civil society observers were, however, ebullient, as exemplified by Flávia Lefevre's reaction: "Civil society won on so many points that I believe it's really incredible, I sincerely do. After it all finished I said I don't know how we got all of those points" (interview, 2015). A contrarian position holds that the "incredible" nature of the Marco Civil is a chimera; the reason that civil society got all of those points was because the digital rights contained in the bill ultimately cohered with rather than checked the logics of informational capitalism.

Other observers aligned with this view. Paulo Santarém, manager of the public consultation for the Ministry of Justice, offered this much more circumspect judgement in our interview:

> *It does not guarantee that the internet is more just*, it does not impede the telcos from offering abusive plans. . . . It does not avoid the diffusion of material that violates the rights of minorities or individuals. For the law, it permits that these discussions occur on clearer terms. That is undeniable. (emphasis added)

It is with no satisfaction that I note how recent history strongly suggests that the Marco Civil's "legal clarity" has done little to uphold digital rights for Brazilians. The failure to establish collective over individual digital rights, to confront the logics of informational capitalism, and to address the inequitable political economy of the internet have returned to haunt Brazil. The impeachment of Dilma Rousseff in a legislative coup d'état and the subsequent election of a neofascist president in Jair Bolsonaro were strongly abetted by the limited liability of Google, WhatsApp, and Facebook, as those platforms were used to disseminate disinformation favoring Bolsonaro's campaign (Avelar, 2019). Listening to one of the last interviews with Lula da Silva before his imprisonment on dubious corruption charges in 2017 was poignant, indeed, that when asked for his biggest regret in politics, his reply was to have never carried out meaningful reform of the communications media (Costa, 2019). Given the role of Globo and other media giants in Brazil as orchestrators of Rousseff's dubious impeachment (Matos, 2016), it is clear why that regret might loom largest. The Marco Civil unfortunately represents just the latest chapter in a long saga of doomed efforts to democratize media in Brazil.

5

Legacy

The Fragile Contingency
of Digital Rights

If the seismic release of the Edward Snowden surveillance revelations proved to be the unlikely catalyst for the Marco Civil's passage into law, the start of its unraveling occurred just five years later and was similarly unforeseen. On October 28, 2018, the election of Jair Bolsonaro broke a run of four successive center-left administrations and heralded the arrival of a neofascist in the Planalto. Given Bolsonaro's glorification of the military dictatorship and open admiration for its bloody repression, it should have come as no surprise that the cause of digital civil rights in Brazil would find itself with a persecutor rather than a champion in the president's office. Indeed, the manner in which his campaign team exploited the reach and affordances of WhatsApp to flood the app's network with disinformation sent a strong signal that the new administration would trample the fragile safeguards afforded by the Marco Civil.

The purpose of this chapter is to consider the fate of the Marco Civil in its first few years "in the wild" after it emerged from its fraught legislative journey in 2016, up until the end of the Bolsonaro presidency in January 2022. The argument advanced throughout this book is that the digital rights enshrined within the Marco Civil were of a piece with the logics of informational capitalism and that, moreover, they must be understood within the context of Brazil's status at the periphery of that global system. Those logics continued to shape the media and communication systems in Brazil during this period and were imbued with even-greater force as informational capitalism became conjoined with the power of far-right populism: a peripheral manifestation of a global phenomenon. Control over information and the means of its diffusion were pursued more aggressively in the interests of consolidating economic and state power while commodification accelerated as the public interest receded ever further from view.

Specifically, this chapter examines the main ways that the fragile gains of the Marco Civil corroded during the Bolsonaro presidency, including systematic attacks on freedom of expression online, disinformation campaigns, the violation of network neutrality through zero-rating plans, legislative proposals to criminalize content moderation, and the continued, industrial-scale violation of privacy rights. Surveying the full scope of the assault on digital rights tests the theory proposed in these earlier chapters that the Marco Civil could not provide a meaningful check on the many injustices implied by informational capitalism. Finally, we cannot analyze developments in Brazil in isolation from the global rise of far-right populism and the extent to which the design, affordances, and business models of social media platforms—driven by and for informational capitalism—have contributed to its ascent. Thus, one last contribution of this chapter will be to consider how the rise of the far-right using social media communication premised on the logics of commodification and control has further amplified the harms of informational capitalism and overwhelmed the limited protections afforded by digital rights.

Opening the "Office of Hate"

Although Bolsonaro's political legacy is now synonymous with the scourge of disinformation, it must be acknowledged that he acted as an accelerant to an existing blaze, not its ignition. According to journalists at Buzzfeed Brazil, their research conducted in 2016 showed that the top 10 "fake news" stories regarding the sprawling political scandal of the Lava Jato (Car Wash) received more online engagement than the top 10 genuine news stories on the same topic (Aragão & Silverman, 2016). Moreover, the single most shared story in fact impugned Bolsonaro by claiming—falsely—that he had been investigated by the Car Wash prosecutorial team. It is essential to recognize that a wave of right-wing populist anger had been growing well before Bolsonaro became a significant national figure.

Communications scholars Stuart Davis and Joseph Straubhaar (2019) chart the rise of *antipetismo* (populist resentment of the governing PT administrations) emerging from the 2013 street protests that convulsed Brazil. The "villanization" of members of the Workers' Party on mainstream and digital media preceded Bolsonaro's presidential campaign. A new constellation of far-right digital actors, including the Movimento Brasil Livre (MBL), which emerged in 2016 to advocate for the impeachment of Dilma Rousseff and described its digital strategy as a "dictatorship of the like" (Fisher & Taub,

2019), became engaged in "a form of populist post-truth communication" (Davis & Straubhaar, 2019). Bolsonaro's campaign team and supporters thus found fertile ground on which to sow their seeds of information chaos.

WhatsApp had already been established as a favored network of anti-petismo during the trucker strikes of May 2018, in which initial protests against fuel strikes were absorbed into right-wing populist movements and made heavy use of the messaging app (Evangelista & Bruno, 2019). The unparalleled reach of WhatsApp also made it one of the preferred tools for Bolsonaro's campaign team. According to research carried out just before the October 2018 election by Datafolha, 66 percent of Brazilian voters had a WhatsApp account, 44 percent of the electorate used the app to find political information, while supporters of Bolsonaro were the heaviest users at 81 percent, compared to 59 percent for the PT candidate Fernando Haddad (G1, 2018). In absolute terms, in 2018, 120 million Brazilian citizens were active WhatsApp users (Nemer, 2021, Disentangling). As discussed in more detail shortly, the heavy adoption of the app owes in large part to the prevalence of zero-rating programs in Brazil, which operate in contravention of network neutrality principles and by exploiting loopholes within the Marco Civil (Belli, 2018).

A wide array of research has revealed the volume of disinformation and misinformation that was circulating on WhatsApp in the buildup to the 2018 elections and the extent to which it skewed in the interests of Bolsonaro's campaign. Analysis undertaken by the *Guardian* newspaper in 2019, for instance, identifies that 42 percent of viral messages shared within right-wing chat groups constituted disinformation, while the same form of content in left-wing groups only reached 3 percent (Avelar, 2019). Another report published during the election campaign by a fact-checking organization showed that 86 percent of false content circulating on WhatsApp targeted the PT candidate Fernando Haddad (Macedo, 2018). Finally, Brazilian researchers Rafael Evangelista and Fernanda Bruno's (2019) analysis of the eight most-circulated pieces of visual disinformation revealed that all promoted anti-PT and/or pro-Bolsonaro themes.

The manner in which this material was created and circulated has also been carefully probed. During the election, investigative work by the journalist Patricia Campos Mello, published to explosive effect in the *Folha de Sao Paulo*, revealed that businesspeople connected to Bolsonaro were paying digital marketing firms to perform "mass blasts" on WhatsApp in contravention of electoral rules (P. Mello, 2018). The digital rights advocacy group Coding Rights later published a report on the role of disinformation in the Brazilian elections of 2018 and profiled several of the data brokers and digital and/or political marketing firms that played a prominent role in these activities. These included Brazilian firms such as Numbr Group but also a subsidiary of notorious international company, Cambridge Analytica (Coding Rights, 2018, p. 46). As Evangelista and Bruno (2018) make clear, even though the laws were changed in time for the 2018 election to permit the use of political advertisements online, the material being disseminated on WhatsApp did not in many cases correspond to official campaign advertisements. The end result of these efforts became apparent from the reaction of an observation team from the Organization of American States that described the scale and reach of disinformation during the 2018 election as "unprecedented" (D. Mello, 2018).

As has been widely observed, the technical architecture of WhatsApp, with its closed groups, pseudonymous participants, and end-to-end encryption, made monitoring disinformation—and any potential interventions by fact-checkers, regulators, or media organizations—extremely challenging (Nemer, 2021, Disentangling). Beyond the coded design, the social dynamics of WhatsApp in which users are unaware of the provenance of "sponsored" content (in a way that is more obvious on Facebook) and also the closed groups that engender greater relationships of trust can also facilitate the spread of disinformation. Ultimately, "Brazilian elections show how a surveillant structure was built on top of a group message service" (Evangelista & Bruno, 2018). Finally, and in a similar vein, Brazilian media studies researcher David Nemer describes the "human infrastructure of fake news" (2021, July 6) whereby in lieu of purely algorithmic amplification, Bolsonaro's disinformation campaign relied upon a pyramid structure of participants with an apex of professional content creators orchestrating the consumption of disinformation by the base.

Owing in large part to the opacity of the circuits of information on WhatsApp, it is impossible to know the extent of the contribution Bolsonaro's disinformation campaigns to his eventual election victory, although many observers consider it to be a significant factor in his gaining the presidency (Davis & Straubhaar, 2019). Certainly, the fact that once in office, Bolsonaro's administration continued to use the same strategies to cement its hold on power suggests that it considered digital disinformation a potent tool.

Again, although it is hard to attribute the source of disinformation that circulates online, analysis by Felipe Soares et al. (2021) identified a correlation between President Bolsonaro's misleading pronouncements on the COVID-19 virus and surges in disinformation on WhatsApp (p. 4), with the authors seeing fit to label WhatsApp as "Bolsonaro's firehose." Such was the extent of Bolsonaro's role in spreading COVID-19 misinformation that a congressional panel in 2021 recommended that he be charged with crimes against humanity (France 24, 2021).

The most direct link to Bolsonaro can certainly be established in the case of the so-called Office of Hate, an unofficial division of social media communication specialists housed within the presidential palace, that was first identified by the Brazilian newspaper *O Estadão* in the first year of the Bolsonaro administration (Melo, 2023). This team, according to João Ozawa et al. (2023), "engaged in government-funded computational propaganda, employing a combination of people and bots to shape discourse" using a variety of media platforms, including WhatsApp. This team promoted the government's agenda and attacked rivals online. An investigation by the Globo newspaper even revealed that the Bolsonaro administration was directing advertising funds for state enterprises like Petrobras to pro-Bolsonaro YouTube channels known as purveyors of fake news (Fantástico, 2020).

Public concern around the surge of information disorder in Brazilian society is evidenced in the Reuters Digital News Report (Newman et al., 2020), in which 84 percent of respondents expressed concern about blurred lines between fake and real in their online news content. This was the highest percentage of any of the surveyed countries. Growing awareness of the prevalence and implications of disinformation online likely played a role in catalyzing a flurry of activity around the topic in the Brazilian legislature from 2018 onward. The nonprofit investigative journalism collective *Agência Pública* recorded no less than twenty proposed laws claiming to combat the scourge of fake news by 2018 (Grigori, 2018). Many of these proposals include such punitive and troublingly vague measures as multiyear prison terms for circulating content that undermine "social peace or the economic order" (Freedom House, 2018) or requirements for users to register using government-issued ID (Lamensch, 2022).

Most recently, these disparate efforts coalesced into a single bill—the Brazilian Internet Freedom, Responsibility, and Transparency Law, colloquially known as the Fake-News Bill. Shorn of the most polemical provisions, many sectors of civil society, including notable digital rights groups, coalesced in favor of the new bill as it became a more general framework for social media governance (Tomaz, 2023) imposing requirements on platforms for identification of promoted content as well as joint platform liability for its publication, the release of regular transparency reports, public education on misinformation, compensation for journalistic content, and immediate removal of content that infringes the rights of minors.

The parallels with the Marco Civil are clear: a bill that was subject to intense pressure from economic sectors (although in this case, from platforms rather than telcos [Twitter blog, 2022]), a reversion from some quite extreme rights-infringing proposals, such as mandatory identification to more moderate rights-affirming ones; a well-intentioned bundle of measures that garnered support of digital rights groups despite doing little to substantively bolster a communication system that advanced public over private interests. Ultimately, like the Marco Civil, the fake news bill softened some of the rougher edges of exploitative practices while maintaining the same fundamental model that incentivizes harm. Indeed, an early proposal to ban data sharing between messaging apps and third parties, mirroring the EU's Digital Services Act, was struck from the bill owing to heavy pressure from US web platforms and the Globo Group (Tomaz, 2023). This analysis of the bill by the same scholar merits reproduction here:

> In the text, there are no attempts to make platforms operate under alternative economic conditions, either with more competition or with meaningful curbs on the profit motive. There is also no indication that policymakers might pursue this in any further effort. This option has also been completely absent from official statements by digital rights advocates, activists, and any other stakeholder involved in the discussion for more than one year. *In this bill, the public interest is explicitly subject to corporate commercial power, which should remain unchallenged.* (p. 263, emphasis added)

In sum, while the Marco Civil contained provisions that could have sanctioned the dissemination of false information online, its general failure to countenance systematic reform of digital communication in Brazil and its specific establishment of limited platform liability effectively enabled the deluge of disinformation that so polluted Brazil's public sphere in recent years.

The next aspect of digital disfunction that merits examination here, and that is directly related to how disinformation was so widely diffused in Brazil, as well as obvious shortfalls in the Marco Civil's protection of digital rights, is the prevalence of zero-rated mobile internet access.

Hero to Zero: Net Neutrality Exposed

One of the most contentious provisions within the Marco Civil, one that was defended by civil society organizations with as much vigor as it was attacked by the telecoms sector, was the safeguard for network neutrality. As I have argued doggedly through these pages, the energies invested in contesting network neutrality were not commensurate with its value as a digital right or as an impediment to profit maximization. From the former perspective, the principle of network neutrality is a fine one, *in principle*. Internet service providers should not be permitted to distort the flow of digital communication and information retrieval based on their own commercial imperatives. However, network neutrality is also a form of regulatory laissez-faire in terms of waving through concentrated market power and permits all manner of inequities to persist while forestalling more substantive efforts at reform. And for the telecoms sector, although network neutrality could stymie certain revenue streams if aggressively applied, the legal certainty implied by the Marco Civil, coupled with the insertion of a clause permitting freedom of business models, meant that it represented more of a speed bump than a cul-de-sac.

Indeed, the extent of the evasion of network neutrality by the telecoms sector in Brazil since the Marco Civil was regulated in 2016 is breathtaking. The means of that evasion was enabled principally by zero-rating. The term "zero-rating" refers to positive discrimination of mobile internet content through billing management (Hoskins, 2019). In practice, this means that access to certain web apps and services are prioritized for users by either offering them free, perhaps, in combination with a data cap for full internet access or with their own more extensive caps. Favored apps overwhelmingly include those owned by dominant platforms, such as Meta's WhatsApp. This contravenes the principle of network neutrality because the service provider makes certain online content more accessible than others and therefore undermines the ideal of an open and nondiscriminatory internet (Marsden, 2016). Although the boundaries are economic rather than technical, service providers are still playing the role of gatekeepers.

Zero-rating has become highly diffused across the global south. For instance, French researcher Toussaint Nothias (2020) shows that Facebook's zero-rated Free Basics program alone was available in fifty-one countries in Africa and Asia. In research I conducted in the year of the Marco Civil's regulation, one-third of all postpay plans offered by the four major mobile wireless carriers in Brazil included zero-rated services, while the figure was 76 percent for prepay (Hoskins, 2019), and earlier research from CETIC (Regional Study Center for the Development of the Information Society) found that fully 75 percent of all Brazilians used prepay plans that included some zero-rated component (2016).

According to the regulation of the Marco Civil in 2016 (Planalto, 2016), violations of network neutrality in Brazil should be addressed by a combination of Brazilian state bodies (Anatel, the telecoms regulator, and the consumer defense and competition authorities Senacon and Cade) under the direction of the Internet Steering Committee, CGI.br. However, zero-rating has continued unabated despite the provisions to safeguard network neutrality in the Marco Civil. The telecoms sector's bet that its gambit of freedom of business models would pay off has apparently been handsomely rewarded. Certainly in 2023, a coalition of Brazilian digital rights organizations (Coalizão Direitos na Rede) petitioned the Ministry of Justice to finally address zero-rating schemes in the context of their flagrant contravention of network neutrality (Urupá, 2023).

As well as violating net neutrality principles, zero-rating has an intimate connection to the scourge of digital disinformation. In 2019 WhatsApp had 136 million users in Brazil, making it the most popular communication platform in the country (Valente, 2019). According to research conducted by the Brazilian Chamber of Deputies in 2019, WhatsApp was the principal source of information for 79 percent of Brazilians (Valente, 2019), while data I gathered in 2017, examining every mobile plan offered by the four main mobile telecoms companies, 66 percent of all zero-rated plans featured WhatsApp (Hoskins, 2019). The connection here is not coincidental. As Tales Tomaz makes clear: "The dominant position of services such as Facebook and WhatsApp in Brazil is connected to a vast array of political economic affordances, such as the sizeable resources they have for agreements with telecoms and mobile operators for zero-rating" (2023, p. 263). Ethnographic research by legal anthropologist Jeffrey Omari (2020) also reveals the social significance and extent of WhatsApp use in Brazil and the degree to which that is enabled by zero-rating.

The nature of the zero-rating arrangements results in what Evangelista and Bruno (2019) refer to as "perceptive confinement." As Brazilians in lower-income classes are reliant upon mobile internet connections on prepay plans, they will often find themselves dependent upon WhatsApp—and other zero-rated apps—as their only information sources once their meager data plans are exhausted (Urupá, 2023). Indeed, data published by Anatel in 2020 shows that 55 percent of all mobile internet plans are prepay (Gomes, 2020). As the preceding section revealed, given that WhatsApp is one of the main channels of disinformation in Brazil, this can result in an even-higher exposure to distorted and misleading content and an inability to access information sources that might debunk it. As Brazilian telecoms scholar Luca Belli describes it, "fact-checking is too expensive for the average Brazilian" (2018).

In sum, the prevalence of zero-rated mobile internet access in Brazil and its relationship to disinformation demonstrate another stark failing of the Marco Civil, one that can be traced across two dimensions. The first is that by presenting network neutrality as a de facto first amendment for the internet, it came at the expense of market-based reforms. While admirable in principle, network neutrality helps to cement the status quo of Google's and Facebook's market dominance with all the well-documented harms that entails. The second failing lies in the specific manner of its legislation, which permitted an egregious loophole too readily exploited by the telecoms sector to allow zero-rating to proliferate in Brazil, in turn massively enabling the corruption of its public sphere. The next section turns to the broader issue of connectivity and concentration in Brazil and the legacy of the Marco Civil in addressing Brazil's stubborn inequalities in internet access.

Access Stymied: Concentration > Communication

In terms of establishing the obligations of the Brazilian state vis-à-vis the internet, the Marco Civil contained several provisions oriented toward boosting access. The first clause of article 27, for instance, dictates that all policies for digital culture should "promote digital inclusion," while the second demands they should also "look to reduce inequalities, especially between different regions of the country, in terms of access to ICTs" (Planalto, 2014). Most categorically, article 4 states that the first objective of internet use in Brazil should be "the right of Internet access for all."

The reality, however, of how those provisions actually promoted digital inclusion in Brazil represents another disappointment. The failure of the Marco Civil to include political economic measures has done nothing to alter the fact that the market for fixed and wireless internet provision in Brazil has remained stubbornly concentrated, while the goal of increasing connectivity has been left to market mechanisms, resulting in the status quo of economic over civic logics.

Indeed, state connectivity programs in Brazil have a consistent and inglorious record of not realizing their objectives. A fund for the universalization of telecoms connections in Brazil FUST (Telecoms Services Universalization Fund), created as part of the General Telecommunications Law passed in 1997 and based on diverted telecoms profits was never used (Bailey & Pretto, 2010, p. 267). The same law imposed on the state the obligation to "guarantee access to telecommunications to the whole population" (Planalto, 1997). Remaining in the pre–Marco Civil era, the National Broadband Plan (PNBL) was launched in 2010, but by 2014 its incentives were responsible for only 8 percent of new fixed broadband connections and 1 percent of wireless (Bruno, 2014).

Unfortunately, the provisions in the Marco Civil have done little to produce more positive outcomes. In 2017 the government announced a national connectivity plan to succeed the ill-fated PNBL and to unfreeze the FUST funds (BNAmericas, 2017, October 18), while the fact that this was then rebooted in 2023 as a "national policy for digital inclusion" by communications minister Juscelino Filho suggests it represented another chapter of disappointment (BNAmericas, 2023, June 15).

It must be noted that despite the limited role of the state and the failure to achieve its lofty connectivity goals, significant gains have been made in establishing broader levels of connectivity in Brazil. The research arm of the Brazilian Internet Steering Committee publishes an annual report on internet access in Brazil. Its 2017 edition reveals that 61 percent of all Brazilian households had some internet access (ICT Households 2017, 2017), while five years later that had increased to 80 percent (ICT Households 2022, 2022). The COVID-19 pandemic would likely have acted as a significant accelerant for connections, as school closures and domestic lockdowns would increase the need for internet access. However, other data reveals the limitations of market-led increases in internet access and the continuation of a stubborn digital divide that overlays Brazil's deep social stratification. The same source reveals that in 2021, 58 percent of Brazilians only accessed the internet through their phone, and only 13 percent of the two lowest social classes—D and E—had access to a personal computer at home (Mari, 2021). Dependence on mobile access leaves those citizens vulnerable to the perceptive confinement of zero-rating and unable to develop higher levels of digital literacy as well as to perform remote work, schooling, and acts of citizenship. Meanwhile, the fact that thirty-six million Brazilians did not use the internet at all in 2022 suggests that much work remains to be done on the connectivity file.

The continuation of these digital inequalities recalls the tension between massification and universalization that played out during the Marco Civil debates. The former can be achieved through market mechanisms but will inevitably leave behind those for whom instant profit cannot be realized, while the latter demands an active state working in the public interest to provide the necessary infrastructure and affordable and adequate service *for all.* As the communication-rights advocacy group Intervozes stated in 2020, "inequalities in access to services and the exercise of rights are not overcome by fragile agreements with the market" (Intervozes, 2020).

Stubbornly high concentration in the mobile wireless market in Brazil further reveals the fragility of relying on market logics to produce civic outcomes on the issue of access. Concentrated markets result in less competition, less accountability, and less consumer choice and higher prices (Faustino, 2022). An already concentrated market became even more so when four players were reduced to three in 2022 when the smallest incumbent, Oi, was acquired by its three larger rivals, TIM, Telefonica Brasil, and Claro (Reuters, 2022). The dangers implied by zero-rating are exacerbated through market concentration, and less competition on prices results in greater social exclusion. That such an anticompetitive merger was possible owed in large part to the reform of the General Telecommunications Law pushed through by the Bolsonaro administration in 2019. Those reforms not only green-lit Oi's acquisition but also liberated telcos from their obligations around universalization of service, the topic of great controversy among communication-rights groups (Direitos na Rede, 2021).

Meanwhile, at the content and application layers, the hegemony of US platforms and the high concentration among content and communication providers in Brazil remain unaltered. According to research Intervozes published in 2018, 63 percent of all apps downloaded from the Play Store and 75 percent of the apps downloaded from the App Store in Brazil were owned by one of the major platforms. Of those apps, 80 percent were of American origin, and only Globo and Palco MP3 were Brazilian. In terms of the most visited websites, twenty-three of the top thirty were content publishers (as opposed to banks or institutions, for example), and 70 percent of those were platforms. The remaining 30 percent comprised traditional media, such as Folha and Globo; content aggregators, such as UOL; and clickbait sites, such as *Blastingnews*. The only noncommercial site in the list was Wikipedia (Intervozes, 2018, pp. 164–65). The fact that Intervozes published this research under the banner of "Digital Monopolies" shows how much the landscape had changed in Brazil in terms of an understanding of the harms constituted by informational capitalism. During the Marco Civil process, the concerns of communication-rights and consumer-rights groups were focused almost exclusively on the dangers of state power and traditional media concentration.

The level of concentration has scarcely changed until now with the top 10 consumer-visited websites dominated by US-based platforms with the exception of Globo, UOL, and a Czech adult entertainment site. The next twenty comprise ten Brazilian sites; however, only one of those is a content website with a further four ecommerce, two banks, and three government websites (SimilarWeb, 2023, *Top websites*). The scenario for mobile apps by usage is even more extreme with only two Brazilian apps—one ecommerce and another financial services—in a top twenty comprising entirely US content platforms except for Swedish-owned Spotify (SimilarWeb, 2023, *Top apps*). That means that the arenas of speech, news, and culture online in Brazil are controlled by the most-powerful players within informational capitalism in Brazil: the US web platforms and the traditional media conglomerates. The implication of this degree of concentrated control is that the vast majority of communication that occurs online is subject to extractive and invasive behavioral data collection, and the circulation of news and cultural content is driven by commercial imperatives. Although hardly a unique state of affairs in a global context, the failure of the Marco Civil to promote the public interest provision of communication, its dogged promotion of network neutrality, and its blindness to the political economy of the internet in Brazil certainly bear some responsibility for them. The fact of this level of communicative control leads us to the next logical focus when surveying the state of digital rights in Brazil: freedom of expression online.

Content Immoderation Policies

The enactment of safe harbor rules as part of the Marco Civil was widely interpreted as a triumph for digital rights in Brazil and received as a boon by the web platforms. The conflation of safe harbors with users' freedom of expression online was unchallenged by digital rights groups (a position critiqued in previous chapters). Certainly, in the years following the Marco Civil's regulation in Brazil, the shortcomings of the synonymy of safe harbors and freedom of expression online were fully exposed. Not only were the protections afforded by limited liability exploited by web platforms to circulate disinformation and polarizing political content with near-abandon—especially during the 2018 presidential election—thus despoiling the public sphere but the vulnerabilities of Brazilians' freedom of expression online were also exposed by a number of other threats: repeated judicial shutdowns of communication platforms (premised, in fact, on provisions contained in the Marco Civil), pervasive content removal requests by politicians, and regressive legislative proposals under the Bolsonaro administration.

One of the driving ambitions for the architects of the Marco Civil within the Ministry of Justice was to avoid the shutdown of digital communication platforms by overreaching lower-court judges in Brazil. As one of those individuals stated pithily to me in interview, much of the support for the bill was because "our judiciary, our courts, started to break the internet" (Almeida, interview, 2018). The temporary shutdown of YouTube in 2007 was an infamous case in this regard. Depriving millions of Brazilian citizen-users of access to their preferred communication platforms was an obvious threat to freedom of expression. Unfortunately, the belief that the legal clarity offered by the Marco Civil would prevent such overreach proved to be misfounded.

During 2015 and 2016, four blocking orders were issued against WhatsApp by different judges in Brazil as punishment for the service's failure to comply with requests for information in criminal investigations (Freedom House, 2017). These service suspensions had legal basis in articles 11 and 12 of the Marco Civil, in which the Brazilian security services had codified their demands for information access from overseas-based platforms. One further order was issued against Facebook in 2016 (Internet

Lab, 2023). The disquiet caused by these events led to public hearings at the Brazilian Supreme Court in 2018, as well as draft legislative proposals, to try and prevent future excesses.

An ongoing repository of judicial blocking requests maintained by the Brazilian research group Internet Lab (2023) details only two further attempts at judicial blocks of online services—against Facebook in 2018 and Telegram in 2022—suggesting that the intervention of the Supreme Court was sufficient to deter the use of the Marco Civil as a mass digital gag. Although this was not the intention of its drafters, this was a predictable outcome of the Marco Civil's provisions accommodating the systemic needs of Brazil's security services.

In addition to the shutdown or threat thereof of entire communication platforms in Brazil, citizen-users also have had to contend with the piecemeal but systematic removal of individual pieces of content considered objectionable by Brazilian politicians. The phenomenon of politicians aggressively and self-interestedly policing the online public sphere certainly predated the Marco Civil. Indeed, this was a systemic threat to freedom of expression that the bill was supposed to address. By imposing the requirement of judicial intervention for content removal, article 19 of the Marco Civil would not only eliminate the tendency toward preemptive censorship on the part of the platforms but should also stymie the practice of powerful individuals and entities in Brazil wielding their influence covertly to have "undesirable" material vanish from the internet. However, structural weaknesses were engineered into the Marco Civil to meet the needs of the content-production sector and the Brazilian political class. The controversial inclusion of a carve-out for copyright-infringing content within article 19 meant that there remained ample scope for content removal that infringed freedom of expression. Similarly troubling was a provision that online content deemed damaging to "reputation, honor, and personal rights" could be attended to by specialist courts. And that is even before the prospect of court-mandated content removal being abused as a form of "judicial censorship" (Freedom House, 2013).

The Brazilian Association of Investigative Journalism (Abraji) operates a project called "CTRL+X," which monitors judicial content-removal requests initiated by politicians and political parties in Brazil. According to their data, in the six years prior to the Marco Civil entering into force in 2016, 862 such requests were submitted (all but 200 of them on the grounds of defamation and/or slander and/or offended honor), while in the following six years, 2017–22, the volume of requests increased by almost 50 percent to 1,216 (again, with only 200 submitted for reasons other than defamation, etc.) (Abraji, 2023). It should be noted that the 2018 presidential election was a particularly febrile period, with more than 500 attempts by politicians to remove information critical of them from the internet (with 50 percent of those requests granted by the attending judge). Again, more than 90 percent were submitted on the basis of offended honor, suggesting the significance of the loophole gouged into the Marco Civil (Abraji, 2018).

Zooming out to consider all state content-removal requests—including judicial, executive branch, consumer-protection agencies, and the like, as opposed to those initiated simply by a politician—the information presented by Google in its annual transparency report for Brazil provides another valuable metric for gauging the scope and scale of content removal in Brazil and the impact, if any, of the Marco Civil. Google's data shows that in the five years preceding the Marco Civil entering into force (Google only began collecting detailed records in 2011), the number of content-removal requests was 3,564. In the following five years, 2017–21, the number was 4,901, an increase of almost 38 percent (Google, 2023).

Of course, one cannot infer a causal relationship between these increases and the enactment of the Marco Civil's provisions on content removal, nor should one assume that those content-removal requests necessarily constitute an infringement of freedom of expression, as much of it may represent the good-faith suppression of libel or hate speech. Moreover, that all of the incidents cataloged by Abraji, as well as the vast majority of those disclosed by Google, are the result of judicial or court orders suggest that the provisions of the Marco Civil's article 19 are fulfilling a rights-affirming function by routing content-removal requests through a judicial filter and avoiding back channels (although the nature of the latter form means that their volume is impossible to monitor). One other major factor to consider is the arrival of Bolsonaro in the presidency, and the four years of his rule showed government-initiated content-removal requests that tended to be higher than nearly any of the previous four reporting periods (Google, 2023). Certainly, some of the policy initiatives pertaining to freedom of expression in Brazil that were launched under Bolsonaro stoked a climate of fear and repression.

One measure for the general deterioration of freedom of expression online in Brazil under the Bolsonaro administration comes in the form of Freedom House's "Freedom on the Net" score. It is assigned to every country on an annual basis based on metrics such as violations of user rights and obstacles to access. The average annual score in the four years preceding Bolsonaro's presidency was 69 and dropped 5 points to an average of 64 for those years Bolsonaro was president, 2019–22 (Freedom House, 2023). In a similar vein, the "World Press Freedom Index" maintained by Reporters without Borders, placed Brazil in the red zone (deemed "very serious") in

2021, the first time the country had sunk so low in the rankings for more than twenty years (Reporters without Borders, 2021).

As detailed above, the first iterations of the fake-news bill drafted under Bolsonaro's administration contained restrictive provisions, such as the criminalization of speech, that caused a threat to "social peace or to the economic order," as well as a requirement for social-media platforms to register using government-issued identification. Although the bill has seen many of its harder edges softened through congressional amendments and the subsequent election of a PT government, other measures betrayed the character of the Bolsonaro regime. A 2019 reform of the electoral code included prison sentences for anyone found guilty of uttering false accusations about a political candidate with the goal of damaging their candidacy (Lamensch, 2022), and members of Congress issued new proposals to extend penalties for honor offenses online (Freedom House, 2021).

The most controversial and well-publicized of Bolsonaro's efforts to reshape the internet policy landscape came in the form of efforts made in 2021 to weaponize the Marco Civil's court-order provisions for content removal for social media platforms. Under the proposed legislation, social media platforms would face legal penalties if they removed any content outside of a narrow list prescribed by the new law and that was mandated by a court order. That meant that even removing material that violated terms of service or other internal content policies would be forbidden (Archegas & Muñiz, 2022). Such free-speech extremism would meet the needs of Bolsonaro's *gabinete de odio* (office of hate) and create an environment conducive to the disinformation, hate speech, and harassment that served the president and his allies so well. The administration took to Twitter to project the official line that by adopting these measures, Brazil was "taking the global lead in defending free speech on social networks and protecting the right of citizens to freedom of thought and expression" (Lamensch, 2022). The reality, though, as Brazilians, João Archegas and Lucas Muñiz assert, was much different: "These proposals have a clear goal: shielding Bolsonaro and his friends from a Trump-style 'deplatformization'" (2022). Although in September 2021 Bolsonaro issued a presidential decree to enact these measures, they were overturned by the Supreme Court later that month (Freedom House, 2021).

In terms of how freedom of expression online fared in Brazil since the enactment of the Marco Civil, it seems clear that the bill did not constitute the bulwark its backers claimed. Indeed, in some key respects, provisions in the Marco Civil actively contributed to a backsliding in the state of free expression in Brazil. The platform-penalty clauses in articles 11 and 12 of the Marco Civil were invoked, or at least brandished, with alarming regularity, the platforms abused their limited liability to circulate harmful material, while the provision for court-ordered content removal was arguably overused and then reinterpreted by Bolsonaro in an attempt to engineer a state of free-speech maximalism conducive to his government's disinformation tactics. We would do well then to heed the warning of legal scholar Beatriz Kira (2023), in the context of exploring prospects for platform regulation in Brazil: "It is important to remember that once the bill becomes law, it will outlast the current government. The same tools meant to protect the rule of law could be misused by less democratic governments in the future" (2023).

A Sandbag against a Tsunami

Although the Marco Civil presented privacy as one prong in its conceptual trident, alongside network neutrality and freedom of expression, the protections actually afforded to Brazilian citizens were so tepid that one could scarcely expect anything other than a business-as-usual tsunami of private and state surveillance to ensue. Those privacy protections centered principally on: the inviolability of digital communication content (affording emails the same protections as physical mail); a requirement that government data requests be directed via court orders; and for platforms that user data could only be shared with explicit user consent, while users could also request the deletion of their data on terminating a subscription. Those brittle guardrails, however, were further undermined by additional clauses permitting the disclosure of metadata by platforms with any administrative authority, as well as prolonged data-retention requirements to assist law enforcement and IP-rights holders.

Although the volume of data collection conducted by web platforms in Brazil cannot be precisely qualified nor can the ensuing harm, we must note that at the time of writing, the latest data showed that 99 percent of all social media use occurs on platforms using behavioral advertising models—Facebook, Pinterest, Instagram, YouTube, and Twitter (now X) (Statcounter, 2023)—and that the social media user population in Brazil has increased from 96 million in 2015 to 152 million in 2023 (Data Reportal, 2023). It becomes a straightforward inference, therefore, that because there were no meaningful checks on the commodification of user data in the Marco Civil, the commercialization and manipulation of the online public sphere in Brazil increased considerably.

There is, of course, a similar degree of opacity with regard to the levels of state surveillance and the extent to which the Marco Civil may have limited or driven state appetite for the personal data of Brazilian citizens. However, in the same vein as the data published by Google on state content-removal requests, one highly visible metric for state data collection comes in the form of Facebook's annual transparency reports. These catalog all government requests for user-data disclosure, whether through legal process or emergency measures. Mirroring the Google report, Facebook's data show a dramatic upward trend in Brazilian government access requests. In 2016, the earliest available reporting period, there were 1,740 legal process requests, and by the close of the Bolsonaro administration in 2022, the number of requests had shot up to over 16,000 (Meta Transparency Center, 2023). Such numbers may, of course, suggest that the Marco Civil's provisions on data protection were working exactly as intended, by forcing state data requests through official legal channels. However, in the absence of knowing the volume of extrajudicial requests for user data—explicitly endorsed by the Marco Civil—and keeping in mind the Bolsonaro government's propensity for vigilantism and civic repression—as detailed in this section—these numbers reasonably suggest an alarming uptick in state surveillance.

Indeed, institutional and civil society recognition of the shortcomings of the Marco Civil's privacy provisions, coupled with pressure from noncompliance with the General Data Protection Regulation (GDPR) from the European Union, led to the eventual resolution of Brazil's General Law of Data Protection (LGPD) in 2018. Akin to the Marco Civil, this law was prefaced by two periods of public consultation in 2010 and 2015 and then several years of congressional debate, revision, and inertia.

The LGPD was developed, according to the Intervozes director Bia Barbosa, with the goal of "regulating the market for the massive and indiscriminate collection of citizen data and the treatment, disclosure and in many cases, sale, of this information" (Intervozes, 2018, p. 46). The law certainly introduced a number of positive developments. These included provisions on data portability, informed consent for data collection and treatment, special protections for children and adolescents, the principle of nondiscrimination, and the creation of an independent data-protection authority in 2022, the ANPD (National Data Protection Authority) (Grossman, 2022). All of these represent improvements for Brazilian citizens, for sure, in terms of managing their data privacy. However, across its sprawling sixty-five articles, the LGPD represents a continuum from the Marco Civil by doing nothing to directly confront the exploitative mechanics of data collection that undergird informational capitalism. Indeed, as well as implicitly endorsing the business practices of the platforms, the law does not contain any provision related to national defense or law enforcement, which produced a gaping hole to exploit for surveillance by all actors within the security state (Lemos, 2020).

Another parallel with the Marco Civil lies in the LGPD's failure to confront the behavioral advertising business model. Intervozes in its annual "Right to Communication" report in 2021, surveyed the first year and a half of the LGPD in the wild, and made several critical mentions of massive data breaches in Brazil that the law did nothing to prevent, and its enforcement authority did nothing to penalize (Intervozes, 2021). However, there is no mention of the ongoing harm caused by the surveillance business models of the web platforms. This blind spot was also conspicuous during the policy debates and advocacy around the Marco Civil and is, I have argued repeatedly, a structural weakness of the digital-rights paradigm.

That is not to say, of course, that the Brazilian state does not merit critical scrutiny. Data Privacy Research (DPR), a Brazilian CSO, uses "techno-authoritarianism" as its preferred term to describe "the processes of expansion of state power whose objective is to increase surveillance and control capacities over the population, by violating individual rights or significantly increasing the risks of violation of fundamental rights" (Data Privacy Research, 2023). Signs of such a phenomenon were much in evidence under the Bolsonaro regime.

A report released in 2020 by the same group catalogs a litany of privacy abuses that occurred in just that year. These included a decree issued by the Bolsonaro government that allowed government agencies to share citizen data without the citizen's consent, an agreement by the Brazilian Intelligence Agency (ABIN) and the Brazilian Federal Data Processing Service that would provide the former with the personal data of all driver's license holders in the country, in contravention of constitutional guarantees to confidentiality; the creation by the Ministry of Justice and Public Security of a dossier of public security personnel with "antifascist" sympathies; and hiring by the federal government of an independent contractor to monitor and classify journalists it deemed as oppositional (Data Privacy Research, 2020). This buccaneering approach to state surveillance and the disregard for privacy protocols were made explicit by Bolsonaro at a widely reported incident at a cabinet meeting in 2020, when he disparaged the state security services and claimed, "Information systems: mine works. Mine, particularly, works" (Lamensch, 2022). Another major development that demands mention and occurred a year earlier was the creation of the Citizen Base Registry (Soprana, 2019), which allowed for the creation of a unified database of citizen information, including biometric data, drawn from repositories of data across the Brazilian state. Such a centralization of citizen data was widely seen as deeply troubling given the explicitly neofascist president at the helm of the state (Dias, 2019).

Surveying the state of privacy rights in Brazil since the enactment of the Marco Civil thus highlights the woeful inadequacy of its data-protection provisions. The combination of the rising uptake in social media use coupled with the failure to address the platforms' insatiable appetite for user data meant that the exploitation and harm inherent in their business models only increased. For instance, the surge of disinformation circulating online in Brazil cannot be separated from the platforms' capacity to mine personal data to better target individual users. Meanwhile, the avowedly fascist characteristics of the Bolsonaro administration meant a more militaristic approach to state surveillance, greater centralization of citizen data, and much more user-data disclosure from platforms. The LGPD, Marco Civil's successor as guarantor of privacy rights and a more comprehensive attempt to regulate the market for personal data in Brazil, did precious little to reverse these trends but instead just softened the ragged edges of dataveillance.

Building a "Dictatorship of the Like"

What was largely unanticipated at the time of the Marco Civil's development was a rising wave of far-right populism—that often overlapped with outright authoritarianism—and how that might impact the efficacy of digital rights. That political trend was both a general and a particular phenomenon, with Bolsonaro the local manifestation of a global tide. The provisions in the Marco Civil were ill-equipped for a right-wing authoritarian government in terms of being misused or ignored, while more broadly, the digital rights paradigm could not contend with the challenge of social media being used to stoke polarization and spread disinformation. Indeed, the emphasis on protecting the expressive capacity of citizen-users, while also ignoring the structural inequities of informational capitalism, meant that the digital rights paradigm actually facilitated those communicative pathologies of the far right. Where, for instance, is the boundary between protecting freedom of expression online and protecting against the diffusion of disinformation? While it might be overreaching to claim the existence of some new nexus of power between informational capitalism and an emergent far right, it would also be analytically negligent to ignore the extent to which the logics and mechanics of the former bolstered the political fortunes of the latter, and the implications of the far right's dizzying ascent for the fate of digital rights.

Although populism has long historical roots, accounts of the most recent rise of this radical right-wing version often begin with the seismic events of 2016: the election of Donald J. Trump to the presidency of the United

States and the Brexit referendum in the United Kingdom most notably but also electoral breakthroughs for far-right parties in Europe, such as the Alternative for Germany, and the continued regression of so-called illiberal democracies in Turkey, Hungary, and the Philippines. Although these are all discrete phenomena with diverse local factors at play—including many long-simmering social trends that have little directly to do with technology, such as declining trust in institutions and resentment at increasing wealth inequality—one similar theme that emerges from analysis of their emergence is the role played by social media.

Various accounts have shown how the affordances, design, and business models of social media platforms converge with the goals, tactics, and ideologies of far-right populist groups (Diamond, 2019; Deibert, 2019). These include four main factors: the speed and volume of digital communication and the design of social media interfaces facilitates the spread of disinformation, the architectures of social media create ideational echo chambers, the openness of networks renders them vulnerable to manipulation by bad actors, and the systematic collection of personal data allows for individuals and groups to be targeted with divisive messaging and repressed by authorities.

As a starting point, many studies have shown that the communicative dynamics and architecture of social media is highly conducive to the spread of false, misleading, and harmful information. The sheer volume of material circulating on social media networks and the finite attention and cognitive capacity of citizen-users create the conditions for false information to be shared unwittingly. For instance, the research of Filippo Menczer and Thomas Hills (2020) shows that ultimately, "information overload can alone explain why fake news can become viral," while the absence of contextual information in social media posts is also key (Wardle, 2020). There is also the aspect of human psychology, as an individual encountering a glut of information will tend to favor opinions and news that confirm preexisting beliefs, irrespective of its veracity (Deibert, 2019).

Then, in terms of the design of social media, that confirmation bias is exploited by platforms to "prioritize information in our feeds that we are most likely to agree with—no matter how fringe—and shield us from information that might change our minds" (Menczer & Hills, 2020). Also, as a research team from the University of Southern California has shown, "the reward structure of social media platforms" pushes users to indiscriminately share material in order to win recognition (Madrid, 2023). Finally, in terms of the way that the design of social media platforms promotes the diffusion of harmful content, one must also account for the way that humans are drawn to outrage like moths to a flame and how this psychology is exploited by algorithmic systems to keep users engaged for the maximum extent possible (Council of Europe, 2023).

Those factors provide an explanatory baseline for disinformation online that discounts ideology. What many studies have additionally shown is, and this was clearly the case of Bolsonaro in Brazil, that disinformation circulates more widely in right-wing or conservative communities and that right-wing parties and politicians make greater use of disinformation as a political tactic (Guess et al., 2019; University of Oxford, 2018). Right-wing populists have proven well equipped to exploit popular resentment of economic inequality, while the appeals of populists to emotion over reason and their spurious claims align with the perverted attention economy of social media. As Phillip Howard observes, "only one part of the political spectrum—the far right—is really the target for extremist, sensational and conspiratorial content" (University of Oxford, 2018). The overall significance is that the diffusion of disinformation and fake news helps to erode public trust in society, which provides the political conditions that enable far-right populists to flourish.

In a closely related phenomenon, similar psychological tendencies and communicative architectures promote the creation of echo chambers, especially within far-right political communities. The term refers to the phenomenon of like-minded individuals creating insular spaces of communication where they are not exposed to dissenting views (Jamieson & Cappella, 2008). Echo chambers are considered antithetical to the ideal of democratic communication in which competing ideas can be debated and perhaps reconciled. While the extent of echo chambers online is contested (Dubois & Blank, 2018; Ross et al., 2022), even dissenting voices converge with those who argue that the echo chambers are prevalent and problematic and that persons on the far right are more likely to be ensnared within them. As Yochai Benkler, Robert Farris, and Hal Roberts, researchers at Berkman Klein Center for Internet & Society, make clear in their landmark book on disinformation, "the right wing of the media ecosystem behaves precisely as the echo-chamber models predict—exhibiting high insularity, susceptibility to information cascades, rumor and conspiracy theory, and drift toward more extreme versions of itself" (2018, p. 73). Echo chambers contribute to social polarization, which once again produces the divisions and mistrust that right-wing populists can exploit.

Although the echo chambers theory hinges on the closures possible in social media communication, another point of convergence between far-right goals and social media design lies in the openness of social networks and their vulnerability to manipulation by bad actors. This takes the form of sock-puppet accounts promoting certain posts and the hijacking of trending themes (Wardle, 2020) and is notably perpetrated on behalf of authoritarian governments as well as far-right populist politicians (Deibert, 2019; Diamond, 2019).

In their authoritative annual report on computational propaganda, Bradshaw et al. of the Oxford Internet Institute refer to the situation as "industrialised disinformation," with eighty-one countries found to be engaged in organized manipulation of social media for political ends (2021). The researchers find that governments of these countries engage what they call "cybertroops," or "actors tasked with manipulating public opinion online" (p. 1). These activities include "the use of 'political bots' to amplify hate speech . . . the illegal harvesting of data . . . or deploying armies of 'trolls' to suppress political activism" (p. 1). While democratic societies are certainly not immune to such antidemocratic tactics, the list of those states that demonstrate high cybertroop capacity is dominated by authoritarian governments (p. 17). It is well known that the likes of Rodrigo Duterte in the Philippines and Bolsonaro in Brazil engage in the dark arts of employing cybertroops to harass their perceived political enemies. As per Benkler, Farris, and Roberts, "what makes decentralized networks so effective at circumventing established forms of control can also make them the vehicles of repressive mobs" (2018, p. 346), while the ensuing chill on the freedom of political expression of their opponents is precisely the desired effect for the cybergenerals.

The last point of convergence between the business models of social media and the rise of the global far right hinges upon the systematic data collection that is intrinsic to the way such platforms generate revenue. The collection, analysis, and packaging of the personal data of all platform users—far exceeding that required to operate the platform effectively—is sold to advertisers and data brokers and is used to microtarget individuals and serve them with what are expected to be high return-on-investment advertisements. In addition to advertisers and as was revealed vividly in press reports about Cambridge Analytica's role in the Brexit referendum, firms offering "computational propaganda as a service" number upwards of sixty globally, according to Bradshaw et al. (2021). These groups play a major role in the disinformation ecosystem, one that, as explained in the points above, favors far-right political groups. Moreover, in those societies with authoritarian governments—or simply those with dictatorial tendencies and a disregard for citizen privacy, such as the Bolsonaro regime—the fine-grained data collected by the platforms provide the means to identify and target perceived enemies of the regime (Diamond, 2019, p. 22).

A final addendum worth making here is the arena of policy, in which those far-right populists who have won office attempt to further harness the operations of social-media platforms to advance their political goals. The efforts of Bolsonaro in this regard have already been well detailed in this chapter. Another approach is for populists to rail against Big Tech in public but to actually stall the legislative agenda in the knowledge that the status quo best serves their needs. Trump was an exemplar in this regard as he harnessed popular sentiment against the platforms but actually advanced no policy initiative of any substance (Napoli & Royal, 2022). Duterte is another example: he occasionally accuses platforms of interfering in his agenda (Reuters, 2020) but actually leaves them very lightly regulated so as to continue to exploit their reach and affordances.

Through all of these four points of convergence, we can see that the dominant digital rights paradigm is not capable of safeguarding a digital communication environment that is conducive to democracy nor even to advance the more modest goal of protecting individual rights to freedom of expression and privacy. Enacting protections for freedom of expression as a negative right, particularly, by treating safe harbor rules for platforms as an acceptable proxy for free expression, does nothing to address the deluge of disinformation, hate speech, and algorithmic manipulation that distort digital communication for billions of users. In similar fashion, individual privacy rights are not fit for purpose to mitigate the harms generated by the industrial-scale collection, sorting, and commodification of personal information. In sum, the logics of informational capitalism harnessed to the goals of far-right populists and authoritarians is inimical to democracy. And the congruence between social media design and the emergence of the far right should not be considered happenstance. As Benkler et al. comment: "The major threat to the internet as a democratizing force is not the abuse of the system but its intended use" (2018, p. 345).

Conclusion

Surveying the many ways that the digital rights of the Marco Civil have failed to secure the internet as a medium of democratic communication in Brazil or even to realize their first-order objectives of protecting freedom of expression online, data privacy, network neutrality, and access to the internet is a dispiriting task. However, it is also an essential one. Although the election of Bolsonaro to the presidency of Brazil was a destabilizing, radical, and largely unforeseen political development, the argument developed in this book is that even under standard operating conditions, the Marco Civil was congruent with the logics of informational capitalism and therefore unfit for the task of safeguarding an internet conducive to the exercise of citizenship for Brazilians.

The principal shortcomings of the Marco Civil, all further exposed during the Bolsonaro presidency, are manifold: establishing limited liability for platforms already created the conditions for a flood of disinformation and hate speech even before Bolsonaro and his enablers poured fuel on the flames; network neutrality already smoothed the path for platform dominance even before Brazilian telcos flooded the market with discriminatory and disinformation-enabling zero-rating mobile plans; the right to internet access for millions on the wrong side of a stubborn digital divide was already dependent upon market largesse even before the mobile wireless market became even more concentrated, and platforms and media conglomerates tightened their grip on the content and application layers; freedom of expression online continued to be threatened by judicial shutdowns of communication services, while government content removal premised on the Marco Civil actually increased; and, finally, on the topic of privacy, government data-disclosure requests grew significantly, while the Marco Civil's limited data-protection provisions did nothing to withstand a massive increase in platform data extraction. Moreover, all of these flaws can be cataloged even before one accounts for the corrosive impact of the ascent of far-right populism in Brazil spearheaded by Bolsonaro.

It is also important though to recognize that the Marco Civil was shaped in large part by a global paradigm of digital rights that manifested itself in other parts of the world. As a framework of digital rights, the Marco Civil is not unique in its failure to confront the many threats represented by informational capitalism. Therefore, part of the task of the concluding chapter to this book is to explore the various ways that the digital rights paradigm has developed since the passage of the Marco Civil and to reflect on what a more effective buttress against informational capitalism might look like.

Conclusion

If you consider fake news, how divisive
Brazilian society is with regard to political
discussions in the Internet, somehow it
has lost on the way. . . . Maybe we had a
romantic moment with the Marco Civil
. . . and now we're facing a dire reality.
—Guilherme Almeida

As the former Ministry of Justice chief of staff muses in the epigraph of this chapter, the failure of the Marco Civil to directly confront the harms caused by informational capitalism has returned to haunt Brazil. The critique developed through these pages is that as a bill of digital rights, the Marco Civil was of a piece with the logics of informational capitalism and saw its civic potential severely constrained by the material and discursive powers of the system's most powerful actors. Moreover, the composition and the significance of the Marco Civil can only be properly understood within the context of Brazil's status at the periphery of global capitalism. Certainly, in the years since the law was regulated in 2016 and as the previous chapter attests, numerous developments in Brazil have underscored what limited protections the Marco Civil represents for Brazilian citizens qua internet users.

The election of Lula da Silva and the return of the Workers' Party to the helm of government in 2023 offers hope of a brighter day for communication rights in Brazil. The appointment of a special adviser on digital rights, as announced by Lula's new Ministry of Justice in December 2022

(Cruz, 2022), would have been unthinkable under the previous president, for instance. However, while a PT administration may avoid the egregious rights violations seen during the Bolsonaro presidency, the scourge of far-right sentiment abounds in Brazil, and Bolsonaro may have been vanquished, but he has not vanished. Moreover, the Marco Civil was crafted with only a veneer of civic value by a PT-led government, while numerous opportunities for substantive media reform have been squandered by PT administrations over the years. Ultimately, irrespective of the ideological hue of the government of the day, only a Marco Civil—or its successor—premised on different conceptual foundations could really make a difference for the communication rights of Brazilians.

This reflection does bring up the question: with a Marco Civil differently conceived, could Brazil be facing a different reality with regard to the harms imposed by informational capitalism and its status at the periphery of it? Quite possibly. As indicated at various stages in this book, alternative visions of digital rights were espoused in Brazil during the Marco Civil's public consultation exercises. The Brazilian Pirate Party articulated a detailed and clear vision for a digital rights framework premised on principles of public service and infrastructural and political economic reform of the internet: a direct confrontation, in other words, with the logics of informational capitalism. However, these ideas existed outside of the accepted common sense for digital rights, they did not "hew to a particular set of terms" and were promoted by an actor exogenous to the acceptable policy community (Newman, 2016, p. 26). Accordingly, they were discounted.

Of course, the ills associated with online disinformation, commodification, surveillance, and hate speech do not exist in isolation from Brazil's many other social, political, and economic challenges. However, if the public service provision of digital media had been contemplated within the Marco Civil, if privacy had been conceptualized as a collective good rather than something to be mitigated through individualized "protections," and if the interests of internet and media companies were not conceived as an acceptable proxy for the digital rights of Brazil's citizens, then I contend that Brazil might well have begun to establish a digital media system that bolstered rather than undermined its democracy.

Within the state, too, proposals were made to address some of the infrastructural dimensions of Brazil's peripheral status, within the policy discourse of data sovereignty. These included a national email system, data localization, and new submarine cables. Although obscure and problematic agendas lay behind some of these ideas, they collectively represent the kind of (infra)structural reforms that could start to reprogram the exploitative circuits of accumulation underpinning informational capitalism.

As quoted in the conclusion to chapter 4, Lula lamented the failure to enact media reform as his greatest regret from his time in office. The concentration of ownership, commodification of culture, and control over communication acutely evident in Brazil's media system all played a large role in his dubious corruption charges and the ensuing legislative coup against his successor, Dilma Rousseff. In that light, the Marco Civil represents a sorry continuation of squandered opportunities to enact a more just, equitable, and democratic communication environment for Brazil.

A "Techlash" Tempered

Brazil does not of course exist in a microcosm: a so-called techlash—popular awareness of the destructive impacts of platform power and accompanying calls for reform—has emerged in response to myriad conjoined factors (Smith, 2018). The question of platforms accepting responsibility for the harm caused by the content they circulate is chief among them. A deluge of disinformation, extremist propaganda, revenge porn, trolling abuse, racist rhetoric, and fake news surge daily through the networks of YouTube, Facebook, and X. The destructive impacts for democracy and social justice have been keenly observed. The furor over Cambridge Analytica's furtive access to Facebook user data and its attempt to manipulate millions using highly targeted "dark ads" during the 2016 US presidential election and the UK Brexit referendum represent just the most conspicuous such episodes (Cadwalladr & Graham-Harrison, 2018).

The immense size and market power of the major technology companies have also been subjects of great concern. The concentration of platform ownership enables tax evasion, anticompetitive behavior against smaller companies, systematic privacy violations, a vacuum of political accountability, and near-monopolistic control over vast domains of digital activity. As Tim Wu declared pessimistically of the concentrated power of Big Tech, if left unaddressed, "these are end-states. I don't see what dislodges their dominance, at least not in our lifetimes" (Patel, 2018).

Thus have the harms caused by the concentration and control of informational capitalism moved out of the shadows to become matters of lively public debate. Legislators and regulators around the world have certainly taken note, with proposals to address platform power being debated in jurisdictions throughout the European Union and North America.

What is apparent from these legislative proposals is that the paradigm of digital rights that was dominant during the development of the Marco Civil—premised on a trident of network neutrality, digital-data protections, and freedom of online expression—has lost some its legitimacy as a means to safeguard internet users qua citizens from harm, or in creating anything that resembles a democratic medium of communication. Network neutrality is a foundational principle for protecting access to information, innovation, and expressive rights, but it does almost nothing to mitigate the commodification, concentration, and commercialization of the internet. Safe harbors as a proxy for freedom of expression are a fine legal principle in theory but in practice have actually enabled platforms to better profit from the flow of toxic content online. Finally, individual data protections in the context of pervasive surveillance and commodified data relations represent little more than a sandbag against a tsunami. The deficiencies of these measures as civic safeguards are detailed in the critique here, and implicitly at least, this appears to have permeated mainstream thinking on how to address the harms of platform power.

Indeed, the techlash has seen the paradigm of digital rights characterized by individualist, technical fixes premised on protecting the expression, creativity, and freedom of users, seemingly superseded by a slate of more "muscular," interventionist measures. Enacting greater content liability is an area of concerted focus. The fact that in the United States, the birthplace of the "light touch" internet policy paradigm, proposals to reform section 230 (the hallowed and original liability protection for web publishers) have garnered bipartisan support are strong signs that safe harbors are no longer synonymous with users' freedom of expression.

In other developments, in 2017 Germany passed the controversial Network Enforcement Act (NetzDG) that imposes stricter takedown requirements on platforms for unlawful content with financial penalties for noncompliance. Similar proposed moves by other European countries paved the way for the European Union to implement the Digital Services Act (DSA) in 2023, seen by many as the most ambitious effort yet to hold platforms more responsible for hosting harmful content, as well as imposing additional restrictions on ad-targeting (Flew & Martin, 2022). Indeed, in terms of user privacy, the EU's landmark GDPR, adopted in 2018, broke new ground by mandating opt-in for tracking and data portability. This framework of data-protection measures provided the template for a slew of similar laws around the world at the level of the nation-state in the cases of Brazil's General Law of Data Protection or Canada's Consumer Privacy Protection Act but also at the subnational level in the cases of California and Virginia.

A surge of "neo-Brandeisian" initiatives designed to address the market power of platforms has also been observed. The EU's Digital Markets Act (DMA), for instance, attempts to mitigate the gatekeeping power of platforms by mandating interoperability and transparency. By using antitrust rules to impose operational obligations upon—as in the DMA—or even a partial breakup of the major platforms, the rationale of advocates is that competition and accountability would be enhanced within a market comprising more, smaller service providers (Wu, 2018).

Finally, the fate of journalism has also been an animating feature of several notable pieces of platform regulation. Once again, the EU blazed the trail with its 2019 copyright directive that prevented platforms from displaying unlicensed content from publishers. In 2021, the Australian government advanced the publishers-versus-platforms frame by passing the News Media and Digital Platforms Mandatory Bargaining Code, designed to address the conjoined challenges of platform gatekeeping power, the monopolization of digital advertising revenue, and the crisis of sustainable journalism (Flew & Martin, 2022). This model has since been studied by many other jurisdictions, notably, in Canada with its highly contested Online News Act.

An emphasis on digital rights has not, of course, been entirely erased. New digital rights advocacy groups continue to be founded: the Digital Rights Centre in Canada, Digital Rights Watch in Australia, and the Cities Coalition for Digital Rights have all emerged since 2016. The COVID-19 pandemic also had a galvanizing effect in terms of underscoring the importance of the right to internet access as well as pitting citizen privacy against the demands of government surveillance. Indeed, although digital constitutionalism should not be considered reducible to digital rights, the literature on the topic emphasizes the importance of rights charters as part of any broader move toward both imposing checks on power and protecting fundamental rights for citizens online (Celeste, 2022; De Gregorio & Radu, 2022; Gill et al., 2015). As Edoardo Celeste (2022) argues, digital constitutionalism refers to any initiative that translates the values of constitutionalism into the digital age. It can be applied to a variety of frameworks designed to protect an array of fundamental freedoms, encompasses a broad range of actors and institutions, and is therefore compatible with even avant-garde interpretations of digital rights (p. 112).

The European Union is considered to be a paradigm of digital constitutionalism in its policymaking (De Gregorio, 2022) and its recent landmark acts, the DSA and DMA, combine a stated commitment to protecting freedom of expression and privacy with more direct checks on the exercise of power by platforms. However, the concurrent emphasis on digital sovereignty might lead one to presume that the real goal of digital constitutionalism for the European Union is in protecting the continent's tech sector rather than the rights of its citizenry. Another bastion of digital constitutionalism, the United Nations Educational, Scientific, and Cultural

Organization (UNESCO), issued an Internet for Trust project designed to guide platform regulation worldwide and comprises five principles. Three of them stipulate that regulation should be "rights-based," multistakeholder, and open and transparent, a clear continuation of the values of the digital rights paradigm (Celeste, 2022).

Overall, however, it is evident that the center of policymaking gravity has shifted from digital rights to more-interventionist forms of platform regulation. These measures do address some of the blind spots of the dominant digital rights paradigm, manifested in a particular form in the Marco Civil: agnosticism to the political economy of informational capitalism and a failure to consider structural reforms to the business models of its most powerful sectors. These measures constitute a proportionate reaction to the increased power and harms of informational capitalism but retain the gulf between problem and response that rendered the previous digital rights paradigm impotent.

Increasing content liability for platforms is a necessary development. However, the mind-boggling volume of material being published and circulated online—as well as any failure to check the incentives and means for spreading harmful content—means that even with automated systems, effective content moderation is rendered a Sisyphean task, just as likely to silence marginalized voices as it is to stem the flood of disinformation. Moreover, the levels of fines for noncompliance considered by the likes of the EU's DSA or Canada's proposed Online Harms Act are simply inadequate in the face of the massive profits generated by platforms.

That same chasm between regulatory fine and platform revenue exists in the case of new privacy frameworks, such as the GDPR (in which the maximum available fine is 4 percent of global revenue). Moreover, despite the fanfare heralding its enactment, the GDPR as global privacy template has not ushered in a brave new world of robust data protection: perhaps no great surprise when it is described as "the most lobbied piece of legislation in EU history," with Google spending 3.5 million euros in one year alone (Renieris, 2023, p. 51). The model of informed consent premised on pop-up windows has led to more consent fatigue than any meaningful check on datafication (Herrle & Hirsh, 2019), while the value of imposing transparency requirements on algorithmic decision-making systems presumes a citizen has any awareness that their "data double" has passed through such black-box processes. This requirement of a citizen being aware that their rights are being violated, as well as channeling any potential for redress at the level of the individual rather than the collective, are, of course, defining weaknesses of the digital rights paradigm. Finally, the costs of compliance with new data-protection frameworks are borne more heavily by smaller service providers leading potentially and perversely to even-greater market consolidation (Doctorow, 2019).

Even the structural reforms contemplated by the recent wave of "hipster antitrust" do not constitute a meaningful check on platform power. Not only have such proposals remained frozen in the ideational realm but on a conceptual level but they also ignore the commercial underpinnings of our digital communication and/or information system. As per Pickard, "Facebook represents a capitalism problem, not just a monopoly problem" (2022, p. 31).

Significantly, in most of its most celebrated iterations, this wave of platform regulation also retains a myopic focus upon the harms caused by informational capitalism within the system's core. These are indisputably real and measurable, but they ignore the even-greater damage wrought at the periphery: amplified ethnic discord contributing to massive violence, such as in Myanmar (Stevenson, 2018); a toxic legion of trolls, bots, and disinformation marshalled by tyrants from the Philippines to Iran (Deibert, 2020); and attempts to manipulate elections in Brazil, Bolivia, and India, among many others. Recent developments within the digital rights movement also continue to exhibit a faux-universalism. Research on a recent edition of the RightsCon conference shows that approximately half of all digital rights organizations boasting a global remit were registered as nonprofits in the United States (Grover, 2022). As Nothias notes, "digital rights activism mostly relies on institutional support with Euro-American funding, where corporate capture lurks around the corner" (2022).

The reforms catalyzed by the techlash ultimately remain deeply inadequate. While they fail to countenance the inequities and exploitations inherent to informational capitalism on a global scale, while they continue to imagine data as a commodity rather than a collective good, while they regulate rather than abolish pervasive surveillance systems, while they ignore the commercialization of online space, and while they fail to imagine a civic-valued, public-oriented alternative to proprietary platforms, they simply fail as civic safeguards. As John Nathan Anderson notes grimly, "playing by the rules of a strictly neoliberal paradigm will unfortunately lead to more of the same" (2013, p. 209).

In essence, the responses to the harms caused by informational capitalism from policymakers, the mainstream media as well as repentant figures from within the technology sector have converged on the notion that we can "step aside and let the more enlightened forces of capitalism fix the problem" (Couldry & Mejias, 2019, p. 187). Meanwhile, voices that call for decommodified data relations, rethinking advertising as the underpinning of the internet, and recasting social networking and search as public utilities remain muted at the margins. As in the case of the Marco Civil, the Pirate Party represents one such actor on the global stage that promotes information justice outside of the digital rights paradigm. As evidenced in the Swedish chapter's election manifesto in 2022 and echoing their Brazilian counterparts, the Pirate Party call for the public provision of digital infrastructure, and an end to the commodification of data relegates them to the margins of the debate (Piratpartiet, 2022). As Russell Newman pointedly observes in the context of the US net-neutrality debates, a form of processing bias is at play whereby "as long as one pursued the debate in these terms, one mattered; when one deviated, one ceased to be seriously considered" (2019, p. 75).

The lessons of the Marco Civil detailed in this study reveal quite starkly that *any concession to informational capitalism negates a civic outcome.* As the system of commodification, surveillance, and control is permitted to continue unabated, thus will the harms inflicted upon our democracies persist. As we grapple with our response to platform power, the stakes now are simply too high to permit the shortcomings of this Magna Carta for the web to be repeated. For that and other reasons, there is a renewed urgency in understanding how and why the digital rights of the Marco Civil failed to achieve their civic potential. This was the overarching inquiry orienting this research, and the contributions generated by interrogating this are addressed in the following section.

Ultimately, this account helps us to recognize how and why the power-brokers of informational capitalism shape digital rights to their advantage, the nature of the material and discursive power wielded by them, the perils of treating digital rights as a matter of consumption, the way dominant discourses silence marginal voices, and the importance of properly contextualizing the periphery. This account presents a cautionary tale but also one in which we can glean insights that could guide more meaningful interventions into informational capitalism. A cause also then, for hope.

Contributions

Analyzing Informational Capitalism

The scale of informational capitalism—from its application of core technologies to its discursive legitimation and global political economy—challenges the scope of any siloed analysis. One of the principal contributions attempted in this book was to propose an analytical framework for informational capitalism that accounts for the sweep of its systemic functions. I have argued in these pages that informational capitalism needs to be understood in terms of the logics that impel the system "forward in its flight into the future" (Dyer-Witheford, 2015, p. 188), the mechanics and dynamics that account for its granular texture and tensions, the zones that constitute its uneven global political economy, and the discourses that legitimate its functions and serve as a corollary to its material power.

More specifically, by employing a wide-angle lens capturing the broad range of actors that comprise informational capitalism, including the media and telecoms sectors and state actors, I address one of the principal blind spots in recent political economy and critical media studies scholarship: the narrow focus on web platforms and data extraction (Couldry & Mejias, 2019; Srnicek, 2017; Zuboff, 2019). Similarly, another important omission within recent scholarship on informational capitalism that is addressed in my framework is a dearth of systematic efforts to conceptualize the zonal geography of informational capitalism, to relate the periphery to the core.

Meanwhile, effective analyses and policy interventions around digital rights must account for the discourses that legitimate informational capitalism. How a concept like network neutrality is discursively constructed, and the way it is defined and the meanings assigned to it shape the possible regulatory and policy decisions made about it. Discourse is thus *constitutive of media policy* (Lentz, 2013). Meaningful reform will not occur through claims for freedom or innovation, for instance. Freedom is perilous conceptual terrain on which to stake any claim for digital rights, owing to the way that as a signifier, freedom has been usurped by the forces of capital. Much-surer footing can be found atop justice, equity, and democracy. These are the signifiers that are grounded in a social critique of capitalism; they can be used to justify substantive reforms that could actually secure civil rights and lack the long history of discursive colonization by capitalism evident in the tenets of the digital discourse.

Discourses, moreover, are not immutable; they are contested, evolving, constitutions of knowledge, meaning, and power. The discourses that legitimate capitalism in the face of future calls for reform will not be the same as those I traced here. However, they will not arrive out of the ether and will share some characteristics and lineage with the digital discourse examined in detail in this study. Similarly, capitalism itself is not static; it undergoes periodic sea changes in response to technological, political, and cultural developments. However, the next iteration of capitalism will not represent a rupture but, instead, a series of continuities, as the inherent logics of commodification and control are realized through a new set of mechanics, built upon those identified here. The sectors of informational capitalism analyzed in this framework will likely evolve rather than disappear, and the ensuing dynamics will reflect that evolution. Finally, as the recent rise of China into the core of informational capitalism demonstrates, the zonal geography of capitalism will shift but not vanish.

Ultimately, by demonstrating the coherence between the dominant paradigm of digital rights and the systemic logics of informational capitalism, I have revealed that not only are alternate approaches desperately required but also that to a large extent such pathways already exist but remain untrodden. In order to establish the internet as a medium of communication that nourishes rather than corrodes democracy, then the unfulfilled promise of proposals that privilege the public over the proprietary, collectivism over the individual, and the citizen over the consumer—such as the Civil Society Declaration from the 2003 Tunis World Summit on the Information Society (WSIS) summit—shows the way.

This tracing of digital rights was, moreover, a vital endeavor for the specific purposes of this study because it revealed how the measures that comprise the Marco Civil were shaped by discourses of long standing that can be traced back to the emergence of informational capitalism. This is significant because it reveals the extent to which the conceptual trident of the Marco Civil (one shared by many other digital rights charters)—network neutrality, freedom of online expression, and digital privacy—were compromised from the outset and could never constitute a meaningful check on the harms of informational capitalism.

Lessons from the Marco Civil's Torturous Passage

Given the high public profile of the Marco Civil and its presumed status as a template for digital rights frameworks in other jurisdictions, it is essential to establish a fulsome account of how this law came to pass, to illuminate some of its unheralded aspects, and to challenge some of its accompanying myths.

The contributions of the Brazilian Pirate Party presented an alternative and much more substantive vision of what digital rights could mean in Brazil. Its vision of digital rights was broadly aligned with the notion of "information justice" (Karpinnen & Puukko, 2020) and was premised upon collectivist principles, broader social justice concerns, and structural reforms to the internet's infrastructure and political economy. This is an important revelation because by virtue of existing outside of it, the Pirates' manifesto helps to make visible the dominant paradigm of digital rights, also showing that alternative visions were articulated at the time by local actors directly involved in the Marco Civil process.

Analyzing the origins of the Marco Civil—notably the public consultation, the blueprint provided by the decálogo, the interpretive community constituted by the bill's architects, and the multistakeholder input—shows that much of the Marco Civil's acclaimed democratic legitimacy was ill-deserved and, in fact, served to obscure the many ways in which the democratic value of digital rights were circumscribed. Similarly, a systematic analysis of the corporate consultation inputs into the Marco Civil casts a light onto the competing tangle of economic interests that delimited the bill's civic potential.

Civil society organizations played a pivotal role in the passage of the Marco Civil, and it is therefore essential to understand how and why this influence was brought to bear. These constitute some of the granular context for the Marco Civil's passage and challenge the assumptions of its universality, deriving as they do from Brazil's status at the periphery. One key takeaway from this analysis is that CSOs should be wary of marriages of convenience with platforms: the benefits of digital rights for technology and media companies should not be seen as a win-win but, instead, a mutually exclusive proposition.

Finally, carefully tracking the corporate maneuvers and political economic configurations that prefigured all of the substantive changes to the constitution of digital rights in the Marco Civil correspond to the dynamics of informational capitalism identified in my analytical framework. Such granular analysis provides a vital layer of understanding to appreciate—and crucially to anticipate—the agendas and power relationships enmeshed in each digital civil right.

Charting the Periphery

Rather than assume that informational capitalism will have uniform effects across the globe and then try to account for any divergence, this book was written from the premise that sociocultural, political economic differences are essential to understand the impact of the system in distinct contexts. In keeping with this premise, I have consistently foregrounded the significance of Brazil's status at the margins of global capitalism in terms of the constitution and contestation of digital rights and their social significance.

Digital rights are most often presented as frameworks with explicitly universal scope. The analysis of the Marco Civil presented here offers a corrective to that approach as it emphasizes the many social, cultural, and political economic contingencies of digital rights that must be accounted for in order to be both culturally appropriate and legislatively viable.

In regards to the way that network neutrality was contested in Brazil as a digital civil right, for instance, one can observe numerous key contextual differences with other societies around the world and, particularly, in informational capitalism's core. The low social value of innovation, the challenge of enlisting public engagement for a technical policy issue, the fraught status of American web platforms engaging in issue advocacy in Brazil, and the economic significance of zero-rating are all particularities that enhance not only our appreciation of the Marco Civil but might also contribute to better understanding similar issues in other peripheral contexts. Without this awareness, academic analyses and policy proposals are rendered tone deaf. More broadly, I have emphasized that the periphery of informational capitalism is a distinct analytical entity with particularities that must be accounted for when surveying the exploitations of and resistances to the system, and especially when examining the formation of communication policy and digital rights. This is an urgent issue given the growing awareness of the egregious harms wrought by informational capitalism at the margins of the system.

Getting Here and the Path Still to Tread

I have certainly struggled with the perceived churlishness of criticizing digital rights, in general, as well as the efforts of the civil society organizations that advocated tirelessly for the Marco Civil, in particular. Network neutrality, for instance, represents a quandary insofar as it is a prerequisite for the internet to function as an open, accessible, and innovative medium of communication and repository of knowledge. However, as argued in these pages, it is also deeply compromised as a digital right and serves other contradictory ends that erode the internet's civic potential. In a similar fashion, I have also analyzed with a critical lens the actions of CSOs in the context of the Marco Civil. From my discussions with individuals at these organizations, I am aware that they championed the Marco Civil in the face of seemingly insurmountable odds and were willing to confront powerful adversaries in their quest to see the bill passed into law. Given that I recognize their good faith actions, I must also acknowledge that it has sometimes been a challenge to critique what I consider to be the inadequacy of the Marco Civil and the misdirected efforts to promote it.

That critique of digital rights represents a diagnosis. Therefore, the logical progression is to develop a prescription; a framework of digital rights that does more than just mitigate harm but that can actively harness the tremendous potential of digital information and communication technologies to contribute to social justice and democracy. Although I point to some of the characteristics of such a framework—collectivist, positive, civic, and adaptable to diverse social contexts—its precise composition represents the looming unanswered question of this text. Sadly, such an ambitious undertaking was beyond the remit of this study, but I hope the insights from these pages may contribute to its realization.

Finally, I am aware that I have succeeded in telling the story of the Marco Civil and its passage only through the actions of organizations and the perspectives of the accomplished individuals embedded within them. There is also, of course, a story from below that needs to be told, from the perspective of the millions of internet users qua citizens in Brazil whose voices were not heard, as it is their experience that ultimately (dis)qualifies the Marco Civil as a set of civic safeguards.

This quote from political economist Matthew Crain from the introduction to this study merits a bookend here: "The point of critical analysis is not to theorize the domination engendered by capitalism, *but to clarify its dynamism in order to support and work toward forms of intervention*" (2013, p. 254, emphasis added). Responding to this clarion call, the most urgent research agenda that could be built out of this book is to create a web of connections between the multiple points of resistance to the systemic injustices and exploitations of informational capitalism.

As stated at the outset of this study, informational capitalism is a hydra, not a monolith, and it engenders multiple discrete forms of resistance. These are represented by the struggles against new cloud computing centers in Latin America, or the efforts to unionize tech workers in the United States, or to create civic data trusts as a counterpoint to smart-city initiatives. Scholarship that can connect these disparate episodes, understand their continuities and particularities, and show how they can inform one another is of vital importance. As understanding the pitfalls of the Marco Civil process experienced by CSOs in Brazil can help inform the practice of similar groups the world over, so can accounts of the myriad other sites of resistance around the globe. This praxis could, as Ronald Deibert notes of social media reform efforts, "show that everyone's efforts are weaving something larger than their own separate struggles" (2020, p. 264).

Finally, peering off into the horizon, one needs to ask: Where does informational capitalism go next? What will be the next metamutation in the evolving phases of capitalism? Whether that system to come is best conceptualized as data colonialism (Couldry & Mejias, 2019), or AI capitalism (Dyer-Witheford et al., 2019), or something yet to be imagined, it will still be premised on a dynamic of control and resistance. Our capacity to anticipate and analyze the form it takes and its means of control will necessarily shape our capacity to resist it.

Appendix

Copyright

One of three main pillars of intellectual property, alongside patents and trademarks, copyright has become a dynamic arena of dispute in the digital age. Although the means of protection for copyright holders differs by jurisdiction, the US template of "lifetime of author" plus seventy years has become a global norm. As the means of replicating and distributing media content became available to millions with the mass diffusion of the internet, copyright holders within the cultural industries responded with a combination of technological and legislative measures to try and safeguard their intellectual property (IP) assets. The Digital Millenium Copyright Act of 1998 passed in the United States is an iconic example of the latter and became the spear tip for a global push toward punitive measures against digital copyright violators. Resistance to copyright maximalism emerged in response, from abolitionists in the form of the Pirate Party, to reformers in the shape of advocates for a global repository of shared knowledge, the Creative Commons. Copyright reform was not included in the Marco Civil and was deemed the topic of "future legislation" by its drafters.

Data Protection and Privacy

Privacy is a venerable concept with a lineage that can be traced back to ancient Greece. In a modern workaday sense, privacy concerns the rights of the individual to control the information that is disseminated about him- or herself. Data privacy was elevated to a major political concern in Germany and Australia during the 1980s regarding national census and identification schemes. Digital-data protection measures have emerged as a means to extend privacy safeguards into the online realm. In the United States, the fight for encryption as a technological means of privacy protection during the crypto wars and consumer groups demands for privacy laws to protect against data collection by online advertisers helped to turn privacy into a public interest concern in the 1990s. Recently, the European Union has provided global leadership in this field, with the GDPR (General Data Protection Regulation).

Data protection is included in article 7 of the Marco Civil with the final form of the law providing citizens with the right to clear information regarding the collection, storage, and use of their data by online service providers. Protections were additionally established to guard against the use of data for purposes beyond the user's express consent, as well as limited rights to the deletion of personal data. Foreign companies that provide services to Brazilian citizens online are also mandated to observe Brazilian law with regard to data protection.

Safe Harbors and Limited Third-Party Liability

The concept of "safe harbors" originated in US legislation. The Communication Decency Act from 1996 and the Digital Millennium Copyright Act of 1998 both enacted provisions for limiting liability of online content providers in the case of publishing copyright infringing or indecent content. Safe harbors were established in part as a means to protect against the danger of preemptive censorship on the part of websites and/or internet service providers (ISPs) in a way that would greatly restrict free expression online.

Limited third-party liability was established in the Marco Civil in article 18, protecting online publishers from liability for civil damages arising from user-posted content. Content must, however, be removed in the event of a court order, and those intermediaries only become liable if they ignore that mandate. Exceptions to this regime were established in the case of sexually explicit or nude content, which must be removed in response to a request from the subject of such images, as well as a much-vaguer carve-out for copyright-infringing content.

Multistakeholderism

The roots of multistakeholder governance of the internet can be traced back to 1992, when Brazil hosted the UN environmental summit ECO 92 in Rio de Janeiro. Secure internet connections were imperative for the event—at a premium in Brazil at this time—and the nascent internet community in Brazil had to collaborate closely with state and business entities in order to pull off the feat. The collaboration of government, private-sector actors, and civic groups in order to establish governance over an issue of shared interest in a consensus-based forum loosely describes multistakeholderism. It is closely associated with modes of internet governance, such as the Internet Corporation for Assigned Names and Numbers (ICANN) and the World Summit on the Information Society (WSIS), but not exclusively so. Multistakeholderism features in the final version of the Marco Civil to the extent that the Brazilian Internet Steering Committee (CGI.br), a multistakeholder body that establishes norms for the internet's use and operation in Brazil, was established as one of the entities responsible for regulating network neutrality, while mechanisms of governance of the internet in Brazil should be multistakeholder in nature.

Network Neutrality

"Network neutrality" was first coined by American law professor Tim Wu in a 2003 essay to describe the normative goal that all data should move freely on the internet without being subject to discrimination based on origin or type. If enacted as communication policy, it would prevent arbitrary prioritization, which is the throttling or blocking of certain digital services or data in a way that would favor the commercial interests of internet service providers (ISPs). This was seized upon by academics and activists as a means to protect innovation and competition on the internet, as well as the speech and information access rights of its users. The principle became the subject of intense policy debate during the first decade of the 2000s in North America, as well as in the European Union.

Article 9 of the final version of the Marco Civil established a seemingly robust set of measures that would oblige all telecommunications providers to treat all data packages with isonomy, irrespective of origin, destination, or type. However, an additional clause in the "fundamental principles of internet use" section of the bill that established a right to the freedom of online business models provided an enormous loophole to evade net neutrality protections.

Notes

Chapter 1. Understanding Informational Capitalism

The epigraph of this chapter is from Mosco (2009, p. 3).

1. In chapters 2, 3, and 4 of this book, the term "web platforms" is used as this is the most widely used term during the events covered in those pages.

Chapter 2. Circumscription

The epigraph of this chapter is from Flyverbom, (2011, p. 160).

1. The scale of the problem was vividly revealed when the congressperson who permitted me access to the Brazilian parliament to observe the final Marco Civil vote was one of the first politicians indicted in the Lava Jato investigation.

2. A bitter irony, given the role that the traditional media in Brazil played in both Dilma Rousseff's impeachment in 2016 and Lula's imprisonment two years later that were widely considered to be illegitimate and politically motivated.

3. An aspect of the Lei Azeredo that was highlighted by Amadeu with his claim that "os bancos querem democratizar o seu prejuizo" (The banks wish to democratize their losses) that became a slogan of cyber activists (Caribé, interview, 2015).

4. Although officially incorporated as a national organization in 2012, the Partido Pirata did operate as a more fragmented entity in Brazil since 2003.

5. A central text of the cyberutopian discourse, published by John Perry Barlow in 1996.

6. The twenty-one-member committee is based on a multistakeholder composition of nine government representatives, each representing a different ministry; four private-sector representatives drawn from the telecoms, hardware, and software industries; four civil society representatives; three representatives

of the "technical and academic community"; and, quixotically, one "renowned Internet expert."

7. The Pirate Party was justified in its concerns, as data from 2010 shows that the most-visited news sites in Brazil were dominated by the Globo, Folha, and Abril media groups (Ceron, 2010). Globo, Folha, and one e-commerce service represent the only Brazilian entities in the top-ten most-visited sites in Brazil, a list that otherwise comprises exclusively US web companies (Mizukami et al., 2014, p. 46).

8. Tim Wu and Christopher Yu were famed within US communication policy circles as antagonists on the topic of network neutrality, with the former advocating for its importance and the later arguing against it.

Chapter 4. Cataclysm

The epigraph is from Anderson, 2013, p. 203.

1. The Five Eyes, in addition to the United States, comprise Great Britain, Australia, Canada, and New Zealand.

2. The CSOs are Associação das Rádios Públicas do Brasil (Arpub); Artigo 19; Associação Software Livre.org; Barão de Itararé; Coletivo Digital; CTS-FGV; Fórum Nacional pela Democratização da Comunicação (FNDC); GPOPAI/USP; IDEC; Instituto Bem Estar Brasil; Instituto Socio Ambiental; Intervozes; Knowledge Commons; Movimento Mega Não; Partido Pirata; and Proteste.

References

Abbate, J. (1999). *Inventing the internet.* MIT Press.

Abraji (Associacao Brasileira de Jornalismo Investigativo). (2018, November 21). *Políticos tentaram ocultar informação mais de 500 vezes durante a campanha.* https://www.ctrlx.org.br/noticia/politicos-tentaram-ocultar-informacao-mais-de-500-vezes-durante-a-campanha.

Abraji (Associacao Brasileira de Jornalismo Investigativo). (2023). *CTRL+X.* https://www.ctrlx.org.br/#/infografico.

Abramovay, P. (2014, February 19). O Marco Civil e a política dos netos. *Huff-Post Brasil.* http://www.brasilpost.com.br/pedro-abramovay/o-marco-civil-e-a-politic_b_4810634.html.

Abramovay, P. (2017). *Sistemas deliberativos e processo decisório congressual: Um estudo sobre a BBaprovação do Marco Civil da Internet.* [Doctoral dissertation, Universidade de Rio de Janeiro]. Rio de Janeiro Biblioteca Depositária: IESP-UERJ.

Academia Brasileira de Letras. (2012). *ABL defende a inclusão dos direitos dos autores como premissa do Marco Civil da Internet* [ABL defends authorial rights as part of the Marco Civil]. https://www.academia.org.br/noticias/abl-defende-inclusao-dos-direitos-dos-autores-como-premissa-do-marco-civil-da-internet.

Affonso Souza, C., & Lemos, R. (2016). *Marco Civil da internet: Construção e aplicação.* Editar.

Affonso Souza, C., Steibel, F., & Lemos, R. (2017). Notes on the creation and impacts of Brazil's internet bill of rights. *The Theory and Practice of Legislation, 5*(1), 1–22.

Akita, H. (2019). *Undersea cables—Huawei's ace in the hole.* Nikkei Asia. https://asia.nikkei.com/Spotlight/Comment/Undersea-cables-Huawei-s-ace-in-the-hole.

Alimonti, V. (2016). National broadband program and broadband for all: Civil society's perspective. In P. Knight, F. Feferman, & N. Foditsch (Eds.), *Broadband in Brazil: Past, present, and future* (pp. 77–100). Figurati.

Amadeu, S. (2008, July 6). *Manifesto em defesa da liberdade e do progresso do conheçimento da Internet brasileira.* Blog de Sérgio Amadeu. http://samadeu .blogspot.com/search?updated-max=2008-07-24T14:20:00-07:00&max-results=20&start=100&by-date=false.

Amadeu, S. (2013, July 16). *Sérgio Amadeu: A Globo quer desvirtuar o Marco Civil.* Vermelho. https://vermelho.org.br/2013/07/16/Sérgio-amadeu-a -globo-quer-desvirtuar-o-marco-civil/.

Amann, E. (2002). Globalisation, industrial efficiency, and technological sovereignty: Evidence from Brazil. *The Quarterly Review of Economics and Finance, 42*(5), 875–888.

Amato, F. (2013, August 15). Operadoras têm internet móvel de qualidade em só 3 capitais, diz Anatel. *G1 (Globo).* http://g1.globo.com/economia /noticia/2013/08/anatel-aprova-internet-movel-de-todas-operadoras-em-so -3-capitais.html.

American Bar Association (ABA). (2021). *ABA-approved law schools.* https:// www.americanbar.org/groups/legal_education/resources/aba_approved _law_schools/.

Anderson, J. (2013). Beyond the series of tubes: Strategies for advancing media reform. In Z. Stiegler (Ed.), *Regulating the web: Network neutrality and the fate of the open internet* (pp. 201–219). Lexington.

Andrejevic, M. (2007). *iSpy: Surveillance and power in the interactive era.* University Press of Kansas.

Appadurai, A. (1990). Disjuncture and difference in the global cultural economy. *Theory, Culture, & Society, 7*(2), 295–310.

Aragão, A., & Silverman, C. (2016, November 16). *The top fake news stories outperformed real news about a major scandal in Brazil, too.* Buzzfeed News. https://www.buzzfeednews.com/article/alexandrearagao/noticias-falsas-lava -jato-facebook-1#.yqb2Eae3EQ.

Archegas, J., & Muñiz, L. (2022, July 12). *Authoritarian challenges to digital rights in Brazil.* The Digital Constitutionalist. https://digi-con.org /authoritarian-challenges-to-digital-rights-in-brazil/.

Avelar, D. (2019, October 30). WhatsApp fake news during Brazil election "favoured Bolsonaro." *The Guardian.* https://www.theguardian.com/.

Avritzer, L. (2017). Civil society in Brazil: From state autonomy to political interdependency. In S. E. Alvarez, J. W. Rubin, G. Baiocchi, & A. Laó-Montes (Eds.), *Beyond civil society: Activism, participation, and protest in Latin America* (pp. 45–62). Duke University Press.

Avritzer, L., & Anastasia, F. (2006). *Reforma política no Brasil.* Editora UFMG.

Azevedo, R. (2014, March 18). *Para garantir marco civil da internet, governo abre mão de data centers.* Veja. https://veja.abril.com.br/blog/reinaldo /para-garantir-marco-civil-da-internet-governo-abre-mao-de-data-centers/.

Bailey, O., & Pretto, N. (2010). The political economy of digital cultures in Brazil. *International Journal of Media and Cultural Politics, 6*(3): 265–281.

Baiocchi, G. (2017). A century of councils: Participatory budgeting and the long history of participation in Brazil. In S. E. Alvarez, J. W. Rubin, G. Baiocchi,

& A. Laó-Montes (Eds.), *Beyond civil society: Activism, participation, and protest in Latin America* (pp. 27–45). Duke University Press.

Balza, G. (2013, September 17*). Em primeira reação concreta à espionagem, Dilma adia visita oficial aos EUA.* UOL Notícias. https://noticias.uol.com .br/internacional/ultimas-noticias/2013/09/17/em-primeira-reacao-concreta -a-espionagem-dilma-adia-visita-oficial-aos-eua.htm.

Barbosa, L., & Wilkinson, J. (2017). Consumption in Brazil—The field of new consumer studies and the phenomenon of the "new middle classes." In M. Keller, B. Halkier, T.-A. Wilska, and M. Truninger (Eds.), *Routledge Handbook on Consumption* (pp. 146–155). Routledge.

Bauman, Z., Bigo, D., Esteves, P., Guild, E., Jabri, V., Lyon, D., & Walker, R. B. (2014). After Snowden: Rethinking the impact of surveillance. *International political sociology, 8*(2), 121–144.

Bell, D. (1976). *The coming of post-industrial society.* Basic Books.

Belli, L. (2018, December 5). *WhatsApp skewed Brazilian election, showing social media's danger to democracy.* The Conversation. https://theconversation .com/whatsapp-skewed-brazilianelection-showing-social-medias-danger-to -democracy-106476.

Benkler, Y. (2006). *The wealth of networks: How social production transforms markets and freedom.* Yale University Press.

Benkler, Y., Faris, R., & Roberts, H. (2018). *Network propaganda: Manipulation disinformation and radicalization in American politics.* Oxford University Press.

Berry, D. M. (2008). *Copy, rip, burn: The politics of copyleft and open source.* Pluto Press.

Beyer, J. L., & McKelvey, F. (2015). Piracy & social change: You are not welcome among us: Pirates and the state. *International Journal of Communication, 9,* 890–908.

Birkinbine, B. J., Gómez, R., & Wasko, J. (Eds.). (2017). *Global media giants.* Routledge.

BNAmericas. (2016, March 16). *Google to lay Rio-Santos subsea fiber cable.* https:// www.bnamericas.com/en/news/google-to-lay-rio-santos-subsea-fiber-cable.

BNAmericas. (2017, October 18). *Brazil unveils new broadband plan.* https:// www.bnamericas.com/en/news/brazil-unveils-new-national-broadband-plan.

BNAmericas. (2023, June 15). *Brazil readies new telecom policies, programs.* https://www.bnamericas.com/en/news/brazil-readies-new-telecom-policies -programs.

Boltanski, L., & Chiapello, E. (2005). The new spirit of capitalism. *International Journal of Politics, Culture, and Society, 18*(3–4), 161–188.

Boltanski, L., & Chiapello, E. (2007). *The new spirit of capitalism.* Verso.

Bottman, D. (2010). *Não Gosto de Plágio.* http://naogostodeplagio.blogspot.com/.

Bourdieu, P. (1991). *Language and social power.* Harvard University Press.

Bourne, R. (2008). *Lula of Brazil: The story so far.* University of California Press.

Bowrey, K., & Anderson, J. (2009). The politics of global information sharing: Whose cultural agendas are being advanced? *Social & Legal Studies, 18*(4), 479–504.

Boyd-Barrett, O. (2015). *Media imperialism*. Sage.

Boyle, J. (2008). *The public domain: Enclosing the commons of the mind*. Yale University Press.

Bradshaw, S., Campbell-Smith, U., Henle, A., Perini, A., Shalev, S., Bailey, H., & Howard, P. N. (2021). *Country case studies industrialized disinformation: 2020 global inventory of organized social media manipulation*. Oxford Internet Institute. https://demtech.oii.ox.ac.uk/research/posts/industrialized-disinformation/.

Bragatto, R. C., Sampaio, R. C., & Nicolás, M. A. (2015). Inovadora e democrática. Mas e aí? Uma análise da primeira fase da consulta online sobre o Marco Civil da Internet. *Politica & sociedade, 14*(29), 125–150.

Bragatto, R. C., Sampaio, R. C., & Nicolás, M. A. (2015). A segunda fase da consulta do Marco Civil da Internet: Como foi construída, quem participou e quais os impactos. *Revista Eptic, 17*(1), 237–255.

Branco, S. (2016, November 1). *Why Brazil needs a new copyright law*. DroitDu. Net. https://droitdu.net/2016/11/why-brazil-needs-a-new-copyright-law/.

Brazil's triple crisis. (2020). *Strategic Comments, 26*(4), x–xi. https://doi.org/10.1080/13567888.2020.1801009.

Brito, F. (2015). *Direito, democracia e cultura digital: A experiencia da elaboracao legislative do Marco Civil da internet*. [Master's thesis, Universidade de São Paulo]. CAPES: Catálogo de *Teses* e Dissertações.

Bruno, L. (2014, September 30). *Programa de banda larga se aproxima do fim cheio de críticas*. Exame. https://exame.com/brasil/programa-de-banda-larga-se-aproximado-fim-cheio-de-criticas/.

Cadwalladr, C., & Graham-Harrison, E. (2018, March 17). Revealed: 50 million Facebook profiles harvested for Cambridge Analytica in major data breach. *The Guardian*. https://www.theguardian.com/.

Câmara dos Deputados. (2013). *Sessão: 359.3.54.O*. https://www.camara.leg.br/internet/sitaqweb/TextoHTML.asp?etapa=3&nuSessao=359.3.54.O&nuQuarto=3&nuOrador=3&nuInsercao=0&dtHorarioQuarto=09:21&sgFaseSessao=CG.

Campbell, J., & Carlson, M. (2002). Panopticon.com: Online surveillance and the commodification of privacy. *Journal of Broadcasting & Electronic Media, 46*(4), 586–606.

Caribé, J. C. (2006, November 7). *A morte da internet no Brasil*. Xô Censura. https://xocensura.wordpress.com/tag/censura/.

Caribé, J. C. (2007, January 9). *Pela liberdade de expressão!* Xô Censura. https://xocensura.wordpress.com/tag/censura/.

Caribé, J. C. (2007, May 4). *A morte da internet no Brasil, Versão 2.0*. Xô Censura. https://xocensura.wordpress.com/tag/censura/.

Carvalho, J. M. (2013). *Cidadania no Brasil: O longo caminho*. Civilização Brasileira.

Carvalho, M. (2006). *A trajetória da internet no Brasil: Do surgimento das redes de computadores à instituição dos mecanismos de governança*. [Master's thesis, Universidade Federal de Rio de Janeiro]. CAPES: Catálogo de *Teses* e Dissertações.

Castells, M. (2000). *The rise of the network society*. Blackwell.

Castro, N. (2013, November 4). Alê Youssef, Hermano Vianna, José Marcelo Zacchi e Ronaldo Lemos discutem o novo no "Navegador." *O Globo Cultura*. https://oglobo.globo.com/cultura/revista-da-tv/ale-youssef-hermano-vianna-jose-marcelo-zacchi-ronaldo-lemos-discutem-novo-no-navegador-10649163.

Celeste, E. (2022). *Digital constitutionalism: The role of internet bills of rights*. Routledge.

Centeno, M. A., & Cohen, J. N. (2012). The arc of neoliberalism. *Annual Review of Sociology, 38*, 317–340.

Ceron, R. (2010). *Most visited news sites in Brazil*. Comscore. https://www.comscore.com/fre/Insights/Infographics/Most-Visited-News-Websites-in-Brazil.

CGI.br. (2009). *Princípios para o uso e governança da internet*. https://principios.cgi.br/.

CGI.br. (2013). *Revista*. https://cgi.br/publicacoes/indice/periodicos/.

Chant, I. (2014, October 16). *Google funds new Brazil—U.S. undersea fiber optic cable*. IEEE Spectrum. https://spectrum.ieee.org/tech-talk/telecom/internet/google-new-brazil-us-internet-cable.

Clarke, J. (2015). Stuart Hall and the theory and practice of articulation. *Discourse: Studies in the cultural politics of education, 36*(2), 275–286.

Coding Rights. (2018, October). *Data and politics Brazilian country report: Analysis of the playing field for the influence industry in preparation for the Brazilian general elections*. Tactical Tech at Publix. https://cdn.ttc.io/s/ourdataourselves.tacticaltech.org/ttc-data-and-politics-brazil.pdf.

Cohen, J. (2019). *Between truth and power: The legal constructions of informational capitalism*. Oxford University Press.

Coleman, D. (2018). Digital colonialism: The 21st century scramble for Africa through the extraction and control of user data and the limitations of data protection laws. *Michigan Journal of Race & Law, 24*, 417–439.

Coleman, S., & Blumler, J. G. (2009). *The internet and democratic citizenship: Theory, practice, and policy*. Cambridge University Press.

Coll, S. (2014). Power, knowledge, and the subjects of privacy: Understanding privacy as the ally of surveillance. *Information, Communication, & Society, 17*(10), 1250–1263.

Comitê Gestor da Internet no Brasil. (2016). *Pesquisa sobre o uso das tecnologias de informação e comunicação nos domicílios brasileiros: TIC domicílios 2016: Survey on the use of information and communication technologies in Brazilian households: ICT households 2016*. CETIC. https://cetic.br/media/docs/publicacoes/2/TIC_DOM_2016_LivroEletronico.pdf.

Comor, E. (2011). Communication: Blind spot of Western economics. In E. Comor (Ed.), *Media, Structures, and Power: The Robert E. Babe Collection* (pp. 43–59). University of Toronto Press.

Comscore. (2012, January 17). *Facebook blasts into top position in Brazilian social networking market following year of tremendous growth*. https://

www.comscore.com/Insights/Press-Releases/2012/1/Facebook-Blasts-into-Top-Position-in-Brazilian-Social-Networking-Market.

Costa, P. (2019). *The edge of democracy*. Netflix.

Couldry, N., & Mejias, U. A. (2019). *The costs of connection: How data is colonizing human life and appropriating it for capitalism*. Stanford University Press.

Council of Europe. (2023). *Information disorder: Freedom of expression*. https://www.coe.int/web/freedom-expression/information-disorder.

Crain, M. (2013). *The revolution will be commercialized: Finance, public policy, and the construction of internet advertising*. [Doctoral dissertation, University of Illinois at Urbana-Champaign]. University of Illinois Institutional Repository.

Crain, M. (2021). *Profit over privacy: How surveillance advertising conquered the internet*. University of Minnesota Press.

Crandall, B. H. (2011). *Hemispheric giants: The misunderstood history of U.S.-Brazilian relations*. Rowman and Littlefield.

Cruz, C. (2022, December 10). *Futuro ministro da Justiça anuncia assessoria especial de direitos digitais*. Telesíntese. https://www.telesintese.com.br/futuro-ministro-dajustica-anuncia-assessoriaespecial-de-direitos-digitais/.

Cukierman, H. L. (2013). Computer technology in Brazil: From protectionism and national sovereignty to globalization and market competitiveness. *Information & Culture, 48*(4), 479–505.

Dahlberg, L. (2010). Cyber-libertarianism 2.0: A discourse theory/critical political economy examination. *Cultural politics, 6*(3), 331–356.

Dantas, C., & Torres, I. (2014, March 14). *House of Cunha*. IstoÉ. https://istoe.com.br/352400_HOUSE+OF+CdUNHA/.

Dantas, M. (2013). *Comunicação, desenvolvimento, democracia desafios brasileiros no cenário da mundialização mediática*. Fundação Perseo Abramo.

Data Privacy Research. (2020). *Retrospective: Techno-authoritarianism*. https://www.dataprivacybr.org/en/documentos/technoauthoritarianism-retrospective-2020/.

Data Privacy Research. (2023). *Defending Brazil from techno-authoritarianism*. https://www.dataprivacybr.org/en/projeto/defending-brazil-from-techno-authoritarianism/.

Data Reportal. (2023). *Digital 2023: Brazil*. https://datareportal.com/reports/digital-2023-brazil.

Davis, S., & Straubhaar, J. (2020). Producing antipetismo: Media activism and the rise of the radical, nationalist right in contemporary Brazil. *International Communication Gazette, 82*(1), 82–100.

Dean, J. (2005). Communicative capitalism: Circulation and the foreclosure of politics. *Cultural Politics, 1*(1), 51–74.

De Gregorio, G. (2022, December 7). *How does digital constitutionalism reframe the discourse on rights and powers?* Ada Lovelace Institute. https://www.adalovelaceinstitute.org/blog/digitalconstitutionalism-rightspowers/.

De Gregorio, G., & Radu, R. (2022). Digital constitutionalism in the new era of internet governance. *International Journal of Law and Information Technology, 30*(1), 68–87.

Deibert, R. J. (2019). The road to digital unfreedom: Three painful truths about social media. *Journal of Democracy, 30*(1), 25–39.

Deibert, R. J. (2020). *Reset: Reclaiming the internet for civil society.* House of Anansi Press.

Deleuze, G. (1992). Postscript on the societies of control. *October, 59,* 3–7.

Delfanti, A., & Söderberg, J. (2015). *Repurposing the hacker: Three cycles of recuperation in the evolution of hacking and capitalism. Ephemera: Theory & Politics in Organization.* https://ephemerajournal.org/contribution/repurposing-hacker-three-cycles-recuperation-evolution-hacking-and-capitalism.

Dencik, L., Hintz, A., Redden, J., & Treré, E. (2022). *Data justice.* Sage.

Devanny, J., & Buchan, R. (2023, August 08). *Brazil's cyber-strategy under Lula: Not a priority, but progress possible.* Carnegie Endowment for International Peace. https://carnegieendowment.org/2023/08/08/brazil-s-cyber-strategy-under-lula-not-priority-but-progress-is-possible-pub-90339.

Diamond, L. (2019). The threat of postmodern totalitarianism. *J. Democracy, 30,* 20–24.

Dias, T. (2012, July 10). *Marco civil deve ser votado hoje. O Estado de São Paulo.* http://link.estadao.com.br/noticias/geral,marco-civil-deve-ser-votado-hoje,10000035293.

Dias, T. (2012, August 14). *Brasil tem a 5a pior lei autoral do mundo. O Estado de São Paulo.* https://link.estadao.com.br/blogs/tatiana-dias/brasil-tem-a-5a-pior-lei-autoral-do-mundo/.

Dias, T. (2019, August 15). *Aqui estão todas as suas informações que o governo vai réunir numa megabase de vigilância. Intercept Brasil.* https://www.intercept.com.br/2019/10/15/governo-ferramenta-vigilancia/.

Direitos na Rede. (2021, August 04). *Bolsonaro e anatel trabalham contra a universalizção da banda larga.* https://direitosnarede.org.br/2021/08/04/bolsonaro-e-anatel-trabalham-contra-a-universalizacao-da-banda-larga/.

DLA Piper. (2022). *Data protection laws of the world: Brazil.* https://www.dlapiperdataprotection.com/index.html?t=law&c=BR.

Doctorow, C. (2019, June 6). Regulating big tech makes them stronger, so they need competition instead. *The Economist.* https://www.economist.com/openfuture/2019/06/06/regulating-bigtech-makes-them-stronger-so-they-needcompetition-instead.

Dolber, B. (2013). Informationism as ideology: Technological myths in the net neutrality debate. In Z. Stiegler (Ed.), *Regulating the web: Network neutrality and the fate of the open internet* (pp. 143–167). Lexington.

Domino, J. (2021, November 11). *Filipinos are left to pick between repressive social media laws—or none at all.* Rest of World. https://restofworld.org/2021/philippines-social-media-regulation/.

Drahos, P., & Braithwaite, J. (2002). *Information feudalism: Who owns the knowledge economy?* New Press.

Dubois, E., & Blank, G. (2018). The echo chamber is overstated: The moderating effect of political interest and diverse media. *Information, Communication, & Society, 21*(5), 729–745.

Duran, R. (2014, February 13). *Lawyers and law schools in Brazil.* The Brazil Business. https://thebrazilbusiness.com/article/lawyers-and-law-schools-in-brazil.

Dyer-Witheford, N. (2015). *Cyber-proletariat: Global labour in the digital vortex.* Pluto Press.

Dyer-Witheford, N., Kjøsen, A. M., & Steinhoff, J. (2019). *Inhuman power: Artificial intelligence and the future of capitalism.* Pluto Press.

Edmundson, A., Ensafi, R., Feamster, N., & Rexford, J. (2018, June). Nation-state hegemony in internet routing. In *Proceedings of the 1st ACM SIGCAS conference on computing and sustainable societies* (pp. 1–11). Association for Computing Machinery.

Ekman, P. (2013, July 11). *A reforma política começa na TV.* Carta Capital. https://www.cartacapital.com.br/blogs/intervozes/a-reforma-politica-comeca-na-tv-1419/.

Elmer, G. (2004). *Profiling machines: Mapping the personal information economy.* MIT Press.

Época. (2013, September 9). *Rival brasileiro para Gmail se chamara Mensageria Digital e estreara em 2014.* http://colunas.revistaepocanegocios.globo.com/tecneira/2013/09/09/rival-brasileiro-para-gmail-se-chamara-mensageria-digital-e-estreara-em-2014/.

Estadão. (2013, November 7). *Teles querem mudar texto do Marco Civil.* https://link.estadao.com.br/noticias/geral,teles-querem-mudar-texto-do-marco-civil,10000032606.

Eubanks, V. (2019). *Automating inequality: How high-tech tools profile, police, and punish the poor.* Picador.

Evangelista, R., & Bruno, F. (2019). WhatsApp and political instability in Brazil: Targeted messages and political radicalisation. *Internet Policy Review, 8*(4). DOI:10.14763/2019.4.1434.

Fairclough, N. (2001). The dialectics of discourse. *Textus, 14*(2), 231–242.

Fairclough, N. (2003). Political correctness: The politics of culture and language. *Discourse & Society, 14*(1), 17–28.

Fantástico. (2013, September 2). *Veja os documentos ultrassecretos que comprovam espionagem a Dilma.* http://g1.globo.com/fantastico/noticia/2013/09/veja-os-documentos-ultrassecretos-que-comprovam-espionagem-dilma.html.

Fantástico (2020, May 31). *Canais de investigados em inquérito das fake news receberam verbas estatais.* https://g1.globo.com/politica/noticia/2020/05/31/canais-deInvestigados-cminquerito-das-fake-news-receberam-verba-estatais.ghtml.

Faustino, P. (2022). *Concentration, diversity of voices, and competition in the media market.* Media 21.

Feenberg, A. (1995). Subversive rationalization. In A. Feenberg & A. Hannay (Eds.), *Technology and the politics of knowledge* (pp. 3–22). Indiana University Press.

Feltrin, R. (2016, October 19). *Globosat completa 25 anos como "case" de sucesso e com receita bilionária.* UOL. https://www.uol.com.br/splash/noticias/ooops/2016/10/19/globosat-faz-25-anos-como-case-de-sucesso-e-com-receita-bilionaria.htm.

Fisher, E. (2010). *Media and new capitalism in the digital age: The spirit of networks*. Palgrave Macmillan.

Fisher, M., & Taub, A. (2019, November 8). How YouTube radicalized Brazil. *New York Times*. https://www.nytimes.com/.

Flew, T., & Martin, F. (2022). *Digital platform regulation: Global perspectives on internet governance*. Palgrave Macmillan.

Flyverbom, M. (2011). *Power of networks: Organizing the global politics of the internet*. Edward Elgar.

Folha de São Paulo. (2013, March 28). *Faturamento das Organizações Globo cresce 16% em 2012*. https://www1.folha.uol.com.br/mercado/2013/03/1253685-faturamento-das-organizacoes-globo-cresce-16-em-2012.shtml.

Font, M. A. (2003). *Transforming Brazil: A reform era in perspective*. Rowman and Littlefield.

Fórum Nacional pela Democratização da Comunicação (FNDC). (n.d.). *Quem somos*. http://www.fndc.org.br/forum/quem-somos/.

Foucault, M. (1972). *The archaeology of knowledge and the discourse on language* (A. M. Sheridan Smith, Trans.). Pantheon.

Fox, E. (1995). Latin American broadcasting. In L. Bethell (Ed.), *The Cambridge history of Latin America 10* (pp. 519–568). Cambridge University Press.

France 24. (2020, July 7). *Brazil's senate approves controversial bill against disinformation*. https://www.france24.com/en/20200701-brazil-s-senate-approves-controversial-bill-against-disinformation.

France 24. (2021, October 20). *Bolsonaro should be charged with crimes against humanity for COVID errors, says senate panel*. https://www.france24.com/en/americas/20211020-bolsonaro-should-be-charged-with-crimes-against-humanity-for-covid-errors-says-senate-panel.

Franklin, M. (2013). *Digital dilemmas: Power, resistance, and the internet*. Oxford University Press.

Fraser, N. (2009). *Scales of justice: Reimagining political space in a globalizing world*. Columbia University Press.

Freedman, D. (2008). *The politics of media policy*. Polity.

Freedman, D. (2012). Outsourcing internet regulation. In J. Curran, N. Fenton, & D. Freedman (Eds.), *Misunderstanding the Internet* (pp. 95–121). Routledge.

Freedom House. (2012). *Freedom of the press 2012: Brazil*. https://www.freedomhouse.org/sites/default/files/Booklet%20for%20Website_0.pdf.

Freedom House. (2013). *Freedom of the net 2013: Brazil*. https://www.refworld.org/reference/annualreport/freehou/2013/en/94528.

Freedom House. (2017). *Freedom of the net 2017: Brazil*. https://freedomhouse.org/country/brazil/freedom-net/2017.

Freedom House. (2018). *Freedom of the net 2018: Brazil*. https://freedomhouse.org/country/brazil/freedom-net/2018.

Freedom House. (2019). *Freedom of the net 2019: Brazil*. https://freedomhouse.org/country/brazil/freedom-net/2019.

Freedom House. (2021). *Freedom of the net 2021: Brazil.* https://freedomhouse
.org/report/freedom-net/2021/brazil.

Freedom House. (2023). *Freedom of the net 2023: Brazil.* https://freedomhouse
.org/report/freedom-net/2023/brazil.

Fuchs, C. (2009). A contribution to the critique of the political economy of
transnational informational capitalism. *Rethinking Marxism, 21*(3), 387–402.

Fuchs, C. (2011). *Foundations of critical media and information studies.* Routledge.

Fuchs, M., Dannenberg, P., & Wiedemann, C. (2022). Big tech and labour
resistance at Amazon. *Science as Culture, 31*(1), 29–43.

Fundação Getulio Vargas (FGV). (2015). *Leading Brazilian multinational enterprises: Trends in an era of significant uncertainties and challenges.* https://emgp
.org/report/leading-brazilian-multinational-enterprises-trends-in-an-era-of
-significant-uncertainties-and-challenges/.

G1. (2012, October 26). *Jornais brasileiros acreditam que sair do serviço Google
News foi boa decisão.* http://g1.globo.com/pop-arte/noticia/2012/10/jornais
-brasileiros-acreditam-que-sair-do-servico-google-news-foi-boa-decisao.html.

G1. (2013, September 1). *Documentos da NSA apontam Dilma Rousseff como alvo
de espionagem.* http://g1.globo.com/politica/noticia/2013/09/documentos-da
-nsa-apontam-dilma-rousseff-como-alvo-de-espionagem.html.

G1. (2013, September 8). *Petrobras foi alvo de espionagem de agência dos EUA,
aponta document.* http://g1.globo.com/politica/noticia/2013/09/petrobras
-foi-alvo-de-espionagem-de-agencia-dos-eua-aponta-documento.html.

G1. (2018, October 3). *Datafolha: Quantos eleitores de cada candidato usam redes
sociais, leem ecompartilham notícias sobre política.* https://g1.globo.com/politica
/eleicoes/2018/eleicao-emnumeros/noticia/2018/10/03/datafolha-quantos
-eleitores-de-cada-candidato-usam-redessociais-leem-e-compartilham-noticias
-sobre-politica.ghtml.

Galloway, A. R. (2006). *Protocol: How control exists after decentralization.* MIT
Press.

Getschko, D. (2009). *Internet: Tempos interessantes.* ComCiência, 110. https://
comciencia.br/comciencia/handler.php?section=8&edicao=48&id=600.

Gill, L., Redeker, D., and Gasser, U. (2015). Towards digital constitutionalism?
Mapping attempts to craft an internet digital bills of rights. *Berkman Center
of Research,* Publication No. 2015–15.

Gillespie, T. (2007). *Wired shut: Copyright and the shape of digital culture.* MIT
Press.

Gilliom, J. (2011). A response to Bennett's' "In defence of privacy." *Surveillance
& Society, 8*(4), 500–504.

Globo domination. (2014, June 7). Economist. https://www.economist.com
/business/2014/06/05/globo-domination.

Godwin, M. (2003). *Cyber rights: Defending free speech in the digital age.* MIT Press.

Goggin, G., Vromen, A., Weatherall, K. G., Martin, F., Webb, A., Sunman, L.,
and Bailo, F. (2017). *Digital rights in Australia.* Sydney Law School Research
Paper No. 18/23. https://ssrn.com/abstract=3090774.

Golumbia, D. (2013). Cyberlibertarianism: The extremist foundations of "digital freedom." *Clemson University Department of English* (September), 1–25.

Gomes, H. (2020, March 19). *Franquia de dados: Anatel avalia proibir bloqueio à internet na pandemia.* Tilt. https://www.uol.com.br/tilt/noticias /redacao/2020/03/19/anatel-e-pressionada-a-proibir-suspensao-do-pacote -de-internet-por-90-dias.htm.

Google. (n.d.). *Global requests for user information: Brazil.* Google Transparency Report. https://transparencyreport.google.com/user-data/overview?user _requests_report_period=series:requests,accounts;authority:BR;time:&lu =user_requests_report_period.

Google. (2023). *Government requests to remove information.* Google Transparency Report. https://transparencyreport.google.com/government-removals /government-requests/BR?lu=country_item_amount&country_item_amount =group_by:requestors.

Greenwald, G. (2013, June 6). NSA collecting phone records of millions of Verizon customers daily. *The Guardian.* https://www.theguardian.com /world/2013/jun/06/nsa-phone-records-verizon-court-order.

Greenwald, G. (2015). *No place to hide: Edward Snowden, the NSA, and the U.S. surveillance state.* Metropolitan Books.

Greenwald, G., Kaz, R., & Casado, J. (2013, July 6). EUA espionaram milhões de e-mails e ligações de brasileiros. *O Globo.* https://oglobo.globo.com/mundo /eua-espionaram-milhoes-de-mails-ligacoes-de-brasileiros-8940934.

Grigori, P. (2018, May 20). *20 projetos de lei no Congresso pretendem criminalizar fake news.* AgênciaPública. https://apublica.org/2018/05/20-projetos-de-lei -no-congresso-pretendem-criminalizarfake-news/.

Grossman, L. (2013). *Futurecom 2013. Convergencia Digital.* http://www .convergenciadigital.com.br/cgi/cgilua.exe/sys/start.htm?UserActiveTemplate =site&infoid=35247#.W19b_dVKiM8.

Grover, R. (2022). The geopolitics of digital rights activism: Evaluating civil society's role in the promises of multistakeholder internet governance. *Telecommunications Policy, 46*(10). https://doi.org/10.1016/j.telpol.2022 .102437.

Guerlanda, N., & Decat, E. (2012, November 26). *Votação do Marco Civil da Internet emperra na Câmara dos Deputados.* Folha de São Paulo. https://m .folha.uol.com.br/tec/2012/11/1190428-votacao-do-marco-civil-da-internet -emperra-na-camara-dos-deputados.shtml.

Guess, A., Nagler, J., & Tucker, J. (2019). Less than you think: Prevalence and predictors of fake news dissemination on Facebook. *Science Advances, 5*(1). DOI:10.1126/sciadv.aau4586.

Guiot, A. P. (2010). A construção da ideologia neoliberal no PSDB (1988–1994). *XIV Encontro Regional da ANPUH-Rio. Rio de Janeiro.*

Gurstein, M. (2014). The multistakeholder model, neoliberalism, and global (internet) governance. *The Journal of Community Informatics, 10*(2).

Habermas, J. (1981). *Theory of communicative action.* Beacon Press.

Haggart, B., & Jablonski, M. (2017). Internet freedom and copyright maximalism: Contradictory hypocrisy or complementary policies? *The Information Society, 33*(3), 103–118.

Hardt, M., & Negri, A. (2000). *Empire*. Harvard University Press.

Harvey, D. (2005). *A brief history of neoliberalism*. Oxford University Press.

Hellegren, Z. I. (2017). A history of crypto-discourse: Encryption as a site of struggles to define internet freedom. *Internet Histories, 1*(4), 285–311.

Herrle, J., & Hirsh, J. (2019, July 9). *The peril and potential of the GDPR*. Centre for International Governance Innovation. https://www.cigionline.org/articles/peril-and-potential-gdpr/.

Hintz, A., and Milan, S. (2011). User rights for the internet age: Communications policy according to "netizens." In R. Mansell and M. Raboy (Eds.), *The handbook of global media and communication policy: General communication & media studies* (pp. 230–241). Wiley-Blackwell.

Holpuch, A. (2013, September 13). Google's Eric Schmidt says government spying is "the nature of our society." *The Guardian*. https://www.theguardian.com/world/2013/sep/13/eric-schmidt-google-nsa-surveillance.

Holston, J. (2009). *Insurgent citizenship: Disjunctions of democracy and modernity in Brazil*. Princeton University Press.

Honorato, R. (2013, September 28). *Tiro do governo vai sair pela culatra, prevê idealizador do Marco Civil*. Veja. https://veja.abril.com.br/tecnologia/tiro-do-governo-vai-sair-pela-culatra-preve-idealizador-do-marco-civil/.

Hoskins, G. T. (2019). Beyond "zero sum": The case for context in regulating zero-rating in the global south. *Internet Policy Review, 8*(1), 1–26.

Human Rights Watch (HRW). (2013). *World Report 2013: Brazil*. https://www.hrw.org/world-0report/2013/country-chapters/brazil.

ICT Households 2017. (2017). *CETIC*. https://cetic.br/media/analises/tic_domicilios_2017_coletiva_de_imprensa.pdf.

ICT Households 2022. (2022). *CETIC*. https://cetic.br/pt/publicacao/pesquisa-sobre-o-uso-dastecnologias-de-informacao-e-comunicacao-nos-domicilios-brasileiros-tic-domicilios-2022/.

Internet Lab. (2023). *Bloqueios*. http://bloqueios.info/pt/#home-content.

Internet Live Stats. (2009). *Brazil Internet Users*. https://www.internetlivestats.com/internet-users/brazil/.

Intervozes. (2018). *A Direito da Comunicação no Brasil*. https://intervozes.org.br/arquivos/interliv013dircom8.pdf.

Intervozes. (2020, February 28). *Acesso à Internet*. https://web.archive.org/web/20200229053750/http:/www.intervozes.org.br/direitoacomuniccao/?page_id=28536.

Intervozes. (2021). *A Direito da Comunicação no Brasil*. https://intervozes.org.br/publicacoes/relatorioireito-a-comunicacao-no-brasil-2021/.

Inverardi-Ferri, C. (2022). Overtime: The cultural political economy of illicit labor in the electronics industry. *Economic Geography*. doi:10.1080/00130095.2022.2142111.

Isin, E., & Ruppert, E. (2015). *Being digital citizens*. Rowman and Littlefield International.

Isin, E., & Ruppert, E. (2019). *Data's empire: Postcolonial data politics*. In D. Bigo, E. F. Isin, & E. Ruppert (Eds.), *Data politics: Worlds, subjects, rights* (pp. 207–229). Routledge.

Jamieson, K. H., & Cappella, J. N. (2008). *Echo chamber: Rush Limbaugh and the conservative media establishment*. Oxford University Press.

Jansen, T. (2012, November 14). Marco Civil: Saiba quais são as semelhanças e diferenças do projeto brasileiro em relação a outros países. *O Globo*. https://oglobo.globo.com/economia/marco-civil-saiba-quais-sao-as-semelhancas-diferencas-do-projeto-brasileiro-em-relacao-outros-paises-6726126.

Jin, D. Y. (2015). *Digital platforms, imperialism, and political culture*. Routledge.

Jordan, T. (2015). *Information politics: Liberation and exploitation in the digital society*. Pluto Press.

Jørgensen, R. (2011). Human rights and their role in global media and communication discourses. In R. Mansell & M. Raboy (Eds.), *The handbook of global media and communication policy: General communication & media studies* (pp. 95–112). Wiley-Blackwell.

Karppinen, K., & Puukko, O. (2020). Four discourses of digital rights: Promises and problems of rights-based politics. *Journal of Information Policy, 10*, 304–328.

Katz, E., & Liebes, T. (1990). Interacting with "Dallas": Cross-cultural readings of American TV. *Departmental Papers (ASC), 159*.

Kelion, L. (2013, October 14). Brazil plans secure email service to thwart cyber-spies. *BBC News*. https://www.bbc.com/news/technology-24519969.

Kimball, D. (2013). What we talk about when we talk about net neutrality: A historical genealogy of the discourse of "net neutrality." In Z. Stiegler (Ed.), *Regulating the web: Network neutrality and the fate of the open internet* (pp. 33–49). Lexington Books.

Kira, B. (2023, April 24). *In Brazil, platform regulation takes center stage*. Tech Policy Press. https://techpolicy.press/in-brazil-platform-regulation-takes-center-stage/.

Kiss, S., & Mosco, V. (2005). Negotiating electronic surveillance in the workplace: A study of collective agreements in Canada. *Canadian Journal of Communication, 30*(4), 549–564.

Knight, P. T. (2014). *The internet in Brazil: Origins, strategy, development, and governance*. Author House.

Kraidy, M. M. (2002). Hybridity in cultural globalization. *Communication Theory, 12*(3), 316–339.

L. S. (2012, December 14). A digital cold war? *The Economist*. https://www.economist.com/babbage/2012/12/14/a-digital-cold-war.

Laclau, E. (2005). *On populist reason*. Verso.

Laclau, E., & Mouffe, C. (2001). *Hegemony and socialist strategy: Towards a radical democratic politics*. Verso.

Lamensch, M. (2022, September 19). *In Brazil, "techno-authoritarianism" rears its head.* CIGI Online. https://www.cigionline.org/articles/in-brazil -techno-authoritarianism-rears-its-head/.

Lemos, R. (2007, May 22). *Internet brasileira precisa de marco regulatório civil.* UOL Notícias. https://tecnologia.uol.com.br/ultnot/2007/05/22 /ult4213u98.jhtm.

Lemos, R. (2010). Prefácio. In S. Branco & W. Brito (Eds.), *O que é o Creative Commons* (pp. 9–17). FGV Editora.

Lemos, R. (2014). O Marco Civil como símbolo do desejo por inovação no Brasil. In G. Leite & R. Lemos (Eds.), *Marco Civil da Internet.* Editora Atlas.

Lemos, R. (2020). *Brazilian General Data Protection Law.* Iapp. https://iapp .org/resources/article/brazilian-data-protection-law-lgpd-english-translation/.

Lentz, B. (2013). Excavating historicity in the US network neutrality debate: An interpretive perspective on policy change. *Communication, Culture & Critique, 6*(4), 568–597.

Lessig, L. (2006). *Code 2.0.* Basic Books.

Lima, H. S. (2015). *A lei da TV paga: Impactos no mercado audiovisual.* [Doctoral dissertation, Universidade de São Paulo].

Litt, D. G., & Monroe-Sheridan, A. R. (2022, February 3). The US-Japan digital trade agreement and "data free flow with trust." *USALI Perspectives, 2*(13). https://usali.org/.

Lyon, D. (2015). *Surveillance after Snowden.* Polity Press.

Macedo, I. (2018, October 26). *Das 123 Fake News Encontradas por Agências de Checagem, 123 Beneficiaram Bolsonaro. Congresso em Foco.* https:// congressoemfoco.uol.com.br/area/pais/das-123-fake-news-encontradas-por -agenciasde-checagem-104-beneficiaram-bolsonaro/.

Machado, A. (2012, November 5). Especialistas defendem direitos autorais. *O Globo.* https://oglobo.globo.com/economia/especialistas-defendem -direitos-autorais-6643528.

Madrid, P. (2023, January 17). *USC Study reveals the key reason why fake news spreads on social media.* USC Today. https://today.usc.edu/.

Maheshwari, N. (2020, June 23). *Traceability under Brazil's proposed fake news law would undermine users' privacy and freedom of expression.* Center for Democracy & Technology. https://cdt.org/insights/traceability-under-brazils-proposed -fakenews-law-would-undermineusers-privacy-and-freedom-of-expression/.

Mainwaring, S. (1999). *Rethinking party systems in the third wave of democratization: The case of Brazil.* Stanford University Press.

Marco da internet ameaça direitos autorais [Marco Civil da internet threatens copyright]. (2012, November 07). *Jornal O Globo.*

Mari, A. (2021, August 23). *Most Brazilians access the web only via smartphones.* ZNet. https://www.zdnet.com/article/most-brazilians-access-the -web-only-viasmartphones/.

Marinoni, B. (2015). Concentração dos meios de comunicação de massa e o desafio da democratização da mídia no Brasil. *Intervozes,* analise 13, 1–27.

Marsden, C. T. (2016). *Net neutrality*. Bloomsbury Academic.

Martínez, G. (2017). Telefónica. In B. J. Birkinbine, R. Gómez, & J. Wasko (Eds.), *Global media giants* (pp. 191–205). Routledge.

Marx, L. (1997). "Technology": The emergence of a hazardous concept. *Social Research, 64*(3), 965–988.

Mastrini, G., & Becerra, M. (2002, April 22). *50 years of media concentration in Latin America: From artisanal patriarchy to large-scale groups*. [Presentation paper]. Panamerican Colloquium, Montreal, Canada.

Mastrini, G., & Becerra, M. (2017). South America. In B. J. Birkinbine, R. Gómez, & J. Wasko (Eds.), *Global media giants* (pp. 257–273). Routledge.

Matos, C. (2016, March 30). *How Brazil's media is hounding out the president*. The Conversation. https://theconversation.com/how-brazils-media-is-hounding-out-the-president-56819.

Mattelart, A., Carey-Libbrecht, L., & Cohen, J. A. (2000). *Networking the world: 1794–2000*. University of Minnesota Press.

Mayer-Schönberger, V., & Cukier, K. (2013). *Big data: A revolution that will transform how we live, work, and think*. Houghton Mifflin Harcourt.

McChesney, R. W. (2013). *Digital disconnect: How capitalism is turning the internet against democracy*. New Press.

McKenna, B. J., & Graham, P. (2000). Technocratic discourse: A primer. *Journal of Technical Writing and Communication, 30*(3), 223–251.

McLaughlin, L., & Pickard, V. (2005). What is bottom-up about global internet governance? *Global Media and Communication, 1*(3), 357–373.

Mejias, U. A. (2013). *Off the network: Disrupting the digital world*. University of Minnesota Press.

Mello, D. (2018, October 25). *Spread of fake news in Brazil unprecedented, says OAS*. Agência Brasil. https://agenciabrasil.ebc.com.br/en/politica/noticia/2018-10/spread-fake-news-brazil-unprecedented-says-oas.

Mello, P. (2018, October 18). *Businessmen fund WhatsApp campaign against PT*. Folha de São Paulo. https://www1.folha.uol.com.br/internacional/en/brazil/2018/10/businessmen-fund-whatsapp-campaign-against-pt.shtml.

Melo, P. (2023, November 2). *Grana rolava solta do "gabinete do ódio."* Paraná Portal. https://paranaportal.uol.com.br/noticias/grana-rolava-solta-no-gabinete-do-odio/.

Menczer, F., & Hills, T. (2020, December 1). *Information overload helps spread fake news and social media knows it*. Scientific American. https://www.scientificamerican.com/article/information-overload-helps-fake-news-spread-and-social-media-knows-it/.

Mendes, P. (2013, July 8). Ministra quer marco civil da internet e diz que soberania está em xeque. *G1*. http://g1.globo.com/politica/noticia/2013/07/ministra-quer-marco-civil-da-internet-e-diz-que-soberania-esta-em-xeque.html.

Meta Transparency Center. (2023). *Brazil*. https://transparency.fb.com/reports/government-datarequests/country/BR/.

Miller, R. (2014, February 3). *Google spent $7.3 billion on its data centers in 2013*. Data Centre Knowledge. https://www.datacenterknowledge.com /archives/2014/02/03/google-spent-7-3-billion-data-centers-2013.

Ministério da Justiça. (2009). *Primeira fase*. http://pensando.mj.gov.br /marcocivil2009/consulta/. Link no longer works.

Ministério da Justiça. (2010). *Contribuições recebidas*. http://pensando.mj.gov .br/marcocivil2009/debate/. Link no longer works.

Ministério da Justiça. (2010). *Segunda fase*. http://pensando.mj.gov.br /marcocivil2009/debate. Link no longer works.

Miranda, E. (2011, September 22). Aprovada após cinco anos de polêmica, lei da TV por assinatura cria cotas para o conteúdo nacional. *O Globo*. https:// oglobo.globo.com/cultura/aprovada-apos-cinco-anos-de-polemica-lei-da-tv -por-assinatura-cria-cotas-para-conteudo-nacional-2695231.

Mirrlees, T. (2016). U.S. empire and communications today: Revisiting Herbert I. Schiller. *The Political Economy of Communication, 3*(2), 3–27.

Mirrlees, T. (2021, January 20). *Getting at GAFAM's power: A structural and relational framework*. Heliotrope. https://www.heliotropejournal.net/helio /gafams-power-in-society.

Mirrlees, T. (2023). *Ten postulates of a media imperialism framework: For critical research on China's media power and influence in the global south*. Global Media and China. https://doi.org/10.1177/20594364231195934.

Mizukami, P. N., Reia, J., & Varon, J. (2014). *Mapping digital media: Brazil*. Open Society Media Program.

Molon, A. (2013, July 16). *Marco Civil: Pela neutralidade, privacidade e liberdade*. Revista Forum. https://revistaforum.com.br/marco-civil-pela -neutralidade-privacidade-e-liberdade/.

Moreira, S. (2016). Media ownership and concentration in Brazil. In E. M. Noam (Ed.), *Who owns the world's media? Media concentration and ownership around the world* (pp. 606–640). Oxford University Press.

Morozov, E. (2011). *The net delusion: The dark side of internet freedom*. Public Affairs.

Mosco, V. (2005). *The digital sublime: Myth, power, and cyberspace*. MIT Press.

Mosco, V. (2009). *Political economy of communications*. Sage.

Moulier-Boutang, Y. (2011). *Cognitive capitalism*. Polity.

Moura, J. F., Ximenes, V. M., & Sarriera, J. C. (2014). A construção opressora da pobreza no Brasil e suas consequências no psiquismo. *Quaderns de Psico-logia, 16*(2), 85–93.

Mueller, G. (2019). *Media piracy in the cultural economy: Intellectual property and labor under neoliberal restructuring*. Routledge.

Mueller, M. (2010). *Networks and states: The global politics of internet governance*. MIT Press.

Mueller, M. (2012, June 7). *Threat analysis of WCIT part 2: Telecommunications vs. internet*. Internet Governance Project. https://www.internetgovernance .org/2012/06/07/threat-analysis-of-wcit-part-2-telecommunications-vs -internet/.

Mueller, M., & Wagner, B. (2014). Finding a formula for Brazil: Representation and legitimacy in internet governance. *Internet Policy Observatory, 8*, 1–29.

Murray, J., de Castro Cerqueira, D. R., & Kahn, T. (2013). Crime and violence in Brazil: Systematic review of time trends, prevalence rates, and risk factors. *Aggression and Violent Behavior, 18*(5), 471–483.

Napoli, P., & Royal, A. (2022). Platforms and the press: Regulatory interventions to address an imbalance of power. In T. Flew & F. R. Martin (Eds.), *Digital platform regulation: Global perspectives on internet governance* (pp. 43–68). Palgrave Macmillan.

Nascimento, L. (2014, March 25). *Câmara aprova Marco Civil da internet.* Agência Brasil. https://agenciabrasil.ebc.com.br/politica/noticia/2014-03/camara-aprova-marco-civil-da-internet.

National Oceanic and Atmospheric Administration (NOAA). (2020). *Submarine cables.* https://www.gc.noaa.gov/gcil_submarine_cables.html.

Nemer, D. (2021). Disentangling Brazil's disinformation insurgency. *NACLA Report on the Americas, 53*(4), 406–413.

Nemer, D. (2021, July 6). *The human infrastructure of fake news in Brazil.* Items. https://items.ssrc.org/extremism-online/the-human-infrastructure-of-fake-news-in-brazil/.

Nery, N., & Agostini, A. (2013, September 2). *Governo brasileiro quer e-mail nacional contra "bisbilhotice."* Folha de São Paulo. https://www1.folha.uol.com.br/mundo/2013/09/1335529-governo-brasileiro-quer-e-mail-nacional-contra-bisbilhotice.shtml.

Net closes: Brazil's Magna Carta for the web, The. (2014, March 29). Economist. https://www.economist.com/the-americas/2014/03/29/the-net-closes.

Newman, N., Fletcher, R., Schulz, A., Andi, S., & Nielsen, R. K. (2020). *Reuters Institute digital news report 2021.* Reuters Institute for the Study of Journalism. https://reutersinstitute.politics.ox.ac.uk/digital-news-report/2021.

Newman, R. (2013). *The paradoxes of network neutralities.* [Doctoral dissertation, University of Southern California]. University of Southern California Dissertations and Theses.

Newman, R. (2016). Net neutrality: The debate nobody knows: Network neutrality's neoliberal roots and a conundrum for media reform. *International Journal of Communication, 10*, 20, 5969–5988.

Newman, R. (2019). *The paradoxes of network neutralities.* MIT Press.

Noble, S. U. (2018). *Algorithms of oppression: Data discrimination in the age of Google.* New York University Press.

Nordenstreng, K. (2011). Free flow doctrine in global media policy. In R. Mansell and M. Raboy (Eds.), *The handbook of global media and communication policy: General communication and media studies* (pp. 131–147). Wiley-Blackwell.

Nordenstreng, K., & Thussu, D. K. (Eds.). (2015). *Mapping BRICS media.* Routledge.

Nothias, T. (2020). Access granted: Facebook's free basics in Africa. *Media, Culture, & Society, 42*(3), 329–348.

Nothias, T. (2022, November 14). *How to fight digital colonialism.* Boston Review. https://www.bostonreview.net/articles/how-to-fight-digital-colonialism/.

Nye, D. E. (2007). *Technology matters: Questions to live with.* MIT Press.

Obar, J. A. (2015). Big Data and the phantom public: Walter Lippmann and the fallacy of data privacy self-management. *Big Data & Society, 2*(2). https://doi.org/10.1177/2053951715608876.

O'Brien, D. (2010, April 28). *Is Brazil the censorship capital of the internet? Not yet.* Committee to Protect Journalists. https://cpj.org/2010/04/is-brazil-the-censorship-capital-of-the-internet/.

Observatório da Sociedade Civil. (2014). *Sociedade civil reitera apoio ao Marco Civil da Internet, mas que melhorias no texto.* https://observatoriosc.org.br/sociedade-civil-reitera-apoio-ao-marco-civil-da-internet-mas-quer-melhorias-no-texto/.

O'Maley, D. (2015). *Networking democracy: Brazilian internet freedom activism and the influence of participatory democracy.* [Doctoral dissertation, Vanderbilt University]. Vanderbilt University Institutional Repository.

Omari, J. (2020). Is Facebook the internet? Ethnographic perspectives on open internet governance in Brazil. *Law & Social Inquiry, 45*(4), 1093–1112.

O'Neil, C. (2017). *Weapons of math destruction: How big data increases inequality and threatens democracy.* Penguin Books.

Organisation for Economic Cooperation and Development (OECD). (2013). *OECD communications outlook 2013.* https://www.oecd-ilibrary.org/science-and-technology/oecd-communications-outlook-2013/telecommunication-revenue-as-a-percentage-of-gdp_comms_outlook-2013-table28-en.

Ozawa, J. V., Woolley, S. C., Straubhaar, J., Riedl, M. J., Joseff, K., & Gursky, J. (2023). How disinformation on WhatsApp went from campaign weapon to governmental propaganda in Brazil. *Social Media + Society, 9*(1). https://doi.org/10.1177/20563051231160632.

Padovani, C., Musiani, F., & Pavan, E. (2010). Investigating evolving discourses on human rights in the digital age. *International Communication Gazette, 72*(4–5), 359–378.

Pait, H., & Straubhaar, J. (2018, June 24). *Imperialism, localisation, glocalisation, and patrimonialism: The fight for national control over TV Globo* [Conference presentation]. International Association for Media and Communication Research (IAMCR), Eugene, Oregon, United States.

Palfrey, J., & Gasser, U. (2012). *Interop: The promise and perils of highly interconnected systems.* Basic Books.

Papp, A. (2014). *Em nome da internet: Os bastidores da construção coletiva do Marco Civil.* [Master's thesis, Universidade de São Paulo]. CAPES: Catálogo de *Teses* e Dissertações.

Parsons, C. (2015). Beyond privacy: Articulating the broader harms of pervasive mass surveillance. *Media and Communication, 3*(3), 1–11.

Partido Pirata. (2013, December 13). *Nota 2.0 do Partido Pirata do Brasil sobre o Marco Civil da Internet.* https://partidopirata.org/nota-2-0-do-partido-pirata-do-brasil-sobre-o-marco-civil-da-internet/.

Partido Pirata. (2016, July 22). *Piratas surgem mudanças no CGI.* https://partidopirata.org/por-um-novo-cgi/.

Passarinho, N. (2014, February 12). Aliados de Dilma criam "blocão" e já defendem investigar caso Petrobras. *G1.* http://g1.globo.com/politica/noticia/2014/02/aliados-de-dilma-criam-blocao-e-ja-defendem-investigar-caso-petrobras.html.

Passarinho, N. (2014, February 12). PMDB decide derrubar projetos prioritários para o Planalto na Câmara. *G1.* http://g1.globo.com/politica/noticia/2014/02/pmdb-decide-derrubar-projetos-prioritarios-para-o-planalto-na-camara.html.

Patel, N. (2018, September 4). *It's time to break up Facebook.* The Verge. https://www.theverge.com/2018/9/4/17816572/tim-wu-facebook-regulation-interview-curse-of-bigness-antitrust.

Pettrachin, A. (2018). Towards a universal declaration on internet rights and freedoms? *International Communication Gazette, 80*(4), 337–353.

Pickard, V. (2016). Toward a people's internet: The fight for positive freedoms in an age of corporate libertarianism. In M. Edstrom, A. T. Kenyon, & E. Svensson (Eds.), *Blurring the lines: Market-driven and democracy-driven freedom of expression* (pp. 61–68). Nordicom.

Pickard, V. (2022). Can journalism survive in the age of platform monopolies? Confronting Facebook's negative externalities. In T. Flew & F. R. Martin (Eds.), *Digital platform regulation: Global perspectives on internet governance* (pp. 23–42). Palgrave Macmillan.

Pickard, V., & Berman, D. E. (2019). *After net neutrality.* Yale University Press.

Piratpartiet. (2022). *Election manifesto 2022.* https://piratpartiet.se/en/election-manifesto-2022/#Ansvarsfull-digitalisering.

Planalto. (1997). *Lei no. 9472.* https://www.planalto.gov.br/ccivil_03/leis/l9472.htm.

Planalto. (2014). *Lei no. 12965.* https://www.planalto.gov.br/ccivil_03/_ato2011-2014/2014/lei/l12965.htm.

Planalto. (2016). *Decreto no. 8771.* https://www.planalto.gov.br/ccivil_03/_ato2015-2018/2016/decreto/d8771.htm.

Possebon, S. (2013, March 27). *Grupo Globo cresce 16% em receitas em 2012 e registra R$ 12,7 bilhões de receita líquida.* Teletime. https://teletime.com.br/27/03/2013/grupo-globo-cresce-16-em-receitas-em-2012-e-registra-r-127-bilhoes-de-receita-liquida/.

Pota Pacamutondo, O. (2014). Brazilian telenovelas and their public in Mozambique: Penetrating and influencing daily life. In A. S. Jannusch, C. Dietz, S. Grassi, T. Kutscher, & P. Leutsch (Eds.), *Promoting alternative views in a multipolar world: BRICS and their evolving role in developing media markets* (pp. 69–75). Robert Bosch Stiftung.

Powers, S. M., & Jablonski, M. (2015). *The real cyber war: The political economy of internet freedom.* University of Illinois Press.

Qiu, J. (2016). *Goodbye iSlave: A manifesto for digital abolition.* University of Illinois Press.

Ramos, P. (2013, September 20). *Hospedagem de dados pode ter graves consequências*. Consultor Jurídico. https://www.conjur.com.br/2013-set-20 /pedro-ramos-hospedagem-forcada-dados-graves-consequencias.

Ramos, P. (2014). Neutralidade da rede e o Marco Civil da internet: Um guia para interpretacao [Net neutrality in Brazil: A guide to understanding Marco Civil]. *SSRN*, 1–15. https://ssrn.com/abstract=2496076.

Raymond, M., & DeNardis, L. (2015). Multistakeholderism: Anatomy of an inchoate global institution. *International Theory, 7*(3), 572–616.

Rede Livre. (2014, March 30). *Danilo Gentili, Roger E Lobão Sobre o Marco Civil.* [Video]. YouTube. https://www.youtube.com/watch?v=6EWGHWzvUMQ.

Renieris, E. M. (2023). *Beyond data: Reclaiming human rights at the dawn of the metaverse*. MIT Press.

Reporters without Borders (2021). *2021 World Press Freedom Index: Journalism, the vaccine against disinformation, blocked in more than 130 countries*. https://rsf.org/en/2021-world-pressfreedom-index-journalism-vaccine -againstdisinformation-blocked-more-130-countries.

Reuters. (2018, February 20). *Mudança nas regras de telecomunicações pode liberar venda de ativos indesejados por operadoras.* Epoca Negócios. https:// epocanegocios.globo.com/Empresa/noticia/2018/02/epoca-negocios -mudanca-nas-regras-de-telecomunicacoes-pode-liberar-venda-de-ativos -indesejados-por-operadoras.html.

Reuters. (2020, September 29). *Philippines accuses Facebook of censoring pro government content.* https://www.reuters.com/article/philippines -dutertefacebook-idINKBN26K1CZ.

Reuters. (2022, April 21). *Purchase of Brazil's Oi mobile operations is concluded, says TIM.* https://www.reuters.com/article/tim-oisale-idINS0N2VX066.

Ribeiro, D. (1995). *O povo brasileiro: A formação o sentido do Brasil.* Companhia das Letras.

Ricci, R. (2013). *Lulismo: Da era dos movimentos sociais à ascensão da nova classe média brasileira: de como o discurso anti-institucionalista dos anos 80 deu lugar ao líder da conclusão da modernização conservadora em nosso país.* Fundação Astrojildo Pereira.

Rizzo, A., & Monteiro, T. (2013, June 19). *Abin monta rede para monitorar o Internet.* Estado de S. Paulo. https://sao-paulo.estadao.com.br/noticias /geral,abin-monta-rede-para-monitorar-internet,1044500.

Robins, K., & Webster, F. (1998). Cybernetic capitalism: Information, technology, everyday life. In V. Mosco and J. Wasco (Eds.), *The political economy of information* (pp. 44–75). University of Wisconsin Press.

Rodrigues, C. D. (2006). Civil democracy, perceived risk, and insecurity in Brazil: An extension of the systemic social control model. *The Annals of the American Academy of Political and Social Science, 605*(1), 242–263.

Rodriguez, K., & Pinho, L. (2015, February 25). *Marco Civil da internet: The devil in the detail.* Electronic Frontier Foundation. https://www.eff.org /deeplinks/2015/02/marco-civil-devil-detail.

Roehrich, N. (2021, August 15). *Apricot subsea cable will boost internet capacity, speeds in the Asia-Pacific region.* Engineering at Meta. https://engineering .fb.com/2021/08/15/connectivity/apricot-subsea-cable/.

Rohter, L. (2002, June 23). Ideas & trends; Deep in Brazil, a flight of paranoid fancy. *New York Times.* https://www.nytimes.com/.

Rohter, L. (2010). *Brazil on the rise.* Palgrave Macmillan.

Romer, R. (2013, July 12). *Mudança no Marco Civil não é "adequada nem aconselhável," afirma Demi Getschko.* Canal Tech. https://canaltech.com.br /espionagem/Mudanca-no-Marco-Civil-nao-e-adequada-nem-aconselhavel -afirma-Demi-Getschko/.

Romero, S., & Archibold, A. (2013, September 2). Brazil angered over report N.S.A. spied on president. *New York Times.* https://www.nytimes.com/.

Rosa, B. (2014, March 9). Remessa de teles brasileiras às sedes sobe até 150%. *O Globo.* https://oglobo.globo.com/economia/remessa-de-teles -brasileiras-as-sedes-sobe-ate-150-11828644.

Rosa, F. R. (2019). *Global internet interconnection infrastructure: Materiality, concealment, and surveillance in contemporary communication.* [PhD dissertation, American University]. AU Institutional Repository.

Rose, R. S. (2005). *The unpast: Elite violence and social control in Brazil, 1954– 2000.* Ohio University Press.

Ross Arguedas, A., Robertson, C., Fletcher, R., & Nielsen, R. (2022, January 19). *Echo chambers, filter bubbles, and polarisation: A literature review.* Reuters Institute. https://reutersinstitute.politics.ox.ac.uk/echo-chambers-filter -bubbles-and-polarisation-literature-review.

Rossini, C. (2012, November 9). *New version of Marco Civil threatens freedom of expression in Brazil.* Electronic Frontier Foundation. https://www.eff.org /deeplinks/2012/11/brazilian-internet-bill-threatens-freedom-expression.

Rossini, C., Cruz, F. B., & Doneda, D. (2015). The strengths and weaknesses of the Brazilian internet bill of rights: Examining a human rights framework for the internet. *CIGI: Global Commission on Internet Governance,* no. 19.

Saad-Filho, A., & Morais, L. (2017). *Brazil: Neoliberalism versus democracy.* Pluto Press.

Samuels, D. J., & Lucas, K. (2010). The ideological "coherence" of the Brazilian party system. *Journal of Politics in Latin America, 2,* 39–69.

Santarém, P. (2010). *O direito achado na rede: A emergencia do acesso a internet.* [MA thesis, Universidade de Brasilia]. CAPES: Catálogo de *Teses* e Dissertações.

Santos, F., & Guarnieri, F. (2016). From protest to parliamentary coup: An overview of Brazil's recent history. *Journal of Latin American Cultural Studies, 25*(4), 485–494.

Schiller, D. (1999). *Digital capitalism: Networking the global market system.* MIT Press.

Schiller, D. (2007). *How to think about information.* University of Illinois Press.

Schiller, D. (2014). *Digital depression: Information technology and economic crisis.* University of Illinois Press.

Schiller, D. (2020). Reconstructing public utility networks: A program for action. *International Journal of Communication, 14*, 4989–5000.

Scholz, T. (2016). *Platform cooperativism: Challenging the corporate sharing economy.* Rosa Luxemburg Foundation.

Schoonmaker, S. (2002). *High-tech trade wars: U.S.-Brazilian conflicts in the global economy.* University of Pittsburgh Press.

Schwarcz, L. M., & Starling, H. M. M. (2020). *Brazil: A biography.* Picador.

Segurado, R. (2011). O debate sobre o marco civil da Internet. *IV encontro da compolítica—Associação Brasileira de Pesquisadores em comunicação e poliítica, Universidade do Estado do Rio de Janeiro (UERJ), Rio de Janeiro, 13.* Conference proceedings.

Sell, S. (2013). Revenge of the "nerds": Collective action against intellectual property maximalism in the global information age. *International Studies Review, 15*(1), 67–85.

Shaw, A. (2011). Insurgent expertise: The politics of free/livre and open source software in Brazil. *Journal of Information Technology & Politics, 8*(3), 253–272.

Silveira, S. A. D., Machado, M. B., & Savazoni, R. T. (2013). Backward march: The turnaround in public cultural policy in Brazil. *Media, Culture, & Society, 35*(5), 549–564.

SimilarWeb. (2021). *Top mobile apps in Brazil.* https://www.similarweb.com/apps/top/google/app-index/br/all/top-free/.

SimilarWeb. (2023). *Top websites ranking.* https://www.similarweb.com/top-websites/brazil/.

SimilarWeb. (2023). *Top apps ranking.* https://www.similarweb.com/topapps/top/google/app-index/br/all/top-free/.

Sinditelebrasil. (2014, April). *Marco Civil da Internet.* Brochure.

Slaughter, J. R. (2018). Hijacking human rights: Neoliberalism, the new historiography, and the end of the Third World. *Human Rights Quarterly, 40*(4), 735–775.

Smith, E. (2018, January 20). The techlash against Amazon, Facebook, and Google—and what they can do. *The Economist.* https://www.economist.com/.

Smythe, D. W. (1960). On the political economy of communications. *Journalism Quarterly, 37*(4), 563–572. https://doi.org/10.1177/107769906003700409.

Soares, F. B., Recuero, R., Volcan, T., Fagundes, G., & Sodré, G. (2021). Research note: Bolsonaro's firehose: How COVID-19 disinformation on WhatsApp was used to fight a government political crisis in Brazil. *The Harvard Kennedy School Misinformation Review, 2*(1).

Söderberg, J. (2008). *Hacking capitalism: The free and open source software (FOSS) movement.* Routledge.

Solagna, F. (2015). *A formulação da agenda e o ativismo em torno do Marco Civil da Internet.* [Master's thesis, Universidade Federal do Rio Grande do Sul]. CAPES: Catálogo de *Teses* e Dissertações.

Soprana, P. (2019, August 10). *Governo interliga bases e permite cruzamento de dados biamétricos.* Folha de São Paulo. https://www1.folha.uol.com

.br/mercado/2019/10/governo-cria-base-de-dados-unificada-de-todos-os -brasileiros.shtml.

Sorj, B. (2001). *A nova sociedade brasileira*. J. Zahar.

Sorj, B. (2003). *Brazil@* digitaldivide.com: *Confronting inequality in the information society*. UNESCO.

Sparrow, T. (2013, January 31). Behind the scenes of Latin America's internet "brain." *BBC News*. https://www.bbc.com/news/technology-21178983.

Springer, S. (2012). Neoliberalism as discourse: Between Foucauldian political economy and Marxian poststructuralism. *Critical discourse studies, 9*(2), 133–147.

Srnicek, N. (2017). *Platform capitalism*. Polity Press.

Stahl, T. (2016). Indiscriminate mass surveillance and the public sphere. *Ethics and Information Technology, 18*(1), 33–39.

Statcounter. (2023). *Social Media Stats Brazil*. https://gs.statcounter.com /social-media-stats/all/brazil.

Stevenson, A. (2018, November 6). Facebook admits it was used to incite violence in Myanmar. *New York Times*. https://www.nytimes.com/.

Stiegler, Z. (Ed.). (2013). *Regulating the web: Network neutrality and the fate of the open internet*. Lexington Books.

Straubhaar, J. (2017). Grupo Globo. In B. J. Birkinbine, R. Gómez, & J. Wasko, J. (Eds.), *Global media giants* (pp. 226–238). Routledge.

Streeter, T. (1996). *Selling the air: A critique of the policy of commercial broadcasting in the United States*. University of Chicago Press.

Streeter, T. (2011). *The net effect: Romanticism, capitalism, and the internet*. New York University Press.

Streeter, T. (2013). Policy, politics, and discourse. *Communication, Culture, & Critique, 6*(4), 488–501.

Sum, N. L., & Jessop, B. (2013). *Towards a cultural political economy: Putting culture in its place in political economy*. Edward Elgar.

Takhteyev, Y. (2012). *Coding places: Software practice in a South American city*. MIT Press.

Tarrow, S. (1996). States and opportunities: The political structuring of social movements. *Comparative Perspectives on Social Movements: Political Opportunities, Mobilizing Structures, and Cultural Framings, 90*(2), 41–61.

Tavares, M. (2012, January 26). Anatel aprova controle da net pela Embratel. *O Globo*. https://oglobo.globo.com/economia/anatel-aprova-controle -da-net-pela-embratel-3773580.

Taylor, A. (2014). *The people's platform: Taking back power and culture in the digital age*. Fourth Estate.

Taylor, L. (2017). What is data justice? The case for connecting digital rights and freedoms globally. *Big Data & Society, 4*(2). https://doi.org/10.1177 /2053951717736335.

Telebrasil. (2012, October 10). *Paulo Bernardo recebe título de homem do ano das telecomunicações*. http://www.telebrasil.org.br/sala-de-imprensa

/releases/2361-paulo-bernardo-recebe-titulo-de-homem-do-ano-das
-telecomunicacoes%22.

Telebrasil. (2018). *O desempenho do setor.* http://telebrasil.org.br/panorama
-do-setor/desempenho-do-setor.

Telegeography. (2021). *Submarine cables FAQ.* https://www2.telegeography.com
/submarine-cable-faqs-frequently-asked-questions.

Telesíntese. (2013, April 24). *Teles apresentam proposta de alteração do Marco
Civil da internet.* https://www.telesintese.com.br/teles-apresentam-proposta
-de-alteracao-do-marco-civil-da-internet/.

Thompson, M. (2010). The insensitive internet: Brazil and the judicialization of
pain. *IP Osgoode: Human Rights Issues.* https://www.iposgoode.ca/2010/05
/the-insensitive-internet-brazil-and-the-judicialization-of-pain/.

Thompson, M. (2012). Marco civil ou demarcação de direitos? Democracia,
razoabilidade e as fendas na internet do Brasil. *Revista de Direito Administra-
tivo, 261,* 203–251.

Thussu, D. (2014). The Indian entertainment and media industry: Bollywood
as India's soft power. In A. S. Jannusch, C. Dietz, S. Grassi, T. Kutscher, &
P. Leutsch (Eds.), *Promoting alternative views in a multipolar world: BRICS
and their evolving role in developing media markets* (pp. 69–75). Robert Bosch
Stiftung.

Tiemann, M. (2009, March 7). *President Lula's speech at FISL 10.* Open Source
Initiative. https://opensource.org/node/446.

Tomaz, T. (2023). Brazilian fake news bill: Strong content moderation accountability but limited hold on platform market power. *Javnost—The Public,
30*(2), 253–267.

Toor, A. (2013, September 25). *Cutting the cord: Brazil's bold plan to combat the NSA.* The Verge. https://www.theverge.com/2013/9/25/4769534
/brazil-to-build-internet-cable-to-avoid-us-nsa-spying.

Tozetto, M. (2013, July 7). *Marco Civil da internet obrigará Google e Facebook
a manter dados no Brasil.* IG. https://tecnologia.ig.com.br/especial/2013-07
-11/marco-civil-obrigara-google-e-facebook-a-manter-dados-no-brasil
.html.

Turcotte, J. F. (2016). Creative transformation and the knowledge-based economy: Intellectual property and access to knowledge under informational
capitalism. [PhD dissertation, York University]. York Space Institutional
Repository.

Twitter blog. (2022, February 24). *PL2630/2020 deixou de ser sobre com-
bater as fake news.* https://blog.google/intl/pt-br/novidades/iniciativas
/pl-26302020-deixou-de-ser-sobre-combater-fake-news/.

UNESCO. (2022). *Guidelines for regulating digital platforms.* https://www
.unesco.org/en/internettrust/guidelines.

United Nations. (2013, September 24). *Statement by H. E. Dilma Rousseff, president of the Federative Republic of Brazil, at the opening of the general debate
of the 68th session of the United Nations General Assembly.* https://gadebate
.un.org/sites/default/files/gastatements/68/BR_en.pdf.

University of Oxford. (2018, February 6). *Trump supporters and extreme right "share widest range of junk news."* https://www.ox.ac.uk/news/2018-02-06 -trump-supporters-and-extreme-right-share-widest-range-junk-news.

UOL Notícias. (2007, June 19). *OAB ataca Febraban e pede mais discussão sobre lei de crimes virtuais.* https://tecnologia.uol.com.br/ultnot/2007/06 /19/ult4213u105.jhtm.

UOL Notícias. (2013, July 7). *Neutralidade da rede é inegociável, diz relator do marco civil da internet.* https://www.uol.com.br/tilt/noticias/redacao/2013/08/07 /neutralidade-da-rede-e-inegociavel-diz-relator-do-marco-civil-da-internet .htm.

Urupá, M. (2023, January 4). *Coalizão solicita ao Ministério da Justiça medidas contra zero rating das operadoras.* Teletime. https://teletime.com.br/04/01 /2023/coalizao-solicita-ao-ministerio-dajusticamedidas-contra-zero-rating -das-operadoras/.

Vaidhyanathan, S. (2013). *The Googlization of everything: (And why we should worry).* University of California Press.

Valente, D. (2019, December 10). *WhatsApp é principal fonte de informação do brasileiro, diz pesquisa.* Agência Brasil. https://agenciabrasil .ebc.com.br/geral/noticia/2019-12/whatsapp-e-principal-fonte-de -informacao-do-brasileiro-diz-pesquisa.

Van Dijck, J. (2013). *The culture of connectivity.* Oxford University Press.

Van Schewick, B. (2016). *T-Mobile's binge on violates key net neutrality principles.* Stanford Law School, Center for Internet and Society.

Vaughn, R. G. (1993). Consumer protection laws in South America. *Hastings Int'l & Competition Law Review, 17*(2), 275–322.

Viola, E. J., & Franchini, M. (2018). *Brazil and climate change: Beyond the Amazon.* Routledge.

Waisbord, S. (2010). The pragmatic politics of media reform: Media movements and coalition-building in Latin America. *Global Media and Communication, 6*(2), 133–153.

Wallerstein, I. (1974). *The modern world-system: Capitalist agriculture and the origins of the European world-economy in the sixteenth century.* Academic Press.

Wardle, C. (2020, September 22). *Understanding information disorder.* First Draft. https://firstdraftnews.org/long-form-article/understanding -information-disorder/.

Wasserman, H. (2018). *Media, geopolitics, and power: A view from the global south.* University of Illinois Press.

Web We Want Foundation. (2014, March 24). *Marco Civil: Statement of support from Sir Tim Berners-Lee.* http://webfoundation.org/2014/03 /marco-civil-statementof-support-from-sir-tim-berners-lee/.

Winseck, D. (2017). The geopolitical economy of the global internet infrastructure. *Journal of Information Policy, 7,* 228–267.

Winseck, D., & Pike, R. M. (2008). Communication and empire: Media markets, power, and globalization, 1860–1910. *Global Media and Communication, 4*(1), 7–36.

Wittel, A. (2012). Digital Marx: Toward a political economy of distributed media. *tripleC, 10*(2), 313–333.

Wiziack, J. (2013, November 6). *Com ajuda de Facebook, Rede Globo dá "chega pra lá" em teles.* Folha de São Paulo. https://www1.folha.uol.com.br /poder/2013/11/1367390-analise-com-ajuda-de-facebook-rede-globo-da -chega-pra-la-em-teles.shtml?debug=true.

Wodak, R., & Meyer, M. (2009). Critical discourse analysis: History, agenda, theory, and methodology. *Methods of Critical Discourse Analysis, 2*, 1–33.

Woodcock, B. (2013, September 20). On internet, Brazil is beating US at its own game. *Al Jazeera America.* http://america.aljazeera.com/articles/2013/9/20 /brazil-internet-dilmarousseffnsa.html.

World Bank. (2021). *Charges for the use of intellectual property, payments.* World Bank Data. https://data.worldbank.org/indicator/BX.GSR.ROYL .CD?view=chart&locations=BR.

World Bank. (2021). *Charges for the use of intellectual property, receipts.* World Bank Data. https://data.worldbank.org/indicator/BX.GSR.ROYL .CD?view=chart&locations=BR.

Wu T. (2018). *The curse of bigness: Antitrust in the new gilded age.* Columbia Global Reports.

YouTube blocked in Brazil. (2007, January 9). *LA Times.* https://www.latimes .com/.

Zibechi, R. (2014). *The new Brazil: Regional imperialism and the new democracy.* AK Press.

Zittrain, J. (2008). *The future of the internet and how to stop it.* Yale University.

Zuboff, S. (2019). *The age of surveillance capitalism: The fight for the future at the new frontier of power.* Profile Books.

<h1>Index</h1>

Communication Decency Act, US, 132–133
Communication Rights within the Information Society (CRIS), 50
connectivity, 21
consumption at the periphery, 125–127
contemporary capitalism, 15; informational turn in, 17–18
content-delivery networks (CDNs), 40
content immoderation policies, 196–200
contestation, 97–98, 140–142, 219–220; choice and freedom, 106–107; commodity form and flow, 131–133; consumption at the periphery and, 125–127; copyright law and, 131–134; ground zero for zero-rating, 107–109; of the "law of Facebook," 109–110; military generals and, 123–124; network neutrality and (*see* network neutrality); obstruction, obfuscation, and the telco Rasputin in, 101–102; political appointments and corporate maneuvers in, 98–101; pragmatism and, 137–140; private censorship and, 134–137; red scare rhetoric and, 112–113; safe harbors and, 120–121, 129–131; telcos' agenda in, 104–106; telcos' discursive strategy in, 110–112; turf war in, 113–116; urban favela communities and, 127–128
control, 47; code and, 24–25; IP regime (law), 23–24; surveillance and, 25–27
copyright, 223; infringement of, 131–133, 138, 140; carve-out grand bargain, 133–134
Copyright Treaty, 57
Couldry, N., 22, 26, 29, 36, 40
Council of Europe, 57
counter-protocological attacks, 33
COVID-19 virus, 188, 213
Crain, Matthew, 25, 221
Creative Commons (CC) licensing system, 20, 62, 99
critical discourse analysis (CDA), 9, 11, 43

critical legal studies, 15
critical political economy, 8
CTS-SAL, 71–72
cultural political economy, 9
cultural products, global flow of, 38–39
Cunha, Eduardo, 101–102, 110, 113, 127, 160, 174–176, 182
cyberlibertarianism, 60–61
cybernetic capitalism, 21
cyberutopianism, 65

Dahlberg, Lincoln, 61
Dantas, Marcos, 127
da Silva, Lula Inácio, 55, 60, 98, 178, 184, 211; discourse in support of the Marco Civil, 66–67; election in 2023, 209–210; formation of interpretive community by, 70–72; framing of freedom and development by, 67–69; national data sovereignty and, 149
data access, economic imperative for, 169–171
data colonialism, 22, 36
data enclosure, 151–152
datafication, 21–22, 39
data localization, 146–151, 178–179; efforts at protecting data sovereignty and, 147–148; Google and, 147, 151–152, 153; June Journeys and need for data, 152–154; jurisdictional battles over, 156–157; nuclear options on, 155–156; pretense and reality of data sovereignty and, 148–151; privacy fallacy and, 146–147
data protection, 223–224
data retention, 166–167, 169–171
data sovereignty, 147–148; pretense and reality of, 148–151; triumph of digital rights over, 157–165
data storage, 179–182
Davis, Stuart, 186
Dean, J., 29
"Death of the Brazilian Internet," 60–61
de Hollanda, Ana, 99, 133
Deibert, R. J., 26

GUY T. HOSKINS is a postdoctoral fellow with the Global Media & Internet Concentration Project at Carleton University and a contract lecturer at Toronto Metropolitan University.

The University of Illinois Press
is a founding member of the
Association of University Presses.

———————————————————

Composed in 11.5/13 Adobe Garamond Pro
with Gotham display
by Kirsten Dennison
at the University of Illinois Press

University of Illinois Press
1325 South Oak Street
Champaign, IL 61820-6903
www.press.uillinois.edu

Printed and bound by CPI Group (UK) Ltd, Croydon, CR0 4YY

06/07/2025

14699416-0001